Silent
Heroes

Silent Heroes

Lowell Thomas

Thank you!

Lowell Thomas

Michigan State University
East Lansing

♾ The paper used in this publication meets the minimum requirements of
ANSI/NISO Z39.48-1992 (® 1997) (Permanence of Paper).

Michigan State University
East Lansing, Michigan 48824

Printed and bound in the United States of America.

10 09 08 07   2 3 4 5 6 7 8 9 10

Cover design by Heidi Daley
Book design by Bookcomp, Inc.

Cover art: Background, Tom Stetler; Inset, Leonard Duchene, Roy Komachi,
Henry DeGraw, William Elliott, Don Hawkins; Spine, Richard Tolly

Dedication

More than one veteran, while being interviewed
for this book, said, "The real heroes are
those guys who never came back." This book is
dedicated to those whose lives were lost
on the battlefields defending the United States
of America, and to the families in
Midland County who suffered the agony
of losing a loved one in that defense.

Contents

CONTENTS

x   **CONTENTS**

Acknowledgments

To the men on these pages who shared their memories with me, I will be eternally grateful. Even in their humor, they would sometimes be fighting a lump in their throats, tears building in the corners of their eyes, as their memories returned to some experience in their past when they were exposed to the horrific evils of mankind.

I am also indebted to the following staff members at the *Midland Daily News* who offered encouragement and assistance:

Gordon Hall and Jenny Anderson, publishers, who granted newspaper space to promote the arrival of *Silent Heroes,* and who followed up with advertising for the sale of the book.

John Telfer, editor, who made space for me to interview the veterans, including his own office when all other offices were occupied.

Ralph Wirtz, managing editor and valued friend, who arranged space for writing, a telephone with voice mail and publication of the stories on these pages in the paper.

Stuart Frohm, wire editor, who helped with research and pointed me in the right direction for contacts.

Rodney Curtis, photo editor, with whom I consulted on many of the photos for the paper, Doug Winger, librarian, who assisted with research when needed and always cheerfully made copies of material brought in by the veterans for use in their stories.

The ladies at the front desk: Linda Fike, Jody Jean, Terry Kenny, Kathy Richmond, Jo Szagesh and Bobbie Norling (who also kept the paychecks coming after my stories appeared in the *Midland Daily News*). They willingly and cheerfully received my many telephone calls, greeted my guests at the newspaper office and aided in the collection of photographs.

Gratitude also goes to Dr. Gary Hughes, superintendent, Midland Public Schools, for his encouragement and for following up on some research for me, to Steve Tracy of the Midland County Veterans Service Office, who reinforced my knowledge of geography, and put me in touch with veterans whose stories needed telling. To those who took the time to read the unedited manuscript and thought enough about it to write the endorsements found on the back cover.

To Barbara Prince Sovereen, my editor, who could take a mass of tangled words, unravel them and make them meaningful.

To my best friend and wife, Jane, who was always there, proof-reading, commenting and researching for me, and her neverending encouraging remarks.

And finally, to those Midland County residents who called or e-mailed to lend their support for what I was doing, including those silent heroes whose stories are not published in this book. I was often cheered on by relatives of those whose stories appear on these pages, asking when the book would be available; some as far away as California.

Without these people, the history of sixty-two valiant men in Midland County would not have been recorded.

Lowell Thomas
November 2004

Foreword

Unlike Tom Brokaw's book, *The Greatest Generation,* this is a book that relates stories of individual veterans in one small geographical area in mid-Michigan. Lowell Thomas's efforts could, and should, be duplicated by every town, village and city in every state in this great nation. Heroes, do indeed, walk among us and their stories should, and need to, be told.

This work contains dozens of fascinating stories of former students, office and factory workers and businessmen who answered the call of their nation in times of national emergencies. *Silent Heroes* is a book not dedicated to the strategies or killing machinery of battle, nor stories of professional soldiers, but of ordinary people whose lives were caught up in—and sometimes ended by—the extraordinary experience of war.

Stanley J. Bozich, Director
Michigan's Own, Inc. Military and Space Museum,
Frankenmuth, Michigan

Introduction

Many wars ago, General William Tecumseh Sherman said, "War is hell." Many of the men in Midland County, some of whom many of us have known for years, have been there and back. I didn't know until they opened up as I tested their aging memories for the experiences they shared.

Most of our wars were commanded by U.S. presidents and high officials, but they were won by teenagers and men barely over twenty, as these stories will attest.

My original intent was to interview an equal number of veterans of World War II, and the Korean and Vietnam wars. Somehow it did not work out that way. Many World War II veterans are just now talking about their experiences, and veterans of the other conflicts are still reluctant to discuss them. When they did, I sometimes later found out that details were left out or ignored by a brain that refused to activate those memories.

Silent Heroes began with stories written about a few of Midland County's combat veterans in the early 1980s, and published in the *Midland Daily News*. It wasn't until Tom Brokaw's book, *The Greatest Generation*, that I theorized there must be men in Midland County who would fit the criteria for such a document of recorded history. After only minimal research, my assumption proved accurate. Their stories on these pages have been published in the *Midland Daily News* over the past twenty years; most between 2001 and 2004.

As a freelance writer, I am indebted to the men in this book for the education I have received from them regarding some of history's most horrific events. I am grateful for the marvelous contributions these men have made to the world and, more specifically, to Midland County.

If I wasn't living out the perfect postwar American suburban dream, I didn't know who was.

Yet for me, the dream still retained its nightmare edge. It was an edge I shared with hundreds of thousands of veterans, most of whom never talked about it to anyone, not even their wives and children. Sometimes it was those visions of planes falling from the air around me, with good men in them. Sometimes it was that remembered giant question mark in my mind. Why me? Why, why, why me? Why did I survive when all those others did not?

Those are the words of eighty-five-year-old Colonel Robert Morgan, pilot of the *Memphis Belle*, the famed B-17 of World War II that was the first Flying Fortress to complete twenty-five missions over Europe without a casualty. The words are excerpted, with his permission, from Morgan's autobiography, *The Man Who Flew The Memphis Belle*. Morgan went on to pilot twenty-six additional missions in a B-29 over the South Pacific and Japan before the war ended.

Many of the combat veterans interviewed for this book used similar words to describe their feelings about their war experiences. "I have never even told my family about this. They have no idea what I did in the war," many have said. And many remarked, "I still don't know why I made it when so many others didn't."

As I interviewed them and listened to their stories, I sometimes choked back emotion, just as they did when they shared them. As I put their stories on paper, I again felt the grief as I relived with them some of their war experiences.

Sometimes in an interview, I would ask the insensitive question, "Do you recall any time when you knew you had deliberately killed another man?" One veteran of World War II looked at me, and with pain in his voice said, "Yes." His memory was all too sharp and he began to tear up, waving off the question. I immediately switched the line of questioning.

Silent Heroes portrays the experiences of Midland County veterans during the worst times of their lives—war times. While none of them claim to be heroes themselves, I believe anyone who comes under fire defending the freedoms of the United States of America falls into that category.

Many of the subjects in this book stated, "The true heroes are the ones who never came back." There is truth in that, but without these veterans' stories, the written history of those who did not return would be lost forever.

This book puts human feelings and faces on these wars, and in doing so lends validity to historical facts.

Putting the experiences of Midland County combat veterans on paper brings alive a history found nowhere else and elevates Midland County veterans into their place in world history.

Nothing I had ever seen, read, or been told about war prepared me for the vision these stories would convey. What caught me most off guard was the vision of some of the atrocities man can perform against man. And some Midland county men in this book experienced them.

Theirs is a story largely unrecorded on paper because servicemen thousands of miles from home could record them only on the far reaches of their memories—memories that have faded through time, or they experienced such horrific acts that their brains refused to recall them at all.

Some of the stories contain the zany antics that men do in war time to relieve stress and/or boredom.

As I began this venture in earnest, I met ordinary men whose circumstances forced extraordinary feats; courageous foot soldiers on the front lines, fighter pilots and bomber pilots who, when viewing their aircraft after a mission, wondered how they ever returned without a casualty—or returned at all. Many of their friends did not. There were POWs who suffered extreme cruelty and suffering at the hands of the enemy. It was not just the pain from torment, but the diseases confronting them from lack of medical attention and creature comforts by their captors.

These firsthand accounts of fighting for survival, of success and failures in concentration camps brings an anguish to the pit of the stomach that most of us never experience.

Words cannot possibly express our gratitude to these men who once put their lives on the line so we can enjoy the freedom in a world made so uncertain by those who would destroy us.

My only regret is that more of our brave veterans did not step forward to have their stories told when the opportunity was there. They remain Midland County's silent heroes.

Lowell Thomas
November 2004

The Bolshevik Revolution

1917–1919

Little is remembered in Russia about the Bolshevik Revolution or how America became involved in it. What has been written about it is contained in books by historians, and stored on library bookshelves, seldom referred to by the general public. Few people living today have even heard of this war.

Initially, President Woodrow Wilson stated that the United States would never be involved in the war. Later, he changed his mind and sent 5,500 American fighting men to Russia during 1918 and 1919. And before it was over, more than 300,000 Americans lost their lives in this war.

One Midland man, Oscar Holstrom, was among the involved. He watched his own men fall around him, if not from the fighting, from the frigid cold of the Arctic battlegrounds.

Holstrom, whose story is told in the first pages of this book, concurred. Even though the war ended in late fall 1918, he and his tormented comrades were not returned home until the Fourth of July the following year.

Oscar Holstrom Faced Red Armies During Bolshevik Revolution

The following story was published in the Midland Daily News *on 20 September 1983.*

If someone were to say Americans fought against the Red Armies of Lenin and Trotsky and died in Russia and Siberia, the statement would undoubtedly be met with some skepticism.

But Oscar Holstrom, a Midland County native, now a resident of Provincial House in Midland, testified to the fact. He was there.

He was one of about fifty Americans still alive in 1983 out of 5,500 who were sent to Russia to fight in the Bolshevik Revolution in 1918–19. Fifteen hundred were from Michigan.

They dubbed themselves the Polar Bears. On 3 August 1918, their heavily laden troop transport, which had left England weeks before, slithered up the Dvina River and docked in Archangel, Russia, just thirty-five miles south of the Arctic Circle. For the next nine months the temperatures ranged from minus ten to minus sixty-eight degrees Fahrenheit, and darkness extended from shortly past noon to nine o'clock the following morning.

The stated purpose of the American expeditionary force was to protect military supplies sent to the Russian Allies, the British had said. Unfortunately, the Bolsheviks had taken the supplies before the U.S. troops arrived.

Holstrom was a member of the 339th Infantry, 85th Division, Company F. He was inducted in Detroit, sent to Camp Custer in Battle Creek for training, then transported to England.

From his well-used wheelchair, the still witty and charming Holstrom admitted to his failing memory, but a 320-page book, *Quartered in Hell: The Story of American North Russian Expeditionary Force, 1918–1919,* published in 1982 verifies his experiences.

Other books have been written about the Polar Bears, but this was the first time the veterans themselves were able to relate their experiences in the snow trenches of Russia in one volume. Holstrom himself was contacted by the author in 1979 regarding his experiences.

One veteran wrote,

Lloyd George made a personal agreement with [President] Woodrow Wilson for the loan of the 339th Infantry and with the usual British B.S. and blandishment convinced the military of France, Italy and Czechoslovakia that it was a peaceful mission to be used for guarding the vast supplies in Archangel and Murmansk districts to keep them from falling into the hands of the Germans. There were no supplies. Actually, the British wanted to occupy and conquer the State of North Russia in order to seize the huge pine and fir forests and the platinum in the Northern part.

In another article, in the 9 August 1982 *Detroit Free Press*, Stanley Bozich, director of Michigan's Own, a military museum in Frankenmuth, compared the Polar Bears to disenchanted Vietnam veterans.

He said some of the Polar Bears were bitter over having to fight a war they did not understand.

Holstrom remembered well the atrocious beatings by the Bolos, their nickname for the Bolsheviks. When an American was captured, he was beaten and often left in the frigid wastes to die. Usually, the Yank died from his skull being crushed by a Bolo rifle butt, Holstrom recalled painfully.

One portion of *Quartered in Hell* states, "We are no longer fighting for the Russians. We are fighting to save our own hides. Over the frozen chaos of Russia we carry our dead. We bury them in the only fashion possible, in heaps. There are no songs in our hearts now. War has scarred our vision."

Holstrom remembered a time his unit had hiked all night, a distance of over thirty miles, walking in snow up to their armpits. The following day, he said, "I was holding down a machine gun nest and was overcome by exhaustion and sleep. When I woke up in the snow, my uniform was covered with sawdust where bullets had hit the trees all around me."

Holstrom also remembered the "closest I ever came to stopping breathing . . . I had my rifle slung across my back when a Bolo bullet hit it, splitting it in two. The magazine exploded, and burned my back." He smiled about it later.

By Christmas 1918, the ink on the peace treaty had been dry for a month, but word had not yet reached Holstrom and the others as they huddled for warmth in the Arctic snow. Thousands of American soldiers had already sailed for Europe, then on to America, but the Polar Bears remained and fought for their lives until the following spring. Most of them were not united with their loved ones until the Fourth of July, 1919.

Holstrom has had a varied career. He worked in the oil fields of Michigan, farmed in this area, worked as a blacksmith in Coleman for sixteen years, and retired from the City of Midland Water Department in 1959.

His first wife, Retha Rease, whom he married in 1921, died in 1972. In 1975 he married, at the age of eighty, Nora Mishler.

Holstrom has a son, Larry, in Muskegon, a daughter, Virginia Murray, in North Bradley, and nine grandchildren.

When questioned about his experience of fighting on Russian soil, the warm, wrinkle-faced Holstrom bowed his head and said sadly, "There are so many memories."

World War II

1941–1945

The history of the battles fought by the American and Allied armies in World War II has filled volumes of books and numerous movie and television screens. Little wonder. There was much to write about. Some of it nonfiction, much of it—particularly on the screens—fiction.

The 1999 World Almanac reports that there were 292,131 American battle deaths in World War II, and well over a half-million wounded. But before it would end on that fateful day in August 1945, over fifty million human beings would be dead from the most horrific blood bath in world history. The number included the millions of Jews exterminated by Hitler and those hundreds of thousands of Japanese killed by the only two atomic bombs ever used in fighting a war.

This section of the book includes dozens of stories of valiant Midland County men who penetrated deep into Germany and surrounding countries to help bring the war in Europe to an end in the spring of 1945. Other Midlanders were involved in the desperate struggle to win the islands in the South Pacific, and indeed, in the bombing of Japan itself. Some Midland County men became prisoners of war, suffering physical and mental atrocities at the hands of their captors, both in Europe and in the South Pacific. Still others were among members of the occupation forces on both sides of the world following the signing of the surrender documents in Tokyo Bay in September 1945.

These are their stories.

Frank Andrizzi:
From the Bulge to the Caves

Frank Andrizzi was a twenty-year-old enlistee who had already been in the U.S. Army for a full year when the Japanese "zeros" devastated Pearl Harbor with bombs and gunfire.

He does not remember where he was when Pearl Harbor was stormed, but his first overseas assignment took him in the opposite direction. Landing in Wales, his first job was unloading bombs and shells from ships arriving from the States that would eventually be used in the war effort over Europe.

Another job Andrizzi held was one few people did during war or in peacetime. He taught members of the Women's Army Corps (WACS) how to drive trucks. This was a needed task that would not place women or civilians in a war zone, thus allowing more men to go to the front lines.

From Wales, Andrizzi was assigned to Utah Beach two days after D day on 6 June 1944 as a forward observer with the 90th Infantry Division. The life expectancy of a forward observer was minimal, and Andrizzi was hit in the back of the head with shrapnel. He was evacuated to the 12th Evacuation Hospital in Nancy, France.

After some time in the hospital (he did not recall how long he was there), the army found him fit to return to the war. He rejoined his outfit, and fought for four days trying to cross the Saar River, a rich coal mining region in southwest Germany. The fighting was fierce. Once they had crossed the river, they received orders to pull back. Andrizzi did not even know at the time why the 90th Division received that order.

"We thought it was stupid retreating," Andrizzi recalled, "because we had lost so many good men just trying to get across. But in the military you don't question an order," he said. "You just do it."

The reason soon became evident, however. They were to take part in the Battle of the Bulge, at Bastogne, Belgium, one of the fiercest battles on that side of the globe in World War II.

"When we got there, you can't imagine the number of trucks and tanks along the side of the road that had been hit [by mortar fire], and left there to rot. I don't know how they ever cleaned it all up."

The 90th Infantry Division was at the Bulge for only a day or two, when it moved on to Luxembourg. Andrizzi was not injured at the Bulge, but had been wounded twice before arriving there.

He did not remember exactly where he was at the time of his second injury, but he was sitting on the passenger side of a jeep. His canteen was resting just to the outside of the jeep, and he was resting his right hand on the canteen.

"A sniper in the second story of a building tried to hit me in the back, but hit my hand holding my canteen," he said. He was hospitalized for a second time, and "they sewed me up," as he put it. And for the second time, he returned to battle.

One of the most frightening experiences of fighting in the forests of Germany was the artillery tree bursts. "Tree bursts are when artillery hits the top of trees, and the shrapnel comes down like rain," explained Andrizzi. That was how Andrizzi received the wound in the back of his head.

When asked if at any time he could honestly say he was frightened, Andrizzi's face brightened as he replied, "You know how big a helmet is. A couple times I swear I crawled up inside it. Anyone who says he wasn't scared is lying."

Following the Battle of the Bulge, and because he had had some training in tanks at Ft. Knox, Kentucky, he was reassigned to the 4th Armored Division in the Third Army, commanded by General George Patton. The division fought on into Czechoslovakia.

On the way, they liberated a concentration camp filled with Polish, French and Russian soldiers. "They had been beaten and were close to starving," Andrizzi remembered. "It was terrible how they treated those people."

When asked if he saw the ovens where the prisoners were cremated he nodded slowly, but it was obvious Andrizzi did not want to talk about it. His only overt response was, "Those guys were sure glad to see us."

At one point, Andrizzi remembered a cave he had entered where he found several famous paintings the Germans had looted. "I remember seeing Patton there, but I don't remember where we were. We took the paintings, and eventually I believe they were sent to the States," he said.

As Patton's army went through each village after the Battle of the Bulge, the houses were supposed to display white flags in the windows, indicating the surrender of the village.

"But they still had snipers in the buildings," Andrizzi recalled. "Patton promised the villagers that if the sniping didn't discontinue, he would burn the town to the ground. That didn't stop the snipers, and we burned the whole town down."

"That's what I liked about Patton," Andrizzi said emphatically. "When he said something, he didn't back off. Word got around, and the sniping stopped."

Andrizzi remembered he was sitting on a tank when told the war was over. For his valor, he was later awarded two Purple Hearts along with several other medals as mementos of a long, difficult war in which he had fought.

He was discharged in 1946. After six years, Andrizzi was finally back in civilian clothes.

Glenn Baumann:
A Special Mountain has Special Meaning

He was immediately classified 4D when the nation learned that Pearl Harbor had been invaded by the Japanese on 7 December 1941.

Glenn E. Baumann was attending Eden Theological Seminary in a suburb of St. Louis, Missouri. A 4D classification meant those studying for the ministry could not be drafted into war.

"Four of us in our class of fifteen had some difficulty with that," Baumann reflected. "We discussed our responsibility to the war effort and decided we also had an obligation."

Two of Baumann's classmates chose to quit the seminary and enlist as privates "in protest of the regulation," according to Baumann. A third failed the physical, and Baumann enlisted in the U.S. Navy with the stipulation that he complete seminary and become a chaplain.

Following seminary he was ordained, and after having completed two months of additional schooling in August 1943, he became a navy chaplain. After that he spent six months at Boston Receiving Station for additional military training and awaited the overseas orders he had requested. Baumann was assigned to the 28th Marines, Fifth Marine Division.

The Fifth Division was on orders to Camp Pendleton, California for additional training, then to Hawaii for more of the same. In January 1945, not yet knowing it was heading into combat, Baumann's division made a practice landing on Maui, Hawaii. The next landing would be for real.

On 19 February 1945, Baumann and the Fifth Marine Division stormed the shores of Iwo Jima, a small, then ugly island situated in the Pacific Ocean, midway between Japan and the Mariana Islands. They were about to burst into American history on that day in a historic battle that was to last for thirty-six days and nights.

But the cost of taking Iwo Jima was at a horrific expense in human lives. Nearly 7,000 Americans died on that island in those thirty-six days and nights and over 19,000 were wounded. For the Japanese it was even worse. Over 21,000 of them perished, leaving only 1,000 who quickly ran off to hide in the caves. Many of them, humiliated at the defeat, took their own lives.

Put in perspective, the total of lost and wounded in those thirty-six days, on an area less than five miles from tip to tip and 2.5 miles across at its widest point, represented every man, woman, and child in the city of Midland in 1983, when this story first appeared.

Baumann spoke of Iwo Jima with compassion bordering on pain and admitted, "It has been only within the last five years that I could talk about these experiences without overt emotion." He has never attended any of his division's reunions.

On that historic February day in 1945, Baumann and a Catholic priest were in the ninth wave of marines to hit the beach, wading ankle deep in volcanic ash.

"It was relatively quiet then," recalled Baumann. "The preceding air attack, naval shelling, and the forward troops had driven the Japanese into the natural caves of the island."

Baumann added, "The Catholic chaplain and I lay there on a sand ledge in the open. He turned to me and asked, 'Glenn, where do we go from here?' I responded with, 'I don't know, I've never been here before.'" Baumann chuckled, and added, "Philosophically, I've found myself in that position many times ever since."

One terrifying experience in Baumann's memory was helping to assist a wounded marine on a stretcher from the battlefield to the ship for medical attention.

"When we returned a half-hour later, our command post had been moved. We were told to follow some telephone wires that would lead us to our destination. Along the way we picked up a private, as lost as we were, when suddenly we found ourselves pinned down by machine gun fire. All three of us jumped into a vacant shell hole and waited. When the shelling stopped, I raised my helmet on my fingertips, and the enemy would repeat the action.

"We concluded we had gone in the wrong direction, and had walked closer to the front lines," Baumann added.

"This kept up until dark," Baumann went on, "then the firing stopped." He instructed his cramped partners to sit tight while he made a break for the next nearest cover, telling them that if nothing happened they should follow.

"Nothing happened," he said, "and we headed for the other side of the island. By sheer luck we found our command post in the dark. That night some Japanese soldiers infiltrated our command post and silently killed two of our men."

The following day Baumann was discussing their situation with his commanding officer and several other men when a mortar shell hit a short distance from them.

"The regimental doctor was killed, another man had both arms and legs ripped from his body," Baumann related painfully, "and another had a big gash in his neck." Later he himself received a burning shrapnel wound on one hand.

"If the mortar had landed four feet closer, all of us would have been the fateful recipients of that shell," Baumann reflected.

Baumann was at Mt. Suribachi, the 550-foot extinct volcano, when the most reproduced photograph of World War II was taken—that of six brave marines raising the American flag on the summit.

"It was a sense of joy," he recalled, "but also a real awareness that the fight was far from over."

He was right. The battles on Iwo Jima raged for another month, during which time the death toll on both sides numbered in the thousands.

In April 1945, the war was over for Baumann and the Fifth Marine Division, although they did not know it at the time. They were returned to Hawaii for replacements, additional training, and prepared for their next assignment which was to invade Japan.

Before the assignment came, the atomic bombs had fallen on Hiroshima and Nagasaki, ending the war.

But Baumann's troop ship headed west anyway—straight for Sasebo, on the southernmost island in the Japanese chain, and they became part of the first American forces to occupy Japanese territory without being fired upon.

"When we arrived at the dock, only one Japanese stood there waiting," Baumann recalled. "The rest had fled to the hills. By the third day they discovered no one was going to hurt them, and they gradually returned to the seafront and asked the GIs for candy and cigarettes," he added.

Two and a half months later Baumann returned to the States for discharge, but not before he was asked by top military officials to remain in the service.

After reflecting upon his experiences thoughtfully, Baumann said matter-of-factly, "I chose not to stay in."

The military's loss was Midland's gain. For twenty-three years, the Reverend Glenn Baumann was pastor of United Church of Christ in Midland until his retirement in 1983.

Author's note: The above story was written for the Midland Daily News, *and published on 28 May 1983.*

Stuart Branson:
War Wounds Still Hurt After Sixty Years

World War II was only eight months old when Uncle Sam said he wanted Stuart Branson. The Great Uncle took him all the way to a hospital ship in Europe. Eventually that same Uncle Sam awarded him two Purple Hearts, a Bronze Star for Heroism, and a Certificate of Merit.

He matured a great deal from a twenty-one-year-old in a war-torn world in 1942 to an already aging young man of twenty-four in December 1945.

His military career began with aircraft mechanic school in Texas. "I never viewed myself as a mechanic," Branson said, even though he graduated at the very top of his seven-hundred-member class. "But I was just fresh out of college, and was used to taking tests and dealing with paperwork."

His wise leaders there soon discovered he had ROTC artillery training at Michigan State University, and urged him to go to officer training school in artillery at Ft. Sill, Oklahoma.

Chuckling, Branson recalled, "They said, 'that's what you want to be, isn't it?' Yes sir!"

After three months of intensive artillery training, often labeled the Ninety-day Wonders, he was commissioned a 2nd Lieutenant, and sent to Camp Campbell, Kentucky, where he was assigned to the 12th Armored Division. Then it was back to Camp Barkley, Texas, where the training was specifically to go overseas.

Branson was one of thousands to eventually disembark from Camp Shanks, New York among a convoy of thirty assorted war ships. His was the lead ship. A great deal of "zigging and zagging" took place, according to Branson, to avoid enemy submarines as they crossed the Atlantic. During the eleven-day crossing, the convoy seemed to be exempt from enemy craft of any kind.

The U.S. ships arrived safely in Bristol, England, where the troops were delayed for nearly a month. In October 1943, they were shipped to Cherbourg, France, which had already been captured by the armed forces on D day.

But the fighting was far from over. It was at Cherbourg where Branson was initiated into combat.

"Moving east, we kept getting closer to the sound of the guns. I kept thinking that tomorrow might be the day, and finally the day

arrived." Branson was in combat every day for nearly the next five
months.

As a motor officer, he was in charge of maintaining the tanks to
keep them in fighting condition.

"One day I was approached by my superiors who said they needed
forward observers because they were losing them," he recalled. "A
forward observer is one who can spot the enemy, radio back the

coordinates so the guns can be aimed to most effectively wipe out the enemy. In our case, it was observing for the 105 howitzers. The people manning the guns seldom saw what the forward observers saw, so what was radioed back had to be heavily relied upon to be effective.

"So the colonel came to three of us [forward observers] and said he was going to flip a coin. 'One of you guys is going to be either a ground observer or drive a tank in the infantry, and the other is going to be in a Piper Cub as an air observer.' So I got the ground job. The guy in the Piper Cub was later shot down and killed."

Although Branson was with an artillery unit, he was assigned to the infantry and often went on attacks into a barrage of enemy gunfire, radioing back to the areas where firepower was needed. "It was my job to go to spots, carefully, where I could see the targets, because the Germans were looking for me too. It was my job to determine if what I saw was actually a target. If I saw the enemy sitting around eating lunch, that was not a target. If I saw men working on their tanks, that was a target."

In order for Branson to know exactly where his own guns were located behind him, he asked via radio for a volley of white phosphorous to be fired. This would send over a huge white mark. He then knew in which direction the guns, six to seven hundred yards behind him, had to be adjusted to hit the target.

"There were code names for 'right' or 'left,' then I would tell them 'I think we're on the target now. Fire for effect.' That meant 'all guns come in on that spot.' If I did my job right, that target would be completely demolished." Branson's training, insight and courage, more often than not, accomplished just that, saving the lives of hundreds, perhaps thousands of American GIs.

"When our big guns hit the target, I loved to radio back, 'Arms and legs everywhere.' I never actually saw arms and legs, but that was my way of complimenting them. They knew they had hit the target."

During the five months Branson was doing his job as a ground observer, he was continually looking for the best vantage point to observe. Many times, while in a town, it would be a church steeple. "The disadvantage of that was if the Germans suspected I was there, they would shoot up in the steeple," Branson remarked soberly.

It was in one such steeple that Branson earned his first Purple Heart. "I heard a shot, something hit the church bell behind me, and almost instantaneously, something hit me in the back of the neck."

Branson was not incapacitated, and he eventually made it back to his own unit.

In a still more serious mode, Branson related the story of an executive officer from another battery who had a guilt trip because his major job was to take the incoming calls from the forward observers, interpret the information, and relay it to the gunners. This officer encountered Branson, and insisted he take one turn at being the observer.

Branson showed him where the phone line was laid, and how to follow it up to the observation post. "We always started before dawn to risk being exposed in daylight," he said.

Unknown to anyone, the Germans had found the line during the night, and were waiting for the observer to arrive. They then killed him. "That bothered me for a long, long time," Branson sighed. "The story here is a guy's concern for sharing the risk."

Sometimes Branson's mission would begin in an airplane, and sometimes he would be driving a tank himself.

On one mission, Branson was assigned to fly in a Piper Cub over the area they were about to attack. "It was the quietest, most placid looking countryside one could imagine," he remembered. "There were farms with houses and barns, and looking everything like some place you would want to visit.

"The next day those barns opened up. The Germans had loaded them with 88 mm guns and just blasted our tanks. The tank ahead of me was hit, and the treads were peeled off like an orange. A lot of people were hurt, but I just lucked out," Branson said with some relief.

General Patton's 12th Armored Division, of which Branson was now a member, moved eastward from the southern part of France, and had joined up with the French 1st Army.

About four and a half months prior to the end of the war, the Germans helped Branson earn his second Purple Heart.

"Our column of tanks were going along this little dirt road, and I was in a jeep as forward observer. By this time the Germans knew we were coming. They had set up an 88 mm in the road ahead of us and just started blasting the first tank. The tank caught fire, and the men rolled out in flames." He shook his head at the memory.

Branson jumped off his jeep with his meager first aid kit, knowing it would not be enough.

The second tank in the column had passed Branson's jeep as he was trying to aid the men from the first tank. As the fighting continued, the column began backing up to avoid more disasters. "The second tank, backing up as fast as it could, didn't see my jeep, and crushed it," Branson remembered. "I could see what was going to happen, and I tried to get it out of the way. When I knew I wasn't going to make it, I just rolled out the side." He was unhurt.

As a result of that accident, Branson and three others were left stranded near the front lines. The tank column had already disappeared in the direction from which it had come.

"They aren't going to know there are still people up here," Branson told the others. He agreed to run back to alert the men in the rear. "As soon as I began running, somebody nailed me through the legs. I could hear the bullet go through both legs and into a tire. I still hear the air hissing out of that."

Branson crawled into the nearby ditch, hoping to be swallowed up, and the men with him followed the usual procedure of ripping open his pant legs and opening packets of sulfa to dump on his wounds to help avoid infection. At first they did not even know his second leg was injured.

As dusk approached, so did an American half-track. Seeing the stranded GIs in the ditch, one of the men on the half-track asked, "You men looking for a ride?"

"We thought that was a rather stupid question," Branson remembered, but they assured the half-track man that they were indeed looking for a ride.

"We were so grateful to be rescued by these two guys in the half-track," Branson recalled, "and my one regret is that I never got to appropriately thank those guys."

Years after the war Branson placed a note in his division newsletter explaining the incident, and asked if that scenario fit anyone out there on the half-track because he would personally like to thank them. "I received one response," said Branson, "but from other details he gave me, I knew it wasn't him." Branson wrote back and thanked him for his reply anyway.

Branson was taken to an aid station, then transferred to a hospital in Paris. "This hospital was where they determined if you were fixupable," Branson mused. "If you are, you are fixed up and sent back to the fighting."

It was determined by hospital personnel that Branson's wounds were too serious to return him to battle, and he was sent instead to a hospital in England for further treatment and recuperation.

His last official duties for the military were reading and censoring mail from GIs to their families and loved ones. In the hospital he had to read the letters to determine if some of the information was confidential and cut that information from the document. He explained that it was tear-jerking to read those letters, knowing the GI was minimizing his experience and the suffering he was enduring. "They just didn't want their families to worry," he said.

Branson explained his philosophy that has sustained him all his life. "I just didn't complain about my injuries when I saw how much worse off those other guys were." He spent the last two months of his military career staring at a series of hospital walls.

Two days after Truman and Churchill announced the war had ended in Europe, Branson received an announcement that pleased him just as much. He was going home. The very next day he was carried on a litter to a hospital ship, and began the long, slow trek to his homeland. As the ship sailed into New York harbor, Branson remembered noting that the lights had been turned on again. During the war, the city had been in a blackout period much of the time.

Branson's war wounds still haunted him sixty years later. As a result, he has always had weak legs, and his left foot "doesn't always work right," he said, and he still sometimes had pain resulting from his injuries.

In small, now yellowing, tattered diaries that Branson maintained daily during his wartime experiences, he can pinpoint with accuracy exactly what he was doing on any given day. His poignant memoirs have resulted in a book he has written with the help of his wife, Katherine. He called it *Tender Comrade*.

Milton Buchanan: Nearly Three Years of Continuous Combat

World War II was just over the horizon when Milton (Buck) Buchanan, now a Coleman resident, enlisted for three years in the U.S. Army. It was October 1939, and he was nineteen years old, a year out of Okemos High School, near East Lansing.

Shortly after joining the military, Buchanan was asked where he would like to go. "As far away from home as possible," he said. He had been riding his bicycle nine miles each way to work in a gas station to help support his family. "Jobs were nearly nonexistent," he said. "The $21 per month from the military, plus my meals, clothes and medical benefits looked like a good deal to me."

Little did Buchanan know that the military would take his request seriously, and it would take him to the other side of the world and back within the next six years.

Buchanan was eventually assigned to the 15th Infantry Regiment, 3rd Infantry Division. The 3rd Infantry Division was the most highly decorated division in both World War I and World War II, according to Buchanan.

His regiment had been in China for over thirty years, but war was imminent between China and Japan, and the regiment had just been returned to the States to rejoin the division. Buchanan joined the 15th in Ft. Lewis, Washington. Dwight D. Eisenhower was his regimental commander.

"When war broke out in Europe, Eisenhower was snatched from us and sent overseas," Buchanan said.

Buchanan was soon "snatched" as well. "They were forming a reconnaissance outfit to be sent to North Africa," he stated," and I went with that, transferring out of the 15th Regiment.

"I wanted to be a scout, because a scout is the boss out front," he chuckled. Scouts also made popular targets for enemy troops, because they warned their own troops of the enemy's position. According to other combat veterans, the life expectancy of a scout was measured in minutes.

His experience in North Africa would be the first of five invasions before he would return safely home on American soil.

Buchanan left Ft. Lewis, Washington via truck convoy to Monterey, California. "They dumped us out about fifty miles north

of the Hearst Ranch, and marched us to the ranch," Buchanan remembered.

While there, Buchanan received his first wound, but it was not a war wound. "This rattlesnake was lying out in the sun and I didn't see it. I cut my arm where the bite was, and sucked out the venom myself." Buchanan still carries the scar. But that would not be his last wound of the war.

Days later Buchanan was on a troop train to Norfolk, Virginia, then herded like cattle aboard a troop ship heading for North Africa and the invasion of Casablanca, on the northwest tip of Morocco.

The invasion of Casablanca on 10 November 1942, was the day after Buchanan's twenty-second birthday. "There was so much going on, I didn't realize until a week later I had missed my birthday," he said.

The fighting lasted about two days, according to Buchanan, and then they were trucked north to Rabat, Morocco. They were encamped just outside the sultan's wall.

A few weeks later they were trucked via convoy across the mountains of Algeria and into Tunisia. Tunisia was on the northernmost tip of Africa bordering the Mediterranean Sea.

"While there we got a few licks at Field Marshall Rommel and his troops," Buchanan said. "At night we would go in and blow up their fuel and ammo dumps." Buchanan was on both scouting and combat missions at the time.

Shortly thereafter, his 3rd Infantry Division left for Sicily, a large island off the southwest tip of Italy across a narrow part of the Mediterranean Sea from Tunisia.

He arrived with the 3rd Infantry Division on the beachhead of Sicily on 7 July 1943, aboard amphibious landing craft amidst a barrage of enemy gunfire. As always, he was on point with his radio, informing the men landing behind him as to potential targets.

It was night when his division landed, and some of the men around him thought he had been caught in a bloodbath. "It was dark, and I had been slugging through some crap that I didn't know what it was." Buchanan smiled as he spoke. "As it got daylight, I could see that I had been spooking through a large tomato field. My buddies thought it was blood."

After taking the beachhead, Buchanan's division was assigned to clear a landing field and a tower for C-47s. "Actually, the planes were landing even before the field was secured," related Buchanan. "We were working on the tower when the 47s began landing. Someone had been giving the pilots misinformation, telling them the field was clear to land."

One of the C-47 pilots was a captain Buchanan knew very well—his brother, Bill. "I didn't even know he was in the area," Buchanan stated, indicating his total surprise, "but we were able to have chow together." The two brothers were able to enjoy each other's company for most of one day. Then the C-47s were loaded with troops for Belgium. Buchanan himself, however, was not one of them.

The fighting was fierce as Buchanan's division struggled its way north to Palermo, the capital of Sicily. "The thing that made it tough was the snipers along the way," he said. "A lot of our men got hit."

Once they arrived in Palermo, they boarded a ship heading across the water for the invasion of Italy at Naples. The opposition was as determined to put down its foe as the foe was to reach Naples. The opposition lost the battle.

Buchanan's division landed first on Salerno, where it fought heavy opposition all the way to Naples. Salerno is a seaport in southwest Italy with a population of approximately 85,000.

"We lost a lot of good men on that drive," Buchanan said soberly.

It was just north of Naples where Buchanan earned his first Purple Heart. It was an easy date for him to remember because it was Christmas Day 1942. He was on patrol looking for an enemy radio, and was shot in the right leg by a German soldier who was guarding an antitank gun. "But he got the worst of it," Buchanan said, with understandable satisfaction.

Because of his wound, Buchanan was out of commission for a week and a half at an aide station. Then it was back to the war where he joined his troops heading for Anzio via Monte Cassino.

Moving still further north, they reached a monastery high on a hill, and his division came to a huge wall. "We just couldn't penetrate that wall," Buchanan stated. "Our air force bombed it night and day. There were no civilians there, only the enemy."

By the time the bombing had stopped, the weather had warmed, and the American troops were slogging through mud a foot deep.

The Americans then went around the monastery, moving still north toward Anzio. Anzio was so well fortified that it was nearly impenetrable, according to Buchanan. "We lost over 4,500 men in that battle," Buchanan stated, as he fought a lump in his throat. The invasion of Anzio left an indelible impression on Buchanan. Even his car's license plate now bears the word ANZIO.

Following that horrific battle, Buchanan's division departed Anzio under cover of darkness and fog. Taking a brief break, Buchanan sat down in the pitch darkness. Little known to him, he was sitting under the muzzle of a big enemy gun dug into the mountainside. The gun fired, and Buchanan was knocked unconscious from the concussion. He was deafened for hours following his recovery.

"But the Germans retreated so fast we couldn't keep up with them," Buchanan said. His division then returned to Naples for fresh ammunition, uniforms and weapons. They were to prepare for the invasion of France.

On their way there, however, they unloaded from landing crafts known as LSTs on the island of Corsica, located in the Mediterranean Sea, almost between Italy and France.

"Corsica was nearly a walk-through," Buchanan said. "But we had to make certain there were no enemy troops there, so that when we invaded southern France, we wouldn't be attacked from the rear." They used all the experience they had gained from their previous invasions to take on southern France.

Buchanan's division fought on through the French Riviera on foot, a distance of 1,000 miles. Buchanan and others became lost in the rotation process, and he spent most of three years in a combat situation.

One night as they were approaching Lyon, France, Buchanan's squad was looking for a place to sleep. They hoped for a building of some kind. "Which is really a dumb thing to do," said Buchanan. "You might better stay out in the woods where you can see your enemy."

They found a house with an attached barn, and asked the owner if they might sleep in the barn. The owner, who had been a Ford dealer in France and spoke perfect English, suggested they stay upstairs in the house because there were already German soldiers up there. "No way," said Buchanan, "Not with the enemy up there."

As the Americans began bedding down in the barn, something told Buchanan that this was not a good picture. They were about to sleep in a barn while the enemy was sacked out in comfortable beds in a house only a few feet away.

Buchanan and his squad sneaked into the house, found unused rooms, and made themselves at home.

They also saved this French family from the Nazis in the house. The French did not trust the Germans, and Buchanan and his men freed the French family from a near hostage situation. The French Government awarded Buchanan the Croix de Guerre with Palm. The award is comparable to America's Congressional Medal of Honor.

Going on through to Alsace-Lorraine, Buchanan took shrapnel in his right leg from a German bazooka. He was picked up by a medic jeep and taken to a hospital in Paris. He was picking the shrapnel out of his own leg until he passed out. The next day he was a passenger on a C-47, and flown to a hospital in England where he woke up on a litter.

The war was winding down, and the army thought Buchanan had been beaten up enough by this time. Buchanan was put on a B-17 that happened to be General Eisenhower's personal plane, and flown to Cologne, Germany. On the same plane was his brother Bill, who was on his way home as well. The plane had been in England for repairs, and was returning to Eisenhower. "It was real plush," Buchanan recalled.

His transportation from Germany was aboard the Queen Elizabeth, which had been transformed into a troop ship during the war.

Buchanan was discharged from the army on 9 October 1945, six years and four days after his enlistment.

Less than a month after his discharge, he had a blind date with an Edna Strang from Lansing. Three weeks later they were married. "And we still are," said Buchanan. "Edna is the best thing that ever happened to me."

As recently as May 2002, Buchanan received yet another award from the French government. "The French consulate from Chicago was in East Lansing for the presentation. The award was for the participation in the liberation of France in 1944 and 1945," Buchanan mentioned humbly.

Buchanan retired from the public relations office at Michigan State University in 1984.

Frank Bush Experienced Three Plane Crashes and a UFO

After fifty-six years, Francis (Frank) Bush still pauses, then chokes back the lump in his throat as he relates the story of a World War II mission over Germany that took the life of his best friend. Bush was a 2nd lieutenant in the 8th Air Force, 96th Bomb Group, 337 Squadron, and served as the bombardier on a B-17. The incident took place over Munich, Germany on 25 February 1945, and according to Bush, could have caused an international incident.

It was a cold, wet day at Snetterton Heath Aerodrome in England. The officers went to their briefing in the cold darkness at 3:00 a.m., the other crew members were briefed an hour later. The target was the German High Command at Munich. Bush's Flying Fortress, aptly named *Dinah Mite*, was lead plane for the division, meaning there were up to 1,000 more planes behind it.

Bush said, "Normally, the bombers went in high, with a group of planes called chaff ships out in front, dropping only tinfoil to foul up the German radar." Bush's plane was the lead chaff ship. He added, "This time the planes were going in low, and the chaff ships were carrying some bombs as well."

Bush emptied the bomb bay, while the tinfoil strips continued to fall from the chaff chute. It was then that Bush's plane was hit. The flak hit the radio room and blew it apart, killing the radio operator, Bush's best friend, Robert "Shep" Shepherd. Then flak hit the bomb bay, but Bush wasn't injured. "Why the plane didn't come apart, I don't know," Bush said. "Another burst hit the ball turret, seriously injuring the turret gunner."

The back of the plane was a mess of hanging tubes and cables, according to Bush.

As he remembered it, the front gunner of the Flying Fortress was seriously injured, "Then the controls of the plane were damaged," Bush said. They knew they were going to go down, even though all four engines were still in good running condition. "We threw out everything that wasn't bolted down to make the plane lighter," said Bush. The pilot managed to keep the plane in the air another one hundred miles until they were over Switzerland, about one hundred miles from Munich.

They circled a small town, spotted two bridges they had to miss, then headed for a pasture along the Rhine River.

Bush was standing, bracing himself between the pilot and copilot when the plane hit the ground with a tremendous thud, bounced and skidded to a halt along the Rhine. The right wing tip caught on a boulder and turned the plane ninety degrees. It crashed into a dike next to the river, its nose crushed. Nobody was injured in the crash. They had stopped on Swiss soil, short of the Austrian border by only a few feet. "Thank God for that boulder," related Bush, "or we would have skidded right onto Austrian soil." The Austrians were not known for their hospitality to American troops.

The *Dinah Mite* would never leave the ground again.

Leaving the plane with the copilot, Bush said that it sounded as though they had stepped out into a swarm of bees. "It can't be bees," Bush said to his copilot, "it's February, and the river is frozen over."

The "bees" turned out to be bullets ricocheting off rocks and from the plane itself. The Austrians were firing at them.

After everyone was out of the plane, an Austrian soldier marched them into a small town where the locals slapped them, kicked them and spit upon them. A short time later, members of the Swiss army came to their rescue.

"I guess that if our town had experienced bombs dropping on us from enemy planes for five years, we would have been pretty upset too," Bush remarked, "so we pretty much discounted it."

Thinking back, Bush says he learned the meaning of a premonition that led to the ruin of that day. "The radio operator actually had it, and it was the strangest thing," Bush said reflectively.

He was really totally experienced, and as far as the enlisted men were concerned, they thought he was God. It was his forty-seventh mission.

While we were loading the plane, about four o'clock in the morning, Shep said to me, "Lieutenant, this is going to be a bad one today. If I don't get back, have somebody go talk to my girl-friend, okay?" I just kind of let that go by me, then said, "What was that, Shep?"

Looking seriously at Bush, Shep answered, "If something happens to me today, would you go see Donna when you get out? Or have one of the crew members see her?" Bush remarked that his friend had never talked like that before, and it caught him off guard.

"What are you telling me here, Shep?" asked Bush. The reply was, "This is the day I bite the bullet." Eight hours later Bush's best friend was dead from enemy flack to the neck.

After a lengthy pause, Bush looked up and said, "I still feel it." Another pause. "You know, he only needed three more [missions], and he would have gone home. I never told any of the other crew what he had said to me because I knew it would disturb them."

Four of the nine men on the *Dinah Mite* were either killed or injured. At one point, a crew member drew Bush's attention to blood streaming down his head, but he never knew when or how the injury came.

Bush did not receive the Purple Heart because there was no medical record of his injury even though hospital officials sutured his wound, and his crew members verified its authenticity.

Bush was honorably discharged from the U.S. Air Force as a 1st Lieutenant in September 1945, but that was not the end of his military career or airplane crashes. Five years later he was recalled from the air force reserves to fly during the Korean War in a B-29, but he never flew over Korea.

He was assigned to many parts of the world, serving in the monstrous bomber as an observer, which meant he could navigate, work the radar, or run the bombsight. "I was probably not very proficient in any of the three," he mused.

Bush seemed to have a penchant for plane crashes. Another one occurred while he was in gunnery school for the B-17.

"We were taking off when the communications got screwed up," Bush said. "The copilot raised the landing gear and lowered the flaps, which is just the opposite of what should be done. The plane did a belly landing, and all personnel cleared the craft unharmed, just before it blew up."

Less than a year earlier, Bush, who had dreams of being a pilot himself, was on a routine training flight in a biplane over Bunker Hill Naval Station near Peru, Indiana. On takeoff, a top cylinder exploded directly under the gas tank. "I thought I was going to hit the tower going in," Bush smiled. "I did a wing-over and got it safely on the ground, and got out of there while it was still running because it was still on fire."

Another incident occurred during his tenure with the B-29s, but it didn't result in a crash. Rather, it involved an unidentified flying object. It was early in 1952. The plane was near Mobile, Alabama, flying at 9,000 feet. As they approached the control, they asked for identification from an aircraft near them. There was no response. Control then asked if there were any military planes in the area. "We were the only one, but there was also a commercial craft nearby," stated Bush.

"We were headed west, the commercial plane was headed east. The UFO was between the two of us," Bush went on. "When we picked the object up on our radar, it was also headed east at about five hundred feet below us flying parallel to the commercial plane.

"It was a very black night, and the unidentified craft came up to our altitude. We couldn't see anything except what appeared to be four turbo exhausts. It continued to fly alongside of us, but we couldn't see any identification."

At that point Bush was in the nose of his B-29, and with the use of radar equipment, was taking pictures through the darkness.

"The radar operator was on the master radar control, and reported the object making a thirty-five-degree turn to the right, and was gaining altitude at three times the speed of sound . . . approximately 2,000 miles per hour." The object was never seen again, according to Bush.

"When we landed at Barksdale Field, Louisiana, the intelligence people wanted to interview us. The crew of the commercial airliner was already there. Intelligence told us to keep quiet about the whole incident, and not to even discuss it with the crew," said Bush.

"Two days later we were at Strategic Air Command Headquarters in Nebraska. We were surprised to find the crew of the civilian airliner there also. We were all interrogated by a brigadier general. They confiscated our military cameras and radar film, and again reminded not to discuss this with anyone in any form.

"The best part was that we got all new camera equipment," Bush added, smiling.

When asked how he felt about discussing the incident with this writer, he replied, "That was fifty years ago. What are they going to do?"

It was only two years ago that Bush learned that the U-2 spy plane was being tested in those parts, and they always flew at night.

"Keep in mind," Bush went on, "that this was 1952, ten years before we had one shot down over Russia."

But Bush never heard any more about the identity of the unidentified object in the black skies over Alabama in 1952. He still wonders about it.

Frank Bush and George Marshall: Their Paths Crossed Nearly Sixty Years Ago

When old friends come together they normally reminisce about the good old days and share what they have in common. Francis (Frank) Bush and George Marshall, both of Midland, get together and do the same thing, with one exception—they are not old friends. They are new friends.

Listening in on their conversation was like walking into a time warp. The clock suddenly went back sixty years. "Frank, do you remember the time . . . ?" Marshall would ask. Or Bush would search his memory and ask Marshall, "George, do you remember so and so when he . . . ?" Sometimes laughter engulfed the room as they related some of their antics they prefer not to be publicized.

They were not talking about family and they were not speaking of their high school days. They were talking about a war in which they both fought, side by side, often thirty thousand feet in the air. They would not know each other for another six decades.

On 7 October 2001, the *Midland Daily News* printed the story of Frank Bush and his experiences as a bombardier on a B-17 Superfortress over Europe in World War II. He was the guy who looked down through the bomb sight and selected the precise moment to open the bomb bay doors. Marshall read the story, called Bush and said, "Frank, we need to talk."

Marshall was a ball turret gunner on a B-17 at the same time, over the same air space. He was the guy in the Plexiglas bubble protecting the underbelly of the aircraft with a 50 caliber machine gun. Marshall's story was in the *Midland Daily News* on 19 January 2003.

Over several cups of coffee the two talked, and not necessarily about the "good old days." Some days were very, very bad as their *Daily News* stories attested. But there in Marshall's kitchen, they compared notes on what they had in common. They had more in common than two average school chums who had played four years of high school football together. They were like two offensive guards who played on the same team, but never actually met.

To verify their togetherness experience, both men have the same book, *The Snetterton Falcon*. It resembles a high school yearbook and is a history of the 96th Bomb Group. There is also a picture of Bush's aircraft as it lay on its belly just a few feet from the Austrian border, its props badly bent as it hit the ground. The ball turret was crushed under the weight of the Superfortress.

The two men compared the dates, times and the missions in the book, and concluded they had flown wingtip to wingtip on numerous bombing missions over Germany during 1944. Wingtip to wingtip refers to a distance of three to five feet between the tips of the wings. Marshall logged twenty-five missions, Bush fourteen.

The term is not entirely accurate, however, according to the two veterans. "Sometimes our wingtips would be overlapping," said Marshall. "Flying a very tight formation with dozens of other planes meant we had a more concentrated firepower against German fighters, and they couldn't come in between us," Bush added. One problem with this type of formation, according to the two former aviators, occurred when the planes would encounter turbulent weather. "Our wingtips would actually bump against one another," Marshall stated.

During their original conversation, they learned they were together in Dyerburgh, Tennessee where the flight groups were formed in 1944, and actually flew practice missions together, but not in the same aircraft. They then were sent on the same train to Lincoln, Nebraska for more training, then on to Miles Standish near Boston for shipping out to Liverpool, England. Both Bush and Marshall, along with 5,000 other servicemen, sailed to Liverpool on the USS *Wakefield*. Both were sent on to Stone, Scotland, where they spent Christmas. Marshall left for Snetterton Heath Air Force Base on 3 January, Bush on 5 January. Both were assigned to the 96th bomb group. Still, they never met.

It was soon learned that the bombardier on Marshall's plane, Richard Kasky from Detroit, was in the same training class as Bush, and was Bush's roommate at Midland Air Force Base in Midland, Texas. The two became good friends.

Marshall was assigned to the 413th Squadron while Bush was implanted in the 337th Squadron. The geographical distance between them during that part of the war was less than the width of a city street.

The planes of both men were shot down during the war. Marshall's came down on 15 January 1945 over Augsburg, Germany. Because the plane was so badly shot up, it had to leave the formation, leaving them vulnerable to Nazi fighter planes. One inboard engine had been completely shot away, according to Marshall. "There was just a hole where the engine had been," he said.

Two more engines were soon inoperable, and with only one engine at full power, they could not keep up the speed or altitude to stay with their group. "And as soon as we were out of the flak area, we were attacked by three German 109 fighters," said Marshall. They headed for the English Channel and toward home base. In doing so they flew over the Battle of the Bulge raging just 1,000 feet below them. "We were even getting hit by rifle and hand gun fire, and if we could have bailed out, there were still those enemy fighters around to pick us off," Marshall added.

The pilot of Marshall's plane was finally able to crash land on an English beach, just sixty-five miles from their base. Fortunately there were no casualties on his plane, but as soon as the aircraft came to a halt they fled for their lives because the plane still had a load of fuel and bombs on board. It never did explode as they anticipated it might. They were eventually picked up by friendly troops and returned to their base.

Bush wasn't quite so fortunate. The day his Flying Fortress came down, his best friend was killed by flak. His plane crash landed just a few feet from the hostile Austrian border. As they disembarked from the crippled craft, Austrian ground troops began firing at them. They were miraculously saved by members of the Swiss army and sheltered by the Swiss underground for a week before being returned to their own base.

That was not the only time Bush's aircraft made a crash landing, however. Once was in gunnery school and the crash was due to copilot error. "The copilot raised the landing gear and lowered the flaps on landing, which is just the opposite of what should be done," he said. The crew escaped the disabled plane just before it burst into flames.

While Bush and Marshall shared many experiences, unknown to the other until recently, they have earned the right to enter the time warp of a war in which they fought so long ago. Sometimes new friends are the best of friends.

Harry Clark, Silent Hero

"I am incredibly uncomfortable talking about my Marine Corps Raider career," Harry Clark said as he prefaced our interview. "At the time, a person signed up to do a job to the best of his abilities, and trying to be heroic, well that's bull."

He was a seventeen-year-old high school senior at Lincoln High School in Ferndale. He was on a picnic with his girlfriend, Patti Ann Hutchinson, and four other friends on 7 December 1941. They were listening to the music of Glenn Miller on a battery-powered radio (the leading edge of technology at the time, according to Clark), when an announcer interrupted with the news that Pearl Harbor had been bombed.

"None of us even knew where Pearl Harbor was," Clark said. "And not even the announcer mentioned where it was."

Clark enlisted in the Marine Corps the following spring, but was allowed to stay in school and graduate with his class in June 1942.

After boot camp in San Diego, he volunteered for the 4th Raider Battalion, only to be told he was too little. "I spun the most fabulous yarns to that interviewing major you ever heard," Clark said laughing, including my short career with Golden Gloves boxing. Of course I never told him I had lost every fight," he chuckled. Clark eventually won the debate with the major.

According to Clark, the Raiders considered themselves the most thoroughly trained infantry possible. "None of us expected, realistically, to live through the war. We fought capably as possible, eventually not for Mom, nor apple pie, nor even for the USA, but for each other," he said. "The worst conceivable thing that could happen was not death or even maiming, but that we might fail to measure up to each other."

Raiders were also well armed; they had their choice of submachine guns, antitank guns, knives, and best of all, according to Clark, the 30 caliber Browning automatic rifle.

Completing his Raider training at Camp Pendleton, California, Clark and the 4th Marine Raider Battalion shipped out to the Hebrides, a group of small islands located about halfway between the Fiji Islands and the northern tip of Australia.

As a scout sniper in the battalion intelligence group, Clark went from island to island in the Hebrides, along with a dozen others,

looking for Japanese radio posts. Often the men would launch a small boat in the black of night on a pitching sea, and arrange to be picked up in three or four days.

One such excursion, according to Clark, brought them face to face with cannibals on the island of Malekula. The islanders were already feasting on human flesh.

From the Hebrides, Clark's battalion moved northeast to the Solomon Islands. The fighting was fierce in the Solomons because the Japanese had control of this island chain during 1942 and most of 1943. They had control not only of the islands, but also the sea and air in the area.

"The slot between the islands was constantly contested by American and Japanese navy ships," recalled Clark. "One area off Tulagi and Guadalcanal in the Solomons became known as Iron-Bottom Sound, because so many ships were lost there by both sides."

On the way to Viru Harbor, the Raiders were ambushed three times by Japanese Imperial Marine forces, according to Clark. "These were big men for Japanese; six feet and more tall and in excellent physical condition. They were brave, and determined men who wanted to die for their Emperor," Clark remembered. "We Raiders helped them do just that."

A reporter stated in a story for the *Christian Science Monitor*, that "the trek from Segi Point to Viru Harbor was (in his judgment) the most incredible and exhausting trip made by American military since George Rogers Clark took Vincennes."

Clark continued, "We were in top condition as we traversed the twenty miles of jungle from point to point as the crow flies, and we were totally exhausted. Normally, we could make sixty miles in a day, but because of the terrain the twenty miles seemed a hundred," he said.

From June until August 1943, Clark trudged and fought for his life and for the lives of his fellow Raiders in the jungles of the Solomon Islands.

But Clark did not do all the shooting in the Solomons. He was also shot *at*. A bullet once hit his ring finger, tearing off the cameo ring his mother had given him for graduation. He leaped over a fallen tree and saw the ring only inches from his nose.

"I reached out and put it in my pocket," he remembered. "On our twenty-fifth wedding anniversary my wife had the cameo mounted in a new setting, and I never take it off. Whenever I look at that ring, I think of the two most important ladies in my life."

In that same skirmish, Clark killed several Japanese troops, including some who came charging at him swinging swords.

"In those areas of deep jungle they shot the hell out of us," he said. "Their 90 mm mortars were even knocking the trees down. There were areas almost like fields that had been leveled, then they began with their machine guns. But we were not to be defeated."

Clark did have some remorse for those whose lives he took. After mortally wounding one Japanese officer, Clark went through his pockets, looking for information that might be useful to his battalion. One thing he found was the officer's identification. His name was Ryuki

Yanigahara, and the name and spelling of the name will be embedded in Clark's brain forever. "The thing I learned from that experience was not to know who you have killed," he said. "It gets too personal."

Many years later Clark was an international manager for The Dow Chemical Company, and made a business trip to Japan. "I ran an ad in the Tokyo newspaper stating that I would like to meet with any of the family of the soldier I had killed. I never mentioned why, just that I had some information about their relative," Clark said. "I mentioned in which hotel I was staying, and that I would be there for two weeks. No one responded."

Another experience in the Solomons landed Clark in a hospital in New Zealand. "We were told we were going to attack a Japanese battalion of marines," Clark recalled. "We thought we could take them, but what we didn't know was that it was a heavy weapons regiment." Clark laughed about that later.

Clark was just twenty-five feet from where an enemy mortar landed. "A mortar landing fifteen to twenty feet from a person could shred a man," Clark said. "I was lucky." He bled from his ears and eyes for half an hour, then went back to fighting.

"But we were practically out of ammunition and out of medical supplies, with a lot of wounded we couldn't take care of; and we were essentially out of food, and water was at a premium," remembered Clark. He and his fellow Marines sometimes crawled beyond the front lines to take fish heads and rice from the dead Japanese. This became their only food.

The U.S. Navy tried to bring in food, water and ammunition on Catalinas—small Patrol Bomber Consolidated Aircraft Corporation (PBY) flying boats—but according to Clark, "The Japanese zeros came in out of the clouds and shot up the PBYs."

When he later headed for base camp on Guadalcanal, he had dropped from 148 pounds to just 97 pounds. He had malaria, yellow jaundice, dysentery, thirty-eight ulcers on his left leg, more than fifty ulcers on his right leg (mostly caused by living conditions), and he had a rare, unknown fever. He had not had food for several days.

"That situation was true of almost every one of us, but not with that much weight loss," said Clark. "I was incredibly strong for my size when my weight was over 140, but was incredibly weak when I reached Guadalcanal," he added, "so they sent me to a hospital in New Zealand."

Clark was in the hospital for three weeks when he took it upon himself to go AWOL. "So I went over the hill to Auckland and met a dentist there who fixed his two front teeth that had been chipped off by hitting them on a landing craft in rough water earlier in the war. I also wanted to be with some 'normal' people," Clark admitted.

When the dentist saw Clark's physical condition, he had to admit he was AWOL, and asked that it be kept confidential. He had to explain how he had gotten so run down, and the dentist did his work and kept quiet about it.

He found an old buddy who shared an apartment for three weeks with him in Auckland. "The sharing part was ridiculous," Clark said. "We hadn't been paid for almost a year."

Eventually Clark was sent back to the islands where he once again broke out in sores, and it was concluded that he needed to be in a more temperate climate to survive. Clark reported that the sores on his legs have returned every summer for fifty-eight years until the summer of 2000. He was transported to Oakland Naval Yard Hospital and on to the Navy hospital at Sun Valley, Idaho, where many combat veterans were being sent for medical attention and recuperation.

After a second hospital transfer, Clark requested to return overseas. "I had a horrible guilt complex because I was alive, enjoying life, was looking at white women and so many of my buddies never would," he said, ruefully.

Adding to his frustration was the knowledge that most of his boot camp buddies had been killed trying to get into Tarawa, northeast of the Solomon Islands. "Their fate was caused by a Navy/Marine snafu," Clark remembered. He did not elaborate, as though he really did not want to think about it.

Clark's request was granted, and he was sent to Guam. It was May 1945, and a most dangerous time to be stationed there. Guam had been captured by the 4th Marine Regiment, which had been formed from the Raider Battalion.

On Guam, the marines had a twenty-five percent casualty loss, and an even greater loss from illness, according to Clark.

"I didn't have a death wish," Clark said, but I volunteered for every dangerous assignment that came my way, and came out smelling like a rose. And I just don't know why," he stated glumly. There was a long pause as Clark contemplated what he had just said.

Clark was on Guam when the atom bomb demolished Hiroshima. "I was pleased to hear that news," he remembered. "I would have gone from Corporal to Second Lieutenant if I had led the first platoon to land on the Japanese island of Kyushu. It was a death sentence. I wouldn't have wanted that job for anything."

In an even more serious mood, he adds, "I've never told a stranger [meaning this writer] about all this." I was humbled, and choked back a lump in my throat.

Clark concluded the interview with the following statement, "I left the Marine Corps completely discombobulated. I had knowingly killed several people, and I felt guilty as hell because I had lived through it and so many of my friends didn't."

Jerry Clark Fought in the Battle of the Bulge

The 257th Field Artillery Battalion was formed in January 1943, and included exclusively three hundred men from Michigan, mostly Eastern Michigan. One of those men was Gerald (Jerry) Clark, a Midland County resident for the past fifty-one years.

Continuous and extensive training on various artillery weapons took place at Camp Gordon, Georgia and Camp Forrest, Tennessee. Nearly two years would slip by before the battalion would be sent into one of the fiercest battles of the twentieth century.

In October 1944 the battalion was transported to Weymouth, England for more training, and two months later shipped to a staging area across the English Channel at LaHavre, France. It was Christmas Eve, according to Clark. One of the most historic battles of the war had already begun, and Clark and his battalion were about to be a part of it.

"That night we were told of a German breakthrough which later became known as the Battle of the Bulge," Clark recalled.

Clark's battalion was under the command of General George Patton and his Third Army.

"I can still see Patton, helmeted, standing in his jeep, with his pearl-handled pistols at his belt." Clark smiled at the memory.

The rugged mountains and dense forests of the Ardennes did not dissuade three powerful German armies from trying to break the American line of defense and trap the Allied Forces in Belgium and Luxembourg.

The thinly-spread American line put up fierce opposition from the moment the Germans entered the area. But both sides paid a heavy price for every inch of ground gained. This went on for three days until Allied reinforcements arrived and kept the Germans from reaching their objective.

The fighting continued for another month in the bitter cold and snow. All the Germans accomplished was putting a small bulge in the line—thus, the Battle of the Bulge.

"We were lucky," recalled Clark. "We lost only ten percent of our battalion." Other outfits lost over fifty percent of their men.

The battle took place in the heavily-forested Ardennes region of eastern Belgium and northern Luxembourg. It took place between 16 December 1944 and 25 January 1945. There were 600,000

American men in the battle, which was more than the combined Union and Confederate forces at Gettysburg. In addition, there were 55,000 British troops. On the opposing side were a half-million German soldiers, or the equivalent of twenty-six divisions.

Before it was over, the Americans would have 81,000 casualties, including 19,000 killed. The British lost 200 men, while 100,000 Germans lost their lives or were badly wounded. Both sides lost 800 tanks, and the German air force lost 1,000 aircraft.

Following the fierce fighting at the Bulge, Clark and his battalion spent the next few months traveling behind the advancing infantry, "setting up, firing on targets, moving and firing, moving and firing. I was assigned with my radio truck, along with two others, to travel to the front lines and radio fire directions back to the battalion. In the late stages we entered the city of Bastogne, and mingled with the Battered Bastards of Bastogne. This was a nickname an infantry unit gave itself after being surrounded by the Germans for several days."

One of the early disasters, according to Clark, was having their cook station destroyed by German cannons, and then having to live on C rations for a month. C rations were small boxes of dried food packaged in the States.

"We were deep into German territory when the war ended, and for a brief time, became temporary occupation troops prior to the arrival of those troops who would be assigned that detail. At this time we were in the ancient walled city of Augsburg, not far from Nuremburg, the site of the war trials held at a later date," Clark remembered.

On 22 April 1945, the 257th Field Artillery Battalion was reviewed by the now famous General DeGaulle, presented with four Battalion Stars, and a decoration from DeGaulle himself.

On a cold, wintry day in January 1946, Clark arrived back home in Grand Blanc. The 257th Field Artillery Battalion had been decommissioned.

"But it has always existed in our memories," Clark said with deep feeling.

Clark was a very young man when he experienced the ravages of war. He had just turned eighteen when he first put on a military uniform. "After I got home, I still had to wait a year until I was old enough to buy a beer," he chuckled.

"We are proud survivors even though our grandchildren sometimes ask, 'Which war were you in, Grandpa?'"

Jack Clerc Survived
the Bataan Death March

"It was pretty dull . . . mild compared to what actually happened."

Jack Clerc is referring to the television documentary *Bataan*, an NBC special. It attempted to show the battle of the Allied forces against the Japanese on the Bataan Peninsula in the Philippines during World War II, and the atrocities committed by the Japanese army against American and Filipino soldiers after their capture.

Clerc could also point out errors in the documentary. He should know, for he is a survivor of the infamous Bataan Death March.

Jack Clerc was just twenty-four when he enlisted in the U.S. Air Force in August 1941, and talk of war was still a rumor. Little did he know that eight months later he would be a prisoner of a foreign power, and would spend the following three and a half years as a slave to sadism.

In late December 1941, Clerc's ship, the liner USS *Calvin Coolidge*, docked on the southern shores of the Bataan Peninsula. Another ship was carrying six A-20 dive-bombers in its holds.

"The plan," according to Clerc, "was to get the airplanes to Nickles Field near Manila, assemble them, and assist the ground forces from the air."

But by the time they arrived at Bataan, the fighting was so fierce that all personnel, including the pilots, were issued Springfield rifles and attached to the 31st Infantry Division. The planes never did get assembled.

For two and a half months Clerc's outfit survived on an eighth of its normal food rations. The Japanese had cut off the shipping lanes from Corregidor Island in Manila Bay, and food and ammunition could not reach the near-starving troops. What little ammunition remained was used to shoot birds and small game for food.

On 8 April 1942, Clerc was taken prisoner, and until his release on 21 August 1945, the only battle he fought was for survival—a battle that thousands of American and Allied men lost in the Philippines.

Clerc cannot recall all the horrible incidents that occurred because the fever of malaria blocked many of them from his brain as they happened. But the following ten days are recorded in the history books as the Bataan Death March.

Approximately 60,000 prisoners were corralled by an estimated 200,000 Japanese troops, and were forced to march 120 miles to prison camps along the peninsula. Only 50,000 Americans, Filipinos and other Allied troops made it. The rest died from starvation, disease or mistreatment. Before the war was over, Clerc would drop from 160 pounds to a scrawny, skin-on-bones 87.

"My greatest fear in being captured," Clerc remembered darkly, "was that we had heard that the Japanese didn't take prisoners." For many it would have been better if they had not. They suffered the torture and humiliation only to be killed by a Japanese bullet, bayonet or beating in the end.

"What little food the prisoners had, the Japanese took from us and cut our rations even more," Clerc recalled.

Some literature points out that the Japanese did not realize there were so many American and Allied troops on the peninsula, and they were ill-prepared to feed them all.

Clerc's punishment began the first day when he was struck on the head with a rifle butt for wearing his American combat helmet. Many of the Japanese soldiers at the camp needed no excuse for their brutality.

Walking under the scorching South Pacific sun, water soon became a luxury, as there was little to be had. Whenever the long, slow moving column passed a stream or other body of water, many of the prisoners were shot in the back as they dove for the precious lifesaving liquid.

"Whenever a soldier fell from the ranks from malnutrition or total exhaustion, he immediately received the jab of a bayonet and was left by the roadside," Clerc recalled.

At one point Clerc himself felt he could no longer endure the tormenting sun, and he knew his canteen was empty. As he stumbled and fell, the motivation of knowing what was coming caused him to roll over and get back on his feet. But not before a Japanese bayonet had ripped into one knee.

Some nights the prisoners were forced into wire-enclosed pens already nearly filled with the dead and dying. There was not room for everyone to lie down, and even in their tired and tortured conditions, the new occupants tried to avoid it as squirming maggots covered the ground.

As if harassment from his captors was not enough, Clerc was suffering from an untreated shrapnel wound in one foot that had occurred a few days before his surrender.

Days later, Clerc's unit was marched to a train depot and loaded into boxcars. Breaking into smaller groups, the men were jammed into cars large enough to hold only half as many. The previous occupants had been horses, and the cars had not been cleaned. "In the heat, the stench alone was nearly overpowering," remembered Clerc.

There was no room to sit, and the soldiers were packed so tight some were standing on each other.

Four hours later, the trudging train with its frail cargo reached Camp O'Donnel. Several men had died from suffocation and the unbearable heat beating down on the sides of the steel cars.

Clerc's first thought was of water and rest. There was little of the precious fluid available, but he obtained some in a swap for a package of cigarettes. Clerc then proceeded to find a clump of bushes where he lay down and slept for two days and nights. The throbbing in his shrapnel-torn foot awakened him. He looked down to see it infested with maggots and rot.

Clerc hobbled to a small hut where he knew there were medics. They treated his wound with iodine and bandages they had managed to salvage from the march.

The Japanese, deciding the camp should be enlarged, deployed Clerc and about one hundred others to do the job. They were assigned to dig postholes with sardine cans. But two days later hundreds more prisoners arrived, and once again the living conditions were extremely overcrowded.

At this camp, due to the shortage of food and water, the prisoners were given only two meals per day. The first was a handful of moldy, uncooked rice. The second was a cup of water. What little water they received was carried by the prisoners from a river two miles away.

"But the water was putrid," recalled Clerc, "and a few days later men began dropping like flies from the dysentery-infected river."

During his three-month stay at Camp O'Donnel, nearly 2,000 men died.

On 6 July 1942, those who could still walk trudged northward to Camp Cabanatuan. Those who could not were left to await eternity.

The next fifteen months continued to be a living hell. Although the prisoners received considerably more rice three times daily, water was still scarce, and the living conditions remained crowded. More men died as a result of disease and continued beatings.

It was here that Clerc contacted diphtheria, jaundice, beri beri, scurvy, pellagra, trench mouth, kidney and bowel problems, and eye trouble. In addition, his feet contained jungle rot, and his body continually fought malaria.

Later, Clerc and 599 others were moved to Los Penios Air Strip where they worked for ten months at hard labor to build an airfield for the enemy. Here Clerc received two severe beatings, which left him bruised and bleeding, as well as numerous minor poundings from the hands and rifle butts of his constant tormentors.

Occasionally packages from the American Red Cross arrived, but not always intact. The Japanese soldiers could find excuses to confiscate some of the contents.

"One day when the packages arrived," remembered Clerc, "the Old Gold cigarettes had been removed because they bore an inscription on the back that read, "Our heritage is freedom.'"

Explaining, Clerc continued, "The Japanese, who couldn't read English, thought it to be a vital message from America, and wouldn't allow us to have them. In addition, they took several food items as punishment. So what was meant to be morale boosters ended up being additional harassment."

In July 1944, two hundred of the sick and weak prisoners from the camp were picked for a detail going to Japan. Clerc was among them.

A few days later, an estimated 1,800 starving, beaten and demoralized American men from various prison camps in the Philippines, were lined up at the port area of Manila, waiting to be loaded into the holds of a Japanese cargo vessel.

Before entering the steaming hold, the men were ordered to strip and leave their clothing topside. When Clerc refused to climb down the rope ladder, a bayonet prompted him to jump in on top of his weakened comrades.

"The crowded conditions in the camps and boxcars were a picnic compared to this," Clerc sighed. "Before we were all loaded, men were already dying from suffocation and the constant heat of the blistering sun on the steel deck above us."

The dead remained in the holds for four days until the ship left port and they could be dumped unceremoniously into the South China Sea.

But even with the departure of the dead, the men had to take turns sitting down because of their cramped quarters. For eighteen days and nights their torture continued.

One at a time, the enemy would allow their slaves the privilege of going topside to use the makeshift latrine on the deck. But because of the numbers, it was impossible for everyone to enjoy the luxury of a moment of privacy and fresh air.

Consequently, the holds of the ship soon contained the excrement of hundreds of people, many of them with dysentery.

"One night the ship plowed through a hurricane and the living conditions were indescribable," recalled Clerc.

"The highlight of the trip was the day the Japanese took us up on deck in groups of one hundred, and sprayed us with sea water. I was suffering from pellagra [caused by insufficient vitamin intake that causes the skin to crack] at the time and the salt burned my sensitive skin to the core." He continued, "some of the men were ecstatic, and enjoyed the treat so much that we were all denied our usual ration of a half cup of barley and a half cup of water for one day."

Docking at Mogi on the island of Kyushu, Japan, in the steaming August humidity, the prisoners were fed small portions of rice, and later Clerc was among one hundred to be loaded into train cars once again. But this time they rode in "class." This one had seats. Those fortunate enough to get one, sat semicomfortably for the first time in weeks. Instead of sitting, Clerc crawled under one and slept for twenty-four hours.

The train halted at its destination, and the new arrivals were informed that a truck would carry the severely ill and those unable to walk to their new camp.

Only one truck was waiting to load the sixty-five ill and weak troops. Realizing the vehicle would not hold that many, the captors began beating their prisoners to test the seriousness of their condition.

"I elected to walk to save my already badly pitted hide," Clerc remembered.

Several hours later, Clerc and his remaining buddies arrived at their new home—a small enclosure surrounded by a fifteen-foot tall fence in Tanagawa, near Osaka.

The torture continued, as did the deaths of Americans, along with their everloyal Allied comrades.

The Americans were not allowed to talk with other Americans, and when Clerc was found renewing acquaintances with a former buddy from Bataan, both received the rifle butt routine.

Added to that routine was a new winter sport for the oppressors. In the middle of the night the prisoners were ordered to fall out in formation for a head count.

Shivering in the ankle-deep snow until all troops were accounted for, they were then released to return to the warmth of their beds.

"But if we failed to fall out within the time allotted, we did it until we got it right. Usually it took a number of tries because the seriously ill had to be dragged to the formation by the stronger ones," Clerc continued.

A few days after arriving at Tanagawa, the beleaguered prisoners were informed they would be working at the shipyards to construct a dry dock—a project that would take twenty years.

"We gasped in disbelief," said Clerc, "what little morale we had at the time faded even more."

The senseless brutality, starvation and disease of the American troops and their loyal Allied companions of World War II did not cease until their captors were informed the war was over. It happened on a hot, miserable day in mid-August 1945.

The only thing that kept Clerc going he said, "was the will to live. I decided early on that if only one person survived that living hell, it was going to be me. I also learned how very much the mind controls the body. I found that I could put myself in a trance on notice so that eventually I didn't feel the pain of the beatings."

Christmas has special meaning for Jack Clerc. It was on that day in 1941 that he began the first leg of a journey from Manila to the Bataan Peninsula and into the eye of a living hell.

Following the war, Clerc was confined to a Chicago hospital for nine months, where both his mind and body eventually healed.

A few months later, at the invitation of the U.S. government, he and six others testified at the international war crime trials in Tokyo.

Clerc has never held ill feelings toward the Japanese; not even when he met in the courtroom those who had delivered and carried out orders for the vicious brutality.

"Time heals all wounds," Clerc said philosophically.

Following the year-long trials, Clerc returned to Midland and in 1973, retired from the Saran Plastics Department at The Dow Chemical Company, ending a thirty-seven-year career.

Author's note: After the above story appeared in the Midland Daily News *on 27 December 1982, a copy was sent to Brigadier General Stephen*

M. Mellnik, U.S. Army, Retired. General Mellnik is the author of Philippine
Diary, *which was later turned into a movie that depicted the Bataan Death
March on the screen.*
The following is a copy of the response received from General Mellnik:

Dear Mr. Thomas:

Thank you for your very perceptive and accurate article describing
a Bataan veteran's travail during WWII. It is difficult, if not impossible, for the well-fed American to accept the fact that man's inhu-
manity to man knows no limit. Events in Afghanistan where Soviet
soldiers literally annihilate villages and maim the survivors with
booby-trapped trinkets; events in Cambodia which killed millions
of innocent people; and events in Indo China which caused hundreds of thousands of Vietnamese citizens to take to the sea—these
testify to the fact that the world has not changed since 1941–45.

   And yet, innocent Americans (perhaps we could call them naïve
or ignorant) sign petitions to ban the nuclear weapon, march in
the streets for the same purpose, and applaud equally naïve, ignorant or stupid bishops as they petition the US government to disarm itself and trust the Lord to keep the baddies from doing us
harm.

   Thank you also for your kind comments on *Philippine Diary.* The
book was an attempt to portray what I saw and did during those
exciting and harrowing days.

With kind regards,
Stephen M. Mellnik (signed)
Brig. Gen. US Army, (Ret.)

A Memorable Christmas Day
for Clare Crampton

Clare Crampton was a twenty-year-old working in the paint department at The Dow Chemical Company when the Japanese attacked Pearl Harbor on 7 December 1941.

"Pearl Harbor was a long ways away, and it didn't begin to hit home until the draft began taking some of the local boys," Crampton recalled. It really hit home, however, when his own draft number was picked a year later. After the routine physicals and paperwork at Camp Custer in Battle Creek, he left for Camp Callon, California for his basic training. It was Christmas Day 1942. He was one of the U.S. Army's newest buck privates.

Following three months of basic training, he was transported to Boston and on to New York, where he walked aboard a troop ship headed for North Africa. It was Crampton's first experience on a ship, as well as his first experience in a foreign country. It was here that he began his journey from being a young naïve painter at Dow, to a fighting machine on foreign soil—an experience that took him from his youth to a world that would change forever.

Thirteen days later he saw the port of Oran from the deck of his ship, and witnessed the biggest air raids he was to see in the next three years.

"The Germans bombed our area that night trying to hit U.S. ships, and just about annihilated our outfit," Crampton remembered. "But, fortunately, we were already on shore at what was called, Gobbler's Knob. It was on high ground, and none of us in my bivouac area was hit."

Crampton's antiaircraft artillery outfit was at a disadvantage because much of their guns and equipment had gone down with a ship that had been torpedoed three to four weeks prior. "We were on C rations for three weeks," Crampton chuckled, remembering.

"Hitler had a lot of his SS troopers in North Africa," he recalled. "At the time, they were the best troops, and better trained, of any troops anywhere. One stockade for prisoners of war contained five hundred of them." Crampton and some of his buddies were detailed to transport them by truck across the desert to Tunisia and Algiers.

"I talked to a lot of them, and they could speak English as good as you or I. They had all been to New York or Chicago, or some large U.S. city, learning the language. Some of them had been in various

stockades, and some were even transferred to a stockade near Freeland Airport [near Midland]. They were assigned to work for some of the farmers in the Freeland area."

While in Africa, Crampton and his men began preparations for the invasion of Sicily, an island off the southwestern tip of Italy, with an area of less than 10,000 square miles, and a population of just over four million, according to the 1943 edition of Webster's New World Dictionary.

They set their guns up in the chief city of Palermo, and waited for what turned out to be the worst air raid of their military careers.

"The Germans must have been following us, because that night their planes first dropped flares, then they strafed us, then dropped their bombs.

"We opened up with our big guns, and fired for an hour and ten minutes straight, putting up a barrage for our ships in the harbor." At this point in the interview, Crampton smiled and said, "I may be getting carried away here." Encouraged to do so, he went on.

"Anyway, the German planes first dropped flares that lit up the ground brighter than it is in this room, then they would come back and strafe, then they would come back and bomb their targets. That was us!

"That night our big guns got so hot you could barely put your hands on them. But we brought down two planes, and crippled another that caused it to hit a mountain near Palermo with a full load of bombs. The next morning we saw the hole in the mountainside, and you could bury a whole house in there."

The next morning Crampton's artillery outfit was visited by some brass almost as big as the president himself.

"Old Blood and Guts [General George Patton] came by the next morning, shook our hands, and asked questions about what happened the night before."

Crampton also verified some of the things in the history books about Patton. "Just a couple miles down the road is where Patton slapped a soldier who told Patton he didn't want to fight anymore. It caused quite a stir in the press at the time. But I had a chance to meet him, and he was tough, one of the toughest commands I was ever in."

Crampton had the opportunity to evaluate many commanders. During his tenure in the military, he moved from the 3rd Army to the 5th Army to the 7th Army.

The fighting at Palermo lasted approximately two months, then preparation began for the invasion of Italy itself.

"Looking across the channel, we could almost see Italy on a clear day, so we took our 90 mm guns up the coast to Sicily, and fired across the water to soften up the German ground troops so we could land there. Our guns would fire six miles up and twelve miles down range."

About two weeks later, the invasion of Italy began in earnest. "It was the spring of 1943 when we crossed into Italy near Anzio, and the Germans plastered us," Crampton remembered.

Going up through Italy was a hard ordeal. The weather was bad. It was cold, snowing, sleeting and raining. But we got up around Naples, set our guns up, then we had another round of air raids. The German aircraft just wouldn't let up.

When we dug in, we were blasting holes with dynamite for our gun emplacements, and it got out of hand. Some dynamite caps got thrown in a fire, and I got some in the face. Fortunately, it didn't break anything, but they wanted to give me the Purple Heart. I just told them to forget it. Maybe if I had gotten hit by the enemy, it would have been different. But I did go to the medics. They laid me out on the ground, and took pieces out of my face with a knife.

He could chuckle about it later.

From Anzio, Crampton and his men were transported to the island of Corsica on landing craft. There they set up their guns to protect the LSTs at night while they would patrol the waters between Corsica and Italy, looking for submarines. "We had radar and big antiaircraft guns, and would fire at anything that came over that stretch of water."

As the war heated up in other parts of Europe, Crampton and his outfit were sent into France by way of Marseilles, a seaport in the southeastern section. They were soon moving their equipment to the front lines where they helped quell the fighting there.

They then moved northward into Austria and Germany.

While in Austria, Crampton was driving a canvas covered truck through the streets in one city, when a German sniper shot through the top of the truck. He noticed that the shot was fired from a church steeple. He stopped the truck, and with a couple of other volunteers, got the sniper. "That was the closest I ever got to hand-to-hand combat. It was a weird feeling. Going in we just didn't know how that was going to come out."

Moving through Austria, Crampton and his men went up through one of the winding roads to the Eagle's Nest, the mountain hideout of Hitler. "When we arrived, smoke from our bombs was still in the area, and there was still food on one of the large tables," he remembered.

For months, Crampton slept in pup tents, so he was no stranger to the wet and cold of the out-of-doors. This included the miserable weather during the Battle of the Bulge in Europe, of which he was a part.

During the Bulge, Crampton says that General Patton was

push, push, push. We'd move up a ways, they would shell us, and we would bog down. We might move a quarter mile a day.

We couldn't get much air support because the weather was so bad our planes couldn't get in there. After the weather broke, the air force came in and things moved along a lot faster.

During the Battle of the Bulge you just tried to stay alive, get enough food to eat, and try to keep warm. I still don't know how I got through all that, but I'm here today to tell about it.

Crampton went on with more sadness, talking about the war Hitler had created.

As we were approaching Munich, I went on ahead to scout the area, and came upon the concentration camp at Dachau. I helped open the gates to let the prisoners out. I never saw such awful looking people in my life. They were dressed in rags, and were just skin and bones.

We gave them all the food, candy bars and cigarettes we had, and they came flocking out of there, not knowing even which way to go home.

It has always bothered me since, especially seeing the ovens where the Jewish people were put to death. I couldn't even eat for a few days, but I'm glad to say I helped open the gates at Dachau.

A glow came into Crampton's eyes and he appeared to suppress a lump in his throat as he shared his memories of Dachau.

"It's only been the last few years that I could talk about this," he said, staring at the floor. "It's bothered me that much."

Crampton was discharged from the military in November 1945, and was awarded citations for six major battles in World War II. After nearly sixty years, he still picks out small fragments of metal that keep coming to the surface of his legs, reminders of a terrible war in which he once fought.

Henry DeGraw's Ships Kept Sinking

Many World War II sailors did not survive sinking ships. Henry DeGraw of Midland survived four. The last one nearly took his life, and could have left him an invalid for a lifetime.

On his twenty-first birthday, 25 April 1941, DeGraw enlisted in the U.S. Navy. It was eight months before Pearl Harbor.

After taking his basic naval training at Great Lakes Training Center in Chicago, and Little Creek, Virginia for specialist training and gunnery school, the young recruit was assigned to a transport ship in Baltimore, Maryland. From there they sailed on to New York, Nova Scotia, Iceland, and finally Archangel, Russia.

On the third day out of Iceland, DeGraw's convoy came under fire. Less than two weeks later, an enemy torpedo sank his ship.

For fourteen hours, DeGraw and seven other crewmen bobbed along on a barrel raft in twenty-seven-degree water. A minesweeper eventually picked up DeGraw and his men.

"A minesweeper is a very small ship, without enough room for eight extra men, so they transferred us to an English cruiser, the HMS *Cecilia*," DeGraw recalled. "That was no small task in twelve to fifteen foot waves in the cold North Atlantic.

"The only heat on the ship was in the officers' quarters, so they put us in there to thaw out," he added. "After we thawed out, we helped man the guns on the English cruiser."

"On the way to Russia, we lost three ships I was on," DeGraw said, almost with amazement. "I kept moving from one sunken ship to another.

"But we shot down a number of enemy planes with my gunnery crew, and sank one submarine," DeGraw went on. "We also lost forty out of seventy ships, plus all the cargo." In all that, DeGraw remained unharmed.

He was not so fortunate on another voyage, however. He boarded an American cruiser in Archangel, sailed for Scotland while being buffeted by twenty-five-foot swells, and six weeks later was on a convoy to North Africa.

In a skirmish near North Africa, DeGraw was wounded by shrapnel in both legs, and returned to New York.

After recuperating for two to three weeks, he was assigned to a refrigerator supply ship which anchored at Charleston, Key West, New Orleans, Cuba, and on through the Panama Canal, arriving in

Brisbane, Australia in late June 1944. On their trip halfway around
the world, his crew sank two two-man Japanese submarines.

After harboring in Sidney, Australia for six weeks, they took on
additional weapons, and headed for Fort Moresby, New Guinea.
Eventually they sailed between New Guinea and Australia into the
Coral Sea Battle just as it was winding down, again without incident
to DeGraw.

DeGraw volunteered for undercover surveillance on landing
barges, and helped set up guns along the shores of New Guinea.

"A Japanese radio sending station was causing a lot of problems
for our people," he remembered, "and we didn't know where it was
located." DeGraw was among sixty men to help find the source of

the radio signal. They theorized it was about forty-five miles inland, and it took three days to find it.

Their assumption proved correct. "It was located at a Japanese hospital with about two hundred patients, along with fifteen to twenty doctors, plus sixty people at their radio sending station. Our orders were to find, destroy, and return," DeGraw explained. "Even the nurses came out with a hand grenade in each hand ready to throw them, and they were stark naked. We left nothing standing of the facilities, or anyone alive. But we did lose one man in the operation."

Going back to Buena Harbor, New Guinea to land troops and deliver nitro with a ten-man crew, they found thousands of Japanese bodies floating in the Harbor; the result of a battle known as the River of Blood.

"While delivering troops to Finchaven, New Guinea, our barge took a direct hit by a Japanese aerial bomb," DeGraw continued.

"I had a .45 caliber Thompson machine gun strapped to my back, which saved my life," DeGraw said somberly. "As I was blown up from the ship, unconscious, I came back down over the gunwale, the gun catching on the side. Without that happening, injured and unconscious, I would have drowned. I was later told they picked me up with a helicopter, and with a hook on a line attached to my ammunition belt, they lifted me up. I woke up two days later in Australia."

The incident mangled a number of vertebrae in his upper back and tore four ribs from his spine. The barge sunk, and he never saw the rest of his crew again.

"But they sent my broken-down machine gun to me, and someone stole it before I could add it to my war souvenirs." He smiled and chuckled about that.

Three weeks later DeGraw was flown to a hospital in Oakland, California, then to recuperation camp at Yosemite Park in California.

From December 1943 until May 1944, DeGraw never took a step.

"My parents were notified that I might never walk again, but thanks to doctors who tried new therapy, I recovered," DeGraw said gratefully. (He later worked in the oil fields in Michigan, Texas, Arkansas and New Mexico, and eventually formed his own excavating company called Midway Construction. To this day he walks and exercises without any aids.)

DeGraw was returned to limited duty at Treasure Island, off the California coast, where he was a guard over prisoners and worked in ship's service, an operation much like an army or air force post exchange. Still an avid volunteer, DeGraw had his duffel bag packed and waited to be shipped overseas once again. "They never called my name," he said philosophically.

DeGraw's brother, Everett, was in five island invasions, including Leyte, and was on Iwo Jima when the American flag was raised at Mt. Suribachi. He survived the war without injuries.

Close Calls Became a Way of Life
for Garold Dice

The Citation from 80ᵗʰ Infantry Division Headquarters reads, in part,

> A Bronze Star Medal is awarded to Sgt. Garold E. Dice . . . Field
> Artillery, Army of the United States, for meritorious service in
> France during the period 25 September to 1 December 1944 . . .
> against an enemy of the United States. During [that period] Sgt.
> Dice distinguished himself in performing his duties as Company
> Reconnaissance Sergeant in a superior manner. The outstanding
> skill, tireless efforts and sincere devotion to duty displayed by Sgt.
> Dice reflect great credit upon himself and the armed forces of the
> United States.

The *Midland Daily News* also reported the news of this citation on 7
September 1945.

At eighty-five, Dice, a Midland native, displayed in a plastic case
at least a dozen medals he earned in the European theater of operations during World War II. His aging memory did not allow him to
even remember what all the medals were for, but it was not his intent
to be a hero when he went to war.

When he joined the National Guard at twenty-three, he was
already an old man by military standards. Most of his comrades were
still in their teens. But war was raging in Europe, and Uncle Sam
called him to active duty in April 1941, eight months before Pearl
Harbor.

After three years of extensive training, in myriad military posts
in the States, he finally landed on foreign soil on 11 August 1944,
and would spend the next 265 consecutive days in combat. He had
spent much of his training in the 808ᵗʰ Tank Destroyer Battalion
Headquarters as a reconnaissance sergeant. He also learned to fire the
90 mm gun on the tank destroyer, then a powerful, high-tech instrument of war. A tank destroyer has a medium tank chassis with an
open turret.

When he arrived in Dorchester, England, he was assigned to
General Patton's Third Army, and two weeks later set sail in an LST
landing craft for the short trek across the English Channel. Their destination was Utah Beach, on the western shores of France. The following day, they arrived at a relatively calm beachhead.

"We were supposed to have been in the invasion itself," said the soft-spoken Dice, "but there weren't enough boats to get us all there." Consequently, Dice's 808th Tank Destroyer Battalion arrived on the beach after the major battle, which took place on 6 June 1944.

"The beach was pretty much cleared by the time we got there," Dice said, "except for some snipers."

But it was there that Dice first heard the guns of war being used in actual combat. Prior to this it had been all practice.

"It was our own 155 mm artillery off in the distance," remembers Dice. "They really got our attention, and they fired all night long."

It was also there that Dice saw his first dead German, and his first dead American. "That really made us realize what we were there for," he said thoughtfully.

"Fortunately we didn't have time to dwell on it." Later, he explained, he saw a lot more dead Americans, some of whom were his own buddies.

Staff Sergeant Dice was put in charge of twelve tank destroyers, and had to know at all times exactly where each one was located in the field in order to make them most effective. As reconnaissance sergeant, one job he had was to keep fuel flowing to the monster machines. Because of their size and weight, "they used two gallons to the mile," Dice said. Sometimes he would have to hop in a fuel truck in the middle of the night to rescue one of his destroyers. "This was sometimes difficult because we weren't allowed to use our headlights, and any road sign we came across was written in a foreign language. I still don't know how, but we always found them."

One night Dice was called upon to take medics to an area where a group of engineers were carrying land mines across a creek to put them in place for the enemy. Something had set off one of the mines, blowing up three trucks and killing thirty-eight Americans.

There was a lengthy pause in the conversation as Dice contemplated where to go from there.

He explained that the 90 mm guns on the tank destroyers were similar to a 30 caliber rifle. They both fired with the same velocity. But the similarity ends there. The shell on the 90 mm is two and a half feet long, and three and a half inches across at its base, according to Dice, but the shell is expelled from its muzzle for a distance of six to eight miles.

In his advanced years, Dice did not necessarily remember everything in chronological order, but he could delve deeply into his memory, and knew what happened to him and to those for whom he was responsible. Aiding him were some snapshots and military papers he brought back, reminding him of a horrible war in which he once fought.

Like all other men in a combat zone, Dice had his share of close calls. One experience he recalled included going out by jeep one day to find new gun positions. As they followed vehicle tracks in the dirt road and rounded a curve, one of the jeeps hit a land mine, killed the platoon sergeant and seriously wounded another man. Dice paused, as if sobered by the words that were to come. "The sergeant was expecting a letter any day about the birth of his first child.

"We had received information from the engineers that the mines had all been cleared from the area, but we soon found out differently, and it was too late," said Dice glumly. Dice was approximately three hundred feet from the jeep that hit the mine.

Dice was frequently in situations where rifle bullets were ricocheting all about him. One time as Dice and his outfit were nearing the Austrian border, they encountered a heavy barrage of fire by Austrian and German soldiers. When the latter realized they were outmanned and outgunned, they blew up their own guns. They did not mind being captured, but they did not want the Americans using their guns.

Dice remembered standing behind the kitchen truck at the Battle of the Bulge, "waiting for my pancakes," he chuckled, when a piece of shrapnel whizzed over his left shoulder, hit the truck, and ricocheted past his right shoulder. It happened in an instant, with no time to duck.

The list of close calls for Dice goes on. He remembered standing in an archway—all that remained of a demolished building in one of the dozens of villages he fought through, when an inner voice told him to leave that position. Before he could even cross the street, an enemy artillery shell hit the archway. "It was a dud," he hastened to say, "but if I had stayed there, I wouldn't be talking about it today."

Dice was an unwilling witness to the destruction of one of his own tank destroyers when it took a direct hit from a German 88 mm gun. "The shell hit the open hatch, and with all the fuel and the oil on board it turned it into a blast furnace," Dice remembered with great sadness. No one on the destroyer survived. The four men aboard were all his friends.

During the 265 days Dice was in combat, his battalion walked, rode, crawled and fought through 59 different cities and towns, and traveled the distance from Midland to southern Florida.

Crossing the Danube on pontoons strapped together between Germany and Austria on 26 April 1945, Dice and the 808th Tank Destroyer Battalion prepared for what was to be the last major battle on European soil. It was the battle to capture Regensberg, Germany.

Victory was relatively easy for the destroyer battalion. The German troops were beginning to show an eagerness to end the war. As Dice's battalion would enter a city, German civilians as well as German soldiers would applaud the American troops.

Even four German officers gladly surrendered their command of seventy men to the American troops. When one of the Germans gave a Hitler salute to the American command, his own superior officer ordered him to salute again, American Army style. Then the men were ordered to have their bolts removed from their weapons and placed on a table. This accomplished, the senior German officer ordered the surrender of all his manned outposts.

It was not an uncommon sight to witness small German groups of soldiers walking the streets, looking for someone to surrender to. They had simply lost the will to fight, according to Dice.

Dice also got firsthand knowledge of the environment of the POW camps in Europe. "One day Generals Eisenhower, Patton and Bradley were all there to watch as the prisoners demonstrated how they were tortured by the Nazi sadists operating the camp." Dice has a yellowed newspaper clipping from the *Army Times,* dated 5 May 1945 to substantiate his statement.

A memo from the 808th Tank Destroyer Battalion from Austria, dated 14 May 1945 reported statistics that had made Dice's unit so vital to the war in Europe. It included a list of sixty-five enemy vehicles destroyed and other equipment annihilated, from bazookas to boats to machine guns, and a radio station. The memo went on to mention the capture of 3,664 German prisoners.

Dice returned to American soil exactly one year from the day he left. He enjoyed a thirty-day furlough at home and was scheduled to go to Louisiana for jungle training in preparation for the invasion of Japan. Fortunately, that was not necessary. While he was home, the war ended when the second mushroom cloud rose out of the heart of Nagasaki. The bomb killed tens of thousands of Japanese, along with the will of that warring nation to fight any longer. The atom bomb that had exploded over Hiroshima a few days prior had already killed 100,000 people.

"I had enough points to get out of the army," Dice stated, "But my brothers, Eugene and Robert were still in the service, so I stayed."

Many years after the war, Dice lost one of his good army buddies. It was Louis L'Amour, the author of dozens of best sellers, whose books are still on bookstore shelves. "We enjoyed his verbal stories even then," Dice remembered.

Dice received his honorable discharge a month after the end of the war.

He married Eleanor Gay on 30 October 1942, a year and a half after his regular tour of duty began. Eleanor was deputy county treasurer for Midland County at the time.

Ted Doan: From Failure to Success With a War in Between

With a threat from his fraternity president saying, "You guys are really getting in trouble, and you are all going to flunk out," young Herbert (Ted) Doan and a few of his friends left Cornell University, and joined the U.S. Army Air Corps (later named U.S. Air Force). It was fall of 1942, and World War II was heating up.

"A half-dozen of us volunteered to be pilots. That was stupidity on my part," Doan said, shaking his head. He had always suffered from astigmatism that left him with less than 20/20 vision, and he could not pass the physical for pilot training. But additional mental and aptitude tests told him he had other talents the corps could use. He was sent to Grand Rapids to become a weather technician.

Following the training he was assigned to the 17th Weather Squadron, and sent to New Jersey for transfer to New Caledonia in the South Pacific with 2,500 other troops on one ship. New Caledonia is between eastern Australia and the Fiji Islands.

While running a zigzag pattern to avoid submarines, his ship roared through a typhoon that left nearly everyone except Doan violently ill. "With that many people being seasick, you can imagine the stench on the ship. The ship was a complete mess as all the latrines became plugged up," he chuckled.

Passing through the Panama Canal on Christmas Day, the ship would take forty-five days to travel from New Jersey to its destination. During the next two years Doan would have experience on twenty different islands in the South Pacific.

By the time his ship reached New Caledonia, they were into another typhoon, and had to wait until it blew itself out. But Doan's first real assignment came on the New Hebrides Islands, located between New Caledonia and Guadalcanal. His job was installing and repairing equipment. Doan compares it to radio equipment. Lacking today's sophisticated equipment, it was difficult to get the machinery running and to keep it running, according to Doan.

Doan tested his equipment by sending up a balloon attached to a box containing instruments for recording temperature, air pressure, altitude and humidity. Later the information would be relayed to a machine on the ground. The weather forecasters would then plot the information on a map, and predict where storms were likely to hit so Allied aircraft could avoid them.

After several weeks in the New Hebrides, he was sent to Bougainville in the Solomon Islands. "This was the closest I ever came to actual combat," claimed Doan, but it was not the closest he ever came to a harrowing experience.

"At that time the Americans held only one percent of the island, the Japanese the other ninety-nine percent," Doan declared. "All we had was an airstrip, and that was enough.

"Most of the time the Japanese were just living off the land, with very little food supplies getting through to them. What little ammunition they had they would use at night. They had howitzers, and would lob shells on our tent area. It was as though they could do a lot of damage, but it was mostly for harassment," related Doan.

One night, when the bombardment began, Doan rolled out of bed onto the ground and into a temporary bomb shelter they had dug into the ground and covered with coconut logs.

When he returned to his tent he discovered a hole in his mosquito netting covering his bunk. "I found the shrapnel that had gone through there, and it was a good eight inches long, three inches wide, and real jagged." Had he stayed in his bunk, that chunk of steel could have ripped through Doan's body as easily as it did his mosquito netting.

His next assignment was to repair weather equipment in the Fiji Islands, and then on to radar school in Hawaii.

"Radar was pretty secret stuff back then," recalled Doan, "The school was behind barbed wire fencing. It was at Scoffield Barracks, where the war began in 1941."

Doan remembered the school dates to be in December 1944 and January 1945. It was the only opportunity he had had to call home since he had been in the military.

"I called to wish my family a Merry Christmas," he said, "and learned that my brother-in-law, Ray Rode, had been killed in Belgium just after D day."

After radar school, Doan was assigned to the 21st Bomber Command, which was under General Curtis Lemay's jurisdiction.

One of Sergeant Doan's first jobs was to fly in a B-29 from the Kwajalein Islands on an eighteen-hour mission over the Sea of Japan, and throw parachuted boxes of weather instruments out of the plane at over 30,000 feet. Instruments on the plane would then interpret the information.

"That gave us a weather station over Japan," explained Doan. "It became a substitute for a ground based weather station. This information was important to the B-29s that would eventually bomb Japan."

One of the problems in releasing the boxes, according to Doan, was that the area of the plane from which they had to be released was not pressurized. Bundled in every piece of clothing he could get on, he would be releasing them in minus fifty degree temperatures.

"I was working on a system that would release these boxes automatically," Doan remembered "and I was preparing a patent for the machine to do this. But the war ended, thus ending the need for that kind of equipment.

"I had the idea that every plane in the United States would someday be throwing these things out to check the weather, but new technology overcame the idea."

Doan's war heroes in the South Pacific were those who fought trying to win Iwo Jima.

"The idea of taking that useless bit of landscape was ridiculous," he said forcefully, "and cost up to 5,000 American lives. But it was a bit of landscape that saved many more," including his own.

"Iwo Jima is halfway between Guam and Tokyo, and any crippled plane that couldn't make it all the way back to Guam was saved by that island when they could land there on the way back to their base."

On one of Doan's flights back from Japan, the oil pressure in the engines began to drop. Two of the four engines stopped. "That's pretty bad, and you can limp along for a long way on two engines. Then the third engine started to go, so we all put on our parachutes, and the captain is talking to us, saying we are either going to bail out or ditch the airplane.

"There's a funny thing about being twenty-one or twenty-two," Doan smiled. "It wasn't particularly frightening, and I don't know why that is, but if you had any sense at all, you would be scared to death. I think one of the reasons young people are useful in war is that they think they are immortal. So anyway, I don't look back and think of it as a frightening experience."

His B-29 limped into Iwo Jima, and by the time it landed there was no power coming from the engines at all.

"So I was one of the guys who was saved by the heroism of people like Lovell Sovereen." Sovereen's story is also told in this book.

Because of Doan's specialty in installing and repairing weather equipment, he was frequently sent by himself from island to island in the South Pacific.

"You get to be quite entrepreneurial," Doan said proudly. "You can do all kinds of things when you roam around by yourself. So I would get good navy food, and I got a mattress.

"I had to fix a weather station on a ship in Saipan or Guam, and would say to the guy, 'I'm going to fix your equipment, but I want a mattress.' It was a trading economy. If you wanted something, and you had a service to offer, you could always trade something."

It worked for Doan, and he received a letter signed by Admiral Chester W. Nimitz that addressed the mattress situation. "Of course, the guy who gave it to me was a chief petty officer, and he just faked the signature." Doan later had the letter framed, and kept it for many years. "Sometimes it was a lot of fun and games," stated Doan. Everyone hides their apprehensions in their own way.

The war ended for the United States in August 1945, but Doan's service didn't end until December that year.

"Coming home, the Golden Gate Bridge was the most marvelous sight I had ever seen," Doan remembered with emotion.

Herbert (Ted) Doan used his ingenuity throughout his career, from his return to Cornell to his presidency of The Dow Chemical Company.

Michael Donahue Flew in Thirty Missions Over Europe

"Now that I am in the autumn of my life, . . . I have time now to remember and recall things that happened in the past," related Michael Donahue, a retired Midland dentist. "There are occasions when I become a little nostalgic and I hark back to the days of my youth in the airfields of East Anglia, located north of London, in Merry Old England."

Those were Donahue's words in an essay he wrote for the *2nd Division Air Journal* in 1982 titled, "Moment of Glory."

"Before I grow too old to remember," he goes on, "or I go to the big air base in the sky, I would like to tell about some of the experiences I had when I flew as a radio operator gunner on a B-24 heavy bomber during World War II."

Donahue was just eighteen in March of 1943 in the middle of World War II, when he was drafted into the U.S. Army Air Corps. After training as a radio operator and gunner, he was assigned to the 93rd Bomb Group, 409th Squadron. It joined with England's Royal Air Force, and engaged in an aerial war with the Axis powers in a B-24 Liberator.

In his essay Donahue said it was the aim of these forces to defeat the German war machine by destroying industrial and strategic targets with day and nighttime bombing raids.

"This kind of air war was entirely new, and never before in the history of aerial warfare had a battle been fought like this," he wrote.

On 12 July 1944, Donahue and his crew were awakened at 2:00 a.m. to fly their sixth mission of the war.

"There were twelve enlisted men, or two flight crews, that lived together in a Nissen hut," said Donahue. "The turnover of the men that occupied half of our hut was so frequent that we really didn't have the time to make friends or to get to know them better.

"As time passed and I became a seasoned combat veteran, I realized it was not a good idea to make too many close friends," he continued.

Breakfast was at 2:30 a.m. on this morning, and Donahue and the crews entered the briefing room an hour later.

They soon learned their target for the day was to be Munich, Germany. "They told us that flak would be heavy both coming and going," Donahue stated, "and that there would be 1,200 antiaircraft guns surrounding the target area." All of them would be aimed at the thirty Liberators. They would, however, have P-51 and P-38 fighter planes as escorts. They would also have the company of German fighter planes, which would be pursued and shot down by the more experienced American pilots.

The load was to be 2,700 gallons of gasoline and 5,000 pounds of bombs. The length of the mission was to be ten hours, six of it on oxygen.

"I feared takeoffs," Donahue stated, "because of the full tanks of gas and the heavy bomb load. Any accidental jarring of an arming device or a faulty fuse on a bomb could cause a horrific explosion."

Flying at 30,000 feet, it can be seventy degrees below zero, according to Donahue. The airmen clothed themselves with all the cold weather apparel the military could issue. "Heaters on military aircraft were nonexistent," he recalled.

In the early morning hours, a personnel truck took Donahue and his crew members to their plane. It was a B-24J, call letters 578R, and its name was *Return Engagement*.

"At 9:15 a.m. we reached the French coast . . . and the formation starts to climb to an altitude of 30,000 feet. It was astonishing how the hours spent at high altitude could sap a man's strength.

"The reasons for this are many," Donahue explained. "You are breathing for hours through an oxygen mask, below zero cold, dehydrated, feeling the jarring impact of enemy shells and bullets, and watching your best friends in the next B-24 trapped in their burning plane, unable to get out."

By 10:30 a.m. they were over Germany and by noon taking flak from ground fire. The bomb bay doors opened amid the flak bursts.

"The noise you hear on a bomb run is loud and frightening," remembered Donahue. "First you are aware of the whine of the plane's engines as they strain under the heavy load. Then you hear the rush of wind as it whistles through the open doors. Outside, the exploding shells slam against the side of the plane.

"It was my job to hold the doors open with the manual handle so they don't close. Waist gunners are throwing out chaff, a tinsel-like material used to foul up the enemy radar. As I was watching the glittering tin foil fall to earth, a piece of metal [flak] about the size of my thumb ricocheted around the bombs in the bomb bay, and came to rest on the catwalk before me.

"Although it was a close call, there was really no cause for alarm because when I picked up the shell fragment from the catwalk, I could plainly see that my name was not on it." Nearly sixty years later, Donahue could smile about that.

Donahue's plane survived that mission without incident, but others in his squadron were not so lucky. He mentions a plane on his left wing that received a direct hit and went down. There were no parachutes seen. Two other Liberators were trailing smoke and falling behind the formation, making them vulnerable to enemy attack.

Donahue can relate to those planes in their vulnerable situation. On his fifteenth mission his plane was pretty badly shot up, and it had lost one engine. It could not be feathered due to the loss of oil pressure, so it just windmilled.

"The slow-turning prop had so much drag on the plane that we lost speed and altitude. We had to drop out of the formation," remembered Donahue.

Alone over enemy territory, the crippled plane was a sitting duck. "It was then that a beautiful P-47 Thunderbolt fighter appeared out of the blue sky and flew real close to our right wing," Donahue reflected. "He followed us all the way to the coast of Holland, then dipped his wings, peeled off and was gone. I think about that little brother, hope he survived the war, and is living somewhere in peace."

All of Donahue's missions were not dropping bombs and fearing enemy planes and flak, however. One in particular, he loved to relate.

One beautiful day in September 1944, he and his crew were in a Liberator heading for an airfield about two hundred miles from their base to pick up the entire Glenn Miller Air Force Band, and return it to the airfield for a performance that evening.

"The members of the band and all their instruments were put aboard four waiting B-24 bombers," said Donahue, then added, "The members of the band sat where they could, some on the flight deck, others huddled in the tail section. The plane wasn't designed for passengers."

On the return trip to base, the four bombers flew at top speed in a tight formation, and at tree top level. "It was the wildest, and roughest ride I had ever had in a B-24. The band was scared to death and so was I, even though I had completed thirteen missions at the time," Donahue recalled.

"I was standing at the waist window, watching the pilot of the next plane sock his wing tip into our waist window, when a member of the band staggered up to me and yelled into my ear, 'How the hell do you stand this?' I believe his name was Johnny Desmond, the lead singer of the band." Donahue and his crew members had front row seats for the performance that night. "I think they felt sorry for us," smiled Donahue.

The big band performed in one of the huge airplane hangers on the base. "I heard the popular and well-known arrangements of the Glenn Miller Band, songs like 'Serenade in Blue,' 'String of Pearls,' and 'Little Brown Jug.' It was a thrilling performance and an event I will cherish the rest of my life," said Donahue smiling.

Donahue's thirtieth and final mission, also a successful one, was on 13 January 1945, over Wurms, Germany. He had also completed thirty-four training flights. Thirty combat missions meant a flier could return to the States.

When asked if he ever thought about his own mortality and God, Donahue shared these thoughts:

Oh, sure, and the closer I got to the end of my combat tour (thirty missions), I started thinking, if I can just survive the next four missions, I'm going to go into the priesthood. I was really pretty serious about it.

So I got through the thing, and when I got back to California I went to a priest and explained my promise to God.

He told me that because I had made that promise under such adverse conditions, that I would not be held to it. He really helped me out, and I felt better after that.

Philosophically, Donahue said,

Unlike the infantry or ground soldiers, air battles were fought in the sky. You just can't revisit aerial battlefields. There are no trenches, no memorial plaques, villages, etc.

Evidence of our combat: black blossoms of flak, falling stricken aircraft, airmen hanging from their parachutes, noise of the engines and guns, shouts of the crew members, streaking chunks of metal penetrating aluminum skin and human flesh.

The sky looks as it did before anything happened.

All this vanishes with the same suddenness that it appeared, for the sky holds no memories. Whatever happens there vanishes like fog in the wind.

Images of the battle remain etched in our minds forever. What remains of the battle dwells in the hearts of those who survived.

Jack Donner Learned Many Life Skills as a Military Pilot

In April 1942, Jack Donner was a twenty-four-year-old clerk for Cadillac Motor Company in Detroit.

The following year he was Lieutenant Donner, piloting a B-17, the mighty Flying Fortress of World War II fame. With a crew of ten, he crossed the South Atlantic from West Palm Beach, Florida.

He was one of forty-eight pilots whose keen skills led a steady stream of men into experiences to be forever etched in their memories.

When word had been received that the U.S. Army had secured an airfield in the fertile Foggia Valley in southern Italy, American airplanes from the U.S. and Allied bases began assembling there.

In all, four hundred heavy bombers gathered, including one hundred B-24s, plus dozens of fighter escorts.

Their missions were to fly long-distance bombing runs over southern France, southern Germany, the Balkan States and Hungary, according to Donner. "Some of our targets were seven to eight hours away."

Donner remembers well his final mission. On 29 April 1944, he was piloting his bomber at 38,000 feet toward a target over Italy. Enemy airplanes that came out of nowhere knocked out two of his engines.

With his speed trimmed, and his altitude impossible to maintain, his Flying Fortress was like an eagle with a clipped wing. A short time later, an enemy fighter plane plucked out a third engine.

Despite receiving wounds to his arms, and with his craft fluttering on only one good engine, Donner kept his nearly helpless fortress airborne for another six hours before desperation forced him to ditch in the cold, choppy Adriatic Sea.

Donner and his crew managed to inflate their rubber dinghy and raise a small sail in the rough blue waters at dusk, but their radio operator drowned in the process. Two others had been wounded either in the air fights or during ditching.

The mountain tops of eastern Italy rose on the far horizon, and the now disarmed and crippled crew took turns with paddles.

For three nights and two days the mountains came closer at snail's pace before the cold, wet and hungry crew put ashore on the central coast of the Italian peninsula.

"Once on land, we went in different directions with the hope that some of us would be going the right way and find help," Donner remembered.

For three days Donner walked inland, passing German solders, "who obviously saw me, but for some reason did nothing even though I wore an American uniform."

Donner learned later that one of his crew members had been captured and the search was on for the others. He himself was seized in a haystack attempting to get some rest and still trying to dry out. A rifle was pointed in his direction, and the intruder exclaimed in perfect English, "I think we're looking for you!"

For the next two days he was fed well, treated well, and was allowed to converse with his German, but English-speaking captors.

But his "freedom" was short-lived. He was sent to an interrogation center in Verona where he was imprisoned in a small, white cell "where a single light bulb hanging from the ceiling burned day and night," Donner remembered.

"Between questioning and eating, I slept most of the time because my energy had been absolutely drained," he added. "I have no idea how long I remained there. I lost all track of time."

Donner soon learned the enemy knew a great deal about American soldiers. When he finally had an opportunity, he asked his interrogators, "Where did you get all that information?" Their short but serious reply was, "We subscribe to *Life* magazine."

Shortly thereafter, Donner and 5,000 other American and British prisoners were moved to a POW camp near the Oder River. On the opposite side was Poland.

In January 1945 the Russians, then American allies, were threatening the POW camp location, and the prisoners were to be moved near Berlin. The move included a sixty-two-mile walk. "Hitler wanted to use us as hostages in negotiations with America," Donner surmised.

Halfway to their destination, having walked through snow and subzero temperatures, "the German officers rebelled at Hitler's orders and detoured us to a train depot not far away. They could see the handwriting on the wall."

Loading nearly twice as many men as the boxcars were designed to hold, the prisoners remained on the cold, hay-strewn floor for four days before the train began to move.

Sometime in February the ill, injured, starving, freezing and dead men arrived in Nuremberg. Forty percent of them did not survive the trip.

Before long, the Germans learned that the U.S. forces were pushing from the west and the prisoners were moved once again, this time to a southern camp near Munich. The days were warmer now, and the biting cold ceased to tear at their every fiber.

One year to the day after he had ditched his B-17 in the chilling, choppy blue waters of the Adriatic, Donner said he witnessed the greatest event of his young life.

"General Patton and the Third Armored Division surrounded the POW camp, and ordered its commander to turn over the camp to him the following morning.

"When morning arrived, the dumb jerk wouldn't surrender," Donner chuckled. During the exchange of gunfire, the prisoners fled to safety under their barracks.

"After Patton and his men took over, we were told that we would all be going home soon," Donner recalled happily.

Four days later, when no action had taken place, the impatience of youth took over, and Donner, with two of his fellow prisoners, decided to try a faster way home. They walked away from the camp.

When asked if that was one of the announced alternatives, Donner replied with a smile, "No, but that was the one we took."

Returning to friendly forces required "liberating" a German civilian's car—while the driver was still in it—and being pulled across the Danube River on a barge by a tank.

Eventually, the trio arrived unscathed—the war was still in progress, but winding down in France—and into the hands of the American military.

Upon his return to the States, and to civilian life, Donner began working for his uncle at Miller Furniture in Midland. It was just a year after the store was established in 1945. Donner bought the business in 1960, and retired in 1978, after selling it to his son, Mark.

Author's note: This story was written for the Midland Daily News, *and published on 26 May 1983.*

Case and Donner: Two Neighbors Almost Met in a World War II POW Camp

William (Bill) Case and Jack Donner met fortuitously thirty-nine years ago, but never knew they might have faced each other until Case read a feature story in the *Midland Daily News* about Donner's liberation from a German prisoner of war camp in 1945.

That was nearly four decades ago, and since that time, both men have been making their contributions to the city of Midland.

Donner owned and managed Miller's Furniture on the Circle from 1960 until his retirement in 1978, and Case had been the treasurer of Midland County since June 1979.

Donner had been the pilot of a B-17, the Flying Fortress of World War II and had been forced to ditch in the April-chilled blue waters of the Adriatic Sea many miles off the western coast of Italy. About a week later, Donner was captured by the Germans, and eventually ended up in a prisoner of war camp, along with 1,500 other American and Allied troops.

During this time, Case was an antitank gunner with the 97th Infantry Division assigned to General George Patton's Armored Division of the Third Army.

By early spring of 1945, Patton could see the war beginning to wind down, even though fighting was still going on in parts of Europe and in the Pacific, according to *Crusade in Europe* by General Dwight D. Eisenhower.

In the book, Eisenhower speaks of the victories of the American and Allied fighting men of the Fifteenth Air Force who, "flew the fifteen hundred miles from Italy to attack Berlin," and of General Patton's U.S. Armored Division that conquered the bridgehead of Remagen, near Munich.

"The attacking troops had taken 19,000 prisoners," according to Eisenhower, and by late March, "the fate of the Germans was sealed," the book continues.

It was that same fate that very nearly, but not quite, brought Case and Donner face to face for the first time on foreign soil. A month after Eisenhower's statement, Patton's armored division, including Case, surrounded the POW camp where Donner was held captive.

Case had been with Patton since just before entering combat from the famous Lucky Strike camp near LaHavre, France, a few months earlier.

They had conquered the city of Ruhr, had taken part in the fall of Dusseldorf, and had beaten the enemy at Remagen as they pushed eastward toward the prison camp at Moosburg. Donner later returned to the United States from the same camp.

It was one year to the day after Donner had ditched his huge B-17 that Patton's division surrounded the POW camp, demanding complete surrender of the Germans and release of the prisoners.

When the order was denied, Patton waited until the following morning and began shelling the guard turrets while the incarcerated scampered for safety under their barracks.

"It was the brightest day of my life," Donner related in an earlier *Daily News* story.

For Case, it was just another day in the war. He was doing what he was trained to do. "But each time we scored a victory, especially liberating our own men," Case recalled, "it was like a personal victory. Had it not been for the courageous men like Donner, the war would have lasted much longer."

While their paths crossed in a traumatic situation almost forty years ago, they recently met formally in Case's office under much less stressful circumstances.

Both have actually seen each other frequently, as each had been active in Blessed Sacrament Church for nearly eighteen years, and for many years lived only two blocks apart in Midland. Neither knew they had "met" until their separate stories appeared in the *Midland Daily News*.

Author's note: The above story was written for the Midland Daily News, *and published on 6 September 1983.*

Lyle Eastman Fought in Two Wars Without a Scratch

At the end of December 1943, seventeen-year old Lyle Eastman enlisted in the U.S. Army, and found himself taking his basic training at Camp Tyler, Texas.

He was then assigned to the 33rd Yellow Cross Division (designated by a yellow cross insignia on the shoulder patch), K Company, 3rd Battalion, 130th Infantry Regiment. He soon learned that his outfit was called the Black Hawks. He theorized the nickname came about because they seemed to be assigned all the dirty work. The name seemed appropriate as his story unfolded.

The following February, he and 5,000 other troops left Ft. Ord, California for the Philippines. They stopped in Hawaii only long enough to take on supplies, then it was on to New Guinea for a brief stopover. "We were packed on that ship like cattle in a cattle car," he recalled. "We slept in bunks stacked five high."

They hit the beach in Lingayen Gulf in the Philippines on 15 February 1945 aboard LSTs, and met little resistance until they trudged inland and found the enemy waiting for them in the jungle.

"The Japanese were jungle fighters, and they didn't want to pursue us on the beachhead out in the open," Eastman said. "We soon found out there were lots of them." Although the war ended in August 1945, it was far from over in February of that year, according to Eastman.

"We hired Filipinos as guides who were called headhunters. They would go into the caves and flush out the enemy. These guides would come back with the ears of Japanese soldiers strung around their necks to let us know how many of the enemy they had killed," added Eastman. "We would pay them with food, money, or anything else they wanted.

"We had a tough time finding someone who could interpret for us because they were from a mountain tribe, and the regular Filipinos wanted nothing to do with them and they couldn't understand them either," Eastman recalled.

From the beachhead all the way to Baguio in the northern Philippines, Eastman's Black Hawks took mountain after mountain over a distance of some three hundred miles. Many of the mountains were 3,000 feet high, according to Eastman. "And we did it all on foot," he said, "but we had to push the Japanese out of the islands."

It took six months of jungle fighting for the Black Hawks to reach Luzon.

Luzon had been a large resort area, with theaters, golf courses, and big cathedrals, according to Eastman. "Everything except the cathedrals had been bombed out by the time we got there," he remembered.

Eastman's most anxious moments occurred when they were taking the mountains. "Men were getting killed all around me, and I pulled through without a scratch," he said wonderingly. "A bullet with my name on it never arrived." He was still puzzled by his luck.

"Every draw we went through, the Japanese were waiting for us. We would open up with machine guns, and every time we did a bunch of our guys got killed by return fire."

Eastman was solemn as he recalled his war experience and checked the notes he has brought to the interview. Delving into bad experiences can be painful, and Eastman took time to think as he sorted out his thoughts and his words.

But in spite of his painful experiences, Eastman and his unit remained undaunted by the intense enemy fire from the slopes of Question Mark Hill in the Philippines. His company tried valiantly three times to assault the hills and close with the enemy.

Over fifty percent of his company became casualties as they became weary and fatigued from the prolonged fight, the heat and the rugged terrain over which the fighting took place. The attack ended as they fought on, exhausted, and reached their final objectives. But the encounter lasted four days and had taken its toll on Eastman's company. The Philippines, and Northern Luzon in particular, was now under American control.

Fighting in the jungle near the equator takes a lot out of a man. Eastman knows. He has had that experience.

"One time we ran out of drinking water, and we couldn't get any, and it was one hundred plus degrees day and night," Eastman went on. "We called for an air drop of water. The first flyover they dropped everything *but* water. The second time they dropped it in Japanese territory, so we couldn't even get at it. Some of the men ran to get it, and they got shot. According to Eastman, men wept unashamedly at this cruel trick of fate.

"The way we finally got water was from an engineering battalion in a rear echelon area that brought it to us." The Black Hawks had planned to refill their canteens in a mountain stream that lay ahead, but when they arrived the stream was dry. The Japanese had dammed off the stream above them. Before water arrived, however, some of the American GIs had begun passing out. "Some of the men were also suffering from severe burns from the blistering South Pacific sun," Eastman recalled.

After taking Baguio, a city on the island of Luzon, it was pretty much a mop-up situation for the Black Hawks. "We went on patrols, taking prisoners. The Japanese supplies were cut off. They had no food or ammunition, and they had been living off roots, leaves and whatever they could get their hands on. In short, they were starving," Eastman recalled.

After Baguio was captured a top Japanese general and commander in the Philippines, General Yamashito, surrendered to the Black

Hawks. "Yamashito was the one who commanded the Japanese troops that chased MacArthur out of the Philippines," said Eastman. "He had fled Baguio, and headed for the mountains where he was found in a cave."

Eastman was targeted for the invasion of Japan when word was received that the atom bomb dropped on Nagasaki had ended the war.

"But we were on our way to Japan, and did a landing about fifty miles from Nagasaki just the same as though it was wartime," said Eastman. They landed at Miyazaki on the island of Honshu.

"It was there that I knew for certain I had shot a man, and knew just where I had shot him," Eastman said with certainty. "There were five of us, going into this little town, and there was a bombed out tank. It had a sign there in English that said, 'American Run Bank.' We stood there studying the sign when three Japanese came upon us with knives. One started for me, and I shot him at fifteen feet."

It was the first time in nearly a year and a half of fighting for Eastman, that he was forced to look a man in the eye and shoot him nearly point blank. "It bothered me for a long time, but it was either him or me."

Eastman was in Japan for eighteen months before he received his discharge on 6 February 1947.

But that was not the end of Eastman's military career. Years later he was driving home from work at 3:00 a.m., in a central Florida town when a taxi ran a red light and broadsided him. Unhurt, Eastman wanted to call the police so his insurance would cover his car. The taxi driver tried to persuade him not to call because he already had too many traffic tickets.

"I called anyway, and that was a mistake," said Eastman. "The cops knew this local fellow, and I had an out-of-state license plate." The police listened only to the taxi driver's story, and took Eastman to the local jail. "They had my car towed away, and I never saw it again," he remembered wryly.

The short version of the story is that in order to get out of jail, Eastman had to listen to a pitch from a marine recruiter, then sign up for the military. Korea was looming over the horizon, and the marines needed men, particularly ones with combat experience.

He spent a few weeks in refresher training at Quantico, Virginia, then six months training officers. He was then transferred to Washington, D.C., as a guard at a naval communications station.

Security was tight, according to Eastman. "Not even Harry Truman got in without a picture ID."

Just prior to being sent to Korea, Eastman landed the job he had been looking for; his assignment was with a motor transport company with the 6th Marine Division. "I could drive anything on wheels," Eastman chuckled. In Korea, he was soon driving a jeep for his commanding officer.

When landing from an LST at Inchon, Korea, Eastman drove a cosmoline-covered truck into eight feet of water. "The cosmoline was a waterproofing for the truck," he remembers, "but it took a full day to clean it off."

He was soon transferred to the 7th Regiment of the 1st Marine division, where he drove troops, supplies and ammunition to the front lines.

"Once I got orders to haul 81 mm ammo to Fox Company in an outpost in the mountains," Eastman said. "It was twenty below zero, forty mile per hour winds, and two feet of snow. After delivering the ammunition, it was a toss-up as to whether he should return to his base. It was getting dark, and the weather was not at all favorable. "But I argued with the company commander in the outpost that I had orders to return that day." It was a grueling fourteen miles back down mountain roads only wide enough for a truck.

"I made it safely," Eastman stated, "but that night Fox Company was almost wiped off the map by Chinese gunfire. Had I stayed, I would have been one of them."

Eastman later learned that he had driven past two divisions of Chinese communist troops. "They could have bumped me off at any time," Eastman said seriously, "but they didn't want to give away their position.

"In all, I drove 100,000 miles in that one truck in Korea," Eastman said. In just over a year, his tour of duty expired, and Eastman counted ninety-six bullet holes in the truck. He had been the sole driver. "There were several holes there that had I been in the truck, I wouldn't be here today." The truck has since been memorialized in a museum at Quantico.

His truck also provided him with warm meals, while men in the foxholes were eating them frozen, according to Eastman. "I would warm up a can of beans on the manifold. Half the time they would burn before I got around to removing them. But I just scraped off the burned ones, and ate the rest."

Eastman had several close calls in Korea, as indicated by the quantity and location of bullet holes in his truck, but his only injury came when he was backing down into an ammunition dump to load his truck. He was accelerating out of the dump when his front-wheel drive truck spun on an empty shell casing, causing the steering wheel to spin out of control. The incident broke his arm in three places.

The following day he was driving his truck once again, but with one arm in a cast.

"I have to be the luckiest guy alive," Eastman admitted. "I've been in two wars, and the only injury I ever received wasn't even caused by enemy action."

For his efforts in Korea, Eastman received three battle stars and the Korean War Medal, which he received only recently. It had been approved as long ago as 1953.

Eastman served eight years in two wars and worked thirty years in business before he retired in 1991. He owned Lyle's Service Company, a well-known heating and air conditioning company in Midland.

William Elliott: A Priest and Chaplain after World War II

William (Bill) Elliott, at nineteen years of age, had already spent six months in the U.S. Army Reserves when Uncle Sam said he was needed on a full-time basis.

His basic training consisted of artillery training directly on the guns at Camp Roberts, California, before shipping out from San Francisco to New Caledonia in October 1943. New Caledonia, an island in the South Pacific, is located about a thousand miles off the northeast coast of Australia. Elliott was assigned to the 246th Field Artillery Battalion, Headquarters Battery, Fire Direction Center (FDC). He chuckles as he explains he was assigned to the FDC because he once had a course in trigonometry.

Leaving New Caledonia just weeks later, Elliott's battery was shipped to Fiji, a group of islands near the equator, 1,500 miles north of New Zealand.

In Fiji, Elliott joined the American Division. This division was not formed until the Massachusetts National Guard units arrived in New Caledonia; it was named American for Americans in New Caledonia, according to Elliott. "This division had more actual combat days than any other division in the war," Elliott said matter-of-factly. "But I didn't join them until after they had been through the bitter battle at Guadalcanal in early 1943."

The division was disbanded following the war, but was reinstated for both the Korean and Vietnam Wars. Colin Powell was the commander of the American Division during Vietnam, "and he still wears his American patch whenever he's in full uniform," Elliott smiled proudly.

Elliott's first action after leaving Fiji came when his division entered the small jungle island of Bougainville in the Solomon Islands in 1944. He was there just a year and a day. "There we kept the Japanese busy while keeping two airports open so both the army and navy could use them as a refueling area in the South Pacific."

The major battle occurred when word came down that the Japanese were going to try to take over the airports. "But we had enough information to allow our artillery and the navy artillery to zero in on their positions to hold them back," Elliott remembered.

One day, Elliott was helping casualties back to safety on the island of Cebu, in the Philippine Islands. "We leveled Cebu City from off-

shore before landing," Elliott explained. "Cebu was the gambling region for the Japanese," Elliott said.

He remembers that what was not leveled was used for shelter when the American troops stormed the cities. At one point, he and two others used a pool table in an old bar for cover.

"The Japanese had moved back into the mountains," Elliott recalled, "and that's when the fighting really escalated.

"At one point the whole side of the mountain blew away. We never found out if the Japanese set off the explosion or if our own bombs had hit an ammo dump. But we lost a lot of our men from falling debris.

"That was probably the biggest loss of men in any action we encountered, with the exception of Hill 260 in Bougainville," Elliott added.

Hill 260 had been set up as an observation post when the Japanese moved in and overtook the hill. Elliott was in a position in which he could hear Japanese voices.

He called that information into the FDC, and the officer who answered the phone said, "You're out of your mind." He continued, "At that point the phone went dead, and we lost our whole team up there." A total of eight artillery men lost their lives on Hill 260 that fateful day, according to Elliott, but the infantry had many more casualties.

The Japanese division pulled back and attacked again, but from a different direction. The Americans were ready for them and many Japanese soldiers were captured, according to Elliott.

"The prisoners thought for certain we were going to kill them, and after we convinced them we were not, they would give us any information we wanted," Elliott remembered.

Not all of Elliott's encounters were that serious. He noted that at one point the Australian army was on the same island in the Philippines as the American army. "Of course they drove on the opposite side of the road than we do, and there were several fender benders before we got that all worked out," Elliott chuckled.

Also less serious were movie times. "After a beachhead was secure, we would sometimes pull back a little, put up a screen in the jungle, and we would have a movie," Elliott recalled. "One June [6 June 1944] when we were watching a movie, it suddenly stopped and it was announced that the Allies had landed on Normandy, and the invasion of Germany had begun."

Elliott did not know it at the time, but his older brother, Robert, was in that invasion on the other side of the world. Fortunately, he survived the battle.

Elliott became an ordained Episcopal priest in 1951, and still serves as the chaplain for the Americal Division Veterans.

Orrie Francis: A Quiet Man in a Quiet Air Force

They were known as "The Silent Squadron" in World War II—and for good reason.

They could soar their gliders at treetop level at sixty-five miles per hour with only the sound of the wind brushing their bubble windshield, and land on a dime behind enemy lines to load or unload men and machines of war. It could happen day or night, and nighttime meant only an illuminated compass to guide them into the combat zones.

Relatively few people have had this experience, and Orrie Francis spoke of his adventure forty years later with the modesty and humility of a man who knows he was one among many who shared his experiences.

One month after the war broke out in the Hawaiian islands, Francis, then twenty-one years old, tried to enlist in the U.S. Navy with his older brother, Clifford.

The Navy immediately accepted Clifford, but due to a heart murmur, Orrie was a "reject." As the war raged on, however, the military became "less choosy," according to Francis. He was drafted into the army in October 1942.

His first assignment, after spending a miserable five days at Fort Custer, Battle Creek—"They were all miserable at first!" he remembered—was at Shepard Field in Wichita Falls, Texas. On the way there Francis received news that he had been transferred to the U.S. Air Force.

"That was the best news I'd had since leaving home," Francis chuckled. "Everyone was trying to get into the air force or the Navy."

In the following eight weeks, he learned how to assemble and maintain the CG-4A gliders which would eventually carry up to fifteen fully equipped men or one jeep and four soldiers to the front lines to join other Allied troops in the fighting. The gliders measured a wingspan of eighty-three feet and a body forty-eight feet long.

Francis learned his lessons well. For two years he drew flight pay as crew chief, making him responsible for the safety of his assigned craft and the men and equipment it carried.

Despite the dangers of his assignment, Francis thought of it only as a job he was trained to do.

In May 1943, he was sent to Camp Shanks, New York, where he walked aboard the USS *West Point*, the second largest ship afloat at the time. In the middle of the night the ship set sail for Casablanca in, northern Africa.

But their arrival was delayed for two days, as they skirted and dodged enemy submarines in the waters of the South Atlantic.

"Six months earlier," Francis recalled, "the Germans had been pushed off African soil and the Americans had taken over the air bases."

During that time, the gliders were sent to the African bases in sections, where it was the job of Francis to reassemble the wood-framed, canvas-covered aircraft for the invasion of Sicily, an island off the coast of southern Italy. Following Sicily, the next target would be Italy itself.

In the weeks to follow, Francis and his squadron were being finely tuned for the attacks. His squadron had been in continuous training since its arrival at Casablanca the previous spring.

One training flight nearly proved fatal to the men in Francis's motorless aircraft. They were flying a simulated mission at night over the Mediterranean Sea.

As they were towed through the air at several thousand feet on a three hundred foot nylon line by their "mother ship," another C-47 towing another glider flew so close to Francis's craft from above that it caused his glider to rock and pitch.

"At one point we thought we were going to overturn in the air," Francis remembered.

"But it was pitch dark, we couldn't use lights, and we were under a radio blackout," he said. "We never knew if the other C-47 pilot ever knew we were there."

Francis never saw Sicily or Italy under attack, however. "For some reason, it was decided to send a different squadron over Sicily." But a week later he arrived there and observed the devastation wrought by the American and Allied forces that brought the island to its knees.

In February 1944, Francis's squadron was doubled in strength to include twenty-six tow planes, as many gliders, and four hundred men. It was sent to Barkston-Heath, 130 miles north of London. The purpose was to take advanced training for the D day invasion of Europe. He was a part of the largest airborne invasion task force ever assembled for war.

"There were acres and acres of airplanes, wing tip to wing tip," Francis remembered.

But once again Francis's luck held out and he did not have to risk his life in battle. "By this time the air force had changed the rules," said Francis. "In order for a glider to go up, it now had to have two commissioned officers as qualified pilots and we didn't have that many officers."

All of the men in Francis' squadron were not so fortunate, however. Nearly half of them became fatalities of war, either in training or in actual combat.

Three years after his induction, Francis had his first vacation. He returned home with his many medals, and married Delores Secor in the fall of 1945.

For nearly a year Francis was employed by The Dow Chemical Company, but returned to his farm near Edenville and operated a general store there for seven years. Still living on his farm as of this writing, Francis has been active in township and county politics. He was Edenville Township Supervisor for eight years and retired as the Midland County Drain Commissioner in September 1982, after holding that position for over sixteen years.

Author's note: This story was published in the Midland Daily News *on 25 May 1983.*

Paul Friedrich Told Another Side of the Story

Paul Friedrich's story is a little different. He was only seventeen, and had been drafted into the German Air Force. It was 1944. He was on his way from a small village in southern France, along with hundreds of other German troops, to attend paratrooper jump school in Cologne, Germany. There was no way for him to know at the time that in eighteen years he would be a citizen of the country he was being trained to fight.

The train in which he was riding never arrived at its intended destination. Word had been received that the Americans and their allies had invaded Normandy, and the troop train was detoured to the Brest Peninsula in France.

Six weeks later his capture was inevitable. Being on a peninsula, every escape route had soon been shut off. Bombs from American airplanes were glowing even in the daytime, and the new recruit's food supply was nearly depleted. For the first time in Friedrich's young life, he knew what it meant to unequivocally give up in any situation.

He was taken by American troops to England, later to be shipped to America. But that was not in the cards either. There were no ships heading west across the Atlantic at that time, and Friedrich and his companions were turned over to the British and sent to a prisoner of war camp south of London.

"Some of us would be moved every few weeks to a different camp," reminisced Friedrich, "so that strong friendships could not be established, and escapes could not be planned."

Friedrich spoke openly about the "craziness of war." Some of his nearest relatives were British, and fighting on the other side. "We could have been shooting at each other!" Friedrich exclaimed.

At one POW camp near Sheffield, England, he learned that an uncle lived almost within sight of his camp, and through a local civilian laborer working at the camp, Friedrich got word to him that he was there.

A short time later, his uncle appeared and asked the guards if Friedrich could be released long enough to go out for dinner. "The guard was probably bribed," Friedrich conjectured. One guard even loaned him a civilian suit.

"The British soldiers were poorly paid," Friedrich related, "and they were always bumming smokes, razor blades and many other

things they couldn't afford. But they were always willing to recipro-
cate the favor if they liked you."

The only stipulation for Friedrich was that he had to return at an
appointed hour, and that he would not speak loudly while in public. His English, being very poor at the time, would attract attention.

Apparently the British guards liked Friedrich. They even allowed
him to play on a civilian soccer team on Saturdays provided he did
not talk on or off the field.

It wasn't until his uncle had notified his mother in Stuttgart,
Germany, that she knew he was alive. She thought he was missing
in action. "We often wrote letters home," remembered Friedrich, "but
we didn't know they weren't being delivered."

Although the war ended in Europe in the summer of 1945,
Friedrich remained a prisoner near Hereford, England until
Christmas 1947. The British held the younger men without wives or
families for cheap labor, he remembered. He and his prison colleagues
worked on farms during the day, returning to the POW camp at night.

Soon after his return to Stuttgart, he met Marla Reile. They were
married in 1949. Three years later, the Friedrichs and their two-year-
old son, Bernd, headed for America for the first time.

"Preparing for that was no small task twenty-eight years ago," said
Friedrich. "We had to have a sponsor in America, stringent physicals, a trade, and pay our own transportation."

A sponsor was finally located in Bay City. Friedrich had learned
barbering in a trade school before being drafted, and through the
generosity of his wife's brother who loaned them the money, the
Friedrichs were on their way to a new life.

Their first home was in Bay City, but once there, they faced another
setback. In order for Friedrich to take the state barbering examina-
tion, he had to be a resident of Michigan for at least six months.

To sustain his family, he worked days at a now defunct nursery in
Bay City, and tended bar at Das Michigan Haus, a German restaurant
and bar on the corner of M-84 and Delta Road in Bay County. The
restaurant is also now defunct.

Finally Friedrich was able to take the exam, and he began plying
his trade as part owner of Irish's Barber Shop at 302 East Indian in
Midland.

"I don't know how we ever survived those early years," said
Friedrich, still with some accent. "When we came to America with our
two-year-old, we had no money, no job, and couldn't speak English."

"Young and dumb," mused his wife in the interview in her pleasant German accent.

"After twenty-eight years America is home. America has been good to us and for us," Friedrich concluded seriously.

Author's note: The above story was written for the Midland Daily News, *and was published, in part, sometime in 1983.*

Graham Gould's Violent Experiences
Could Have Blocked Memories

He wishes he could remember more, but those who are experts in how the mind works say the mind sometimes blocks out what it wishes to forget.

That may be true of Graham Gould, a Midland resident for much of his life, who now lives in Tucson, Arizona.

In a telephone interview, he explained that when he enlisted in the Army Air Corps (later named the U.S. Air Force), he was twenty-five years of age, and was dubbed the "old man." The average age of the airmen at the time was just nineteen.

Having taken the extensive pilot training to fly the B-17, Gould flew in thirty-five missions before the war was over.

Based in England, he and his crew flew numerous missions over European territory. On one such flight, his plane was flying in formation on a final bombing run over Munich, Germany when it appeared they had run out of fuel at 25,000 feet. This was to be one of Gould's most harrowing experiences, and it was caused by human error.

By the time the mistake was noted, Gould's aircraft had lost about ten thousand feet in altitude, and the propellers were just "wind-milling," Gould recalled.

"The flight engineer had neglected to switch from the main tanks to the wing tanks, and we dropped our bombs somewhere over Germany, and tried to catch up to the formation, but they were just too far ahead of us by that time. So we headed back to England all alone."

This left Gould and his crew vulnerable to attack by enemy aircraft. Over France, however, fighter escorts came to their rescue, and flew with them back to England, but not before they had taken some flak from antiaircraft ground fire.

Although Gould never experienced having his craft shot down, he was often fired upon by German planes, and from the ground.

"The flak was our worst enemy," he remembered. "Once over France, flak took out two of our engines. We began losing altitude, and threw out everything over the English Channel that had any weight at all, including our flak jackets and ammunition. We landed safely on two engines at a Royal Air Force base."

When asked if at any time he ever had thought of his own mortality, Gould commented, "Never on a mission. I was always too busy.

When we got back, and learned of friends who would never return, it did make one think about it.

"I know there must have been times when I was scared, but you just blank it out of your mind at the time. I just wish I could remember more."

If the experiences above are the worst Gould could remember, it's little wonder his mind won't allow him to recall the others. He was discharged from the military in the fall of 1945.

Gould ended his career in aviation by working for the Federal Aviation Administration at MBS International Airport from 1959 to 1971.

World War II Still Haunts Robert Graves

"It haunts me yet," says Robert (Bob) Graves, when he talks about some of his experiences in World War II. As a nineteen-year-old in 1943, he had one of the most dangerous jobs in the war; disarming bombs and other demolitions, both American and the enemy's.

Chuckling, he said, "If it hadn't been for the air force I wouldn't have had a job." Frequently, after a bomb run by American planes, there were duds on the ground—bombs that had not exploded. Graves's job was to go in and make certain the bombs would not explode as the American troops covered the ground on their way to the front lines. Sometimes he would intentionally explode them, other times defuse them. He often worked alone under enemy fire, ahead of the infantry.

It was not only dangerous work; it was physically and mentally exhausting. "At times we would be working twenty-four hours a day," Graves recalls. His unit, the 113th Ordnance Bomb Disposal Squad (BDS), included 1,100 soldiers plus 135 officers.

According to an army newspaper clipping near the end of the war, "Since D-Day, bomb disposal personnel have removed an average of three-and-a-half tons of munitions and unexploded bombs per man per month. About 1,600 tons of explosives were removed from Paris alone."

The clipping went on to explain that the bomb disposal men "were among the Army's most highly trained specialists, and had to be able to recognize and deactivate between 200 and 300 German fuses, and about 200 types of artillery fuses of all nationalities."

But defusing bombs and other explosives was not on Graves's mind when he graduated from Midland High School (he was in the second class to graduate from what is now Central Middle School).

After basic training he was sent to the automotive school at Aberdeen Proving Grounds in Maryland and learned to drive every vehicle the army used except tanks.

"One day I got called before a board who told me I was slated for judge advocate general (JAG) school. Acting as though he had a choice, Graves told them he was not interested. When asked what he would like to do, he replied, "Something exciting!"

Apparently he did have a choice. "The next day I was told to pack and get ready for my next assignment," related Graves. He and twenty others were picked up around the camp, and above the next

entrance they passed through was a sign that read *You are Entering Bomb Disposal Area: Off Limits.*

"That was on a Friday, and we were ready to go over the hill," Graves related. "Every day we would hear about people in the bomb disposal unit being killed doing their job." As though mind readers, their superiors would not allow them to leave their barracks without supervision. They were even marched to and from the mess hall as a unit. Fourteen intensive weeks later Graves was ready for his first assignment.

"My first job was to defuse a depth charge that was dropped in a corn field instead of Chesapeake Bay," recalled Graves. After a period of time, he found it and successfully disarmed it.

That would not be his last assignment in the States. He and his captain once disarmed a blockbuster bomb that failed to detonate while being tested. "We looked at that huge thing in awe," said Graves. After a great deal of consultation, the two managed to disarm the fuse. "It was scary," he recalled, "and as we began, we looked around and realized we were alone."

At this point, Graves was invited to attend officer training school and become a commissioned officer. He turned it down. "I know if I did I would be sent to the infantry," he said. "The infantry guys just never got the credit they deserved. They did all the dirty work, and were shot at constantly." Holding his right hand to his forehead he said, "I have to give them a big salute."

Graves admitted that his job with the military made him a loner most of his life. "I just never learned to depend on others because what I did I could only depend on myself," he said.

After a year at Aberdeen Proving Grounds, and with minimal experience, Graves was shipped to Europe aboard the Queen Mary along with 5,000 other troops. He remembered it was August 1944.

When they arrived in Scotland, three and a half days later, they were herded onto train cars to England. They crossed the English Channel on LSTs and disembarked on Omaha Beach. The beach had been a part of the D day invasion two months earlier.

"That was the beginning of trying times," Graves recalled. "When I saw all that destruction, walked up that hill and saw all those crosses [where GIs had been buried following the invasion]." He hesitated and tried to choke back the memory. "It's a sight I'll never forget."

After picking up their equipment and being assigned to General Patton's 3rd Army, the troops headed for Paris where Graves was reassigned to the 65th Infantry Division. That was the beginning of eleven months in a war zone for Graves.

"The hardest jobs to do were the German bombs," Graves recalled, "because they were electrically charged when dropped. Others had a time clock."

Graves also mentioned that some German bombs had what was called a Z40. It was designed to blow if removed. He was armed with a microphone attached to an ear phone to detect anything ticking inside the bomb.

"When trying to remove the fuse and it started ticking, I would take off and come back two days later," said Graves. "If it was still there, I would detonate it."

Graves had a similar situation on the Red Ball Express Road in Germany. He was told to defuse the bomb and not blow it because it would damage the road and disrupt the flow of needed supplies for the troops. "I offered them my equipment and told them to do it themselves. I just didn't feel safe removing that fuse." Graves got his way, blew up the bomb, and the engineers were called in to repair the huge hole in the road.

"Thank God, the Germans had very few duds in my area," Graves said. "They were very complicated. American bombs were simple to defuse. If everything looked okay, I merely defused them. If not, I blew them up."

In describing the Battle of the Bulge, Graves said, "It was a mess. We came upon a couple concentration camps and they were terrible. Today they still haunt me." He chose not to go into detail.

"But I would check out the area for mines and bombs before the troops would proceed. I did just enough for safe passage and somebody else would clean up the area," he related.

Graves recalls the Germans had myriad ordnances. One deadly one was called the Bouncing Betty. "It used a trip wire," Graves said. "If walking along and you tripped the wire, the Betty would pop in the air six feet and shower you with steel balls. So when you heard the sound of it going up, you hit the ground right now!"

The Germans were clever in other ways as well, according to Graves. "They began making shoe mines from wood and plastic, so our metal detectors wouldn't pick them up. They were called shoe mines because they were just powerful enough to blow a man's foot off."

Graves also remembers that often the enemy would plant one land mine on top of another, attached by a wire. The wire would detonate both mines. When a mine was found, he had to make certain there was not another underneath.

"On the other hand," he said, "the Germans always laid out a minefield in the same pattern. Once you found one it was easy to figure out after that."

Into the interview this writer asked the insensitive question, "Was there ever a time when you knew you had killed another man?" Graves looked up from his notes, met the writer's eyes and replied slowly, "Yes." A tear formed in the corner of his eye as he waved off the question. "Sometimes my memory is too good," he said, staring off into the room. The questioning immediately took another track.

Graves received assignments anywhere he was needed, all over Europe. "My last job was to go to Enns, Austria to check out a bridge over the Elbe River," he said. "I arrived early in the morning and could hear action that seemed quite close, so I asked a few of our troops there to cover me."

He found explosives under the bridge and disarmed them. Around noon, he recalled, German soldiers began crossing the river in his direction. "They wanted to surrender because the Russians were after them. The Russians came along soon, but nothing happened. It was V-E Day in Europe, and I would soon be going home."

Like many GIs, Graves had his lighter days too. "Near the end of the war there was a brewery in Germany that had been shut down due to artillery shelling," he grinned, "and my job was to go in and remove the duds so they could open it up and supply our troops with good old German beer."

Chuckling, Graves continued, "I took my time, and when I left each day I filled five gallon water cans with beer and took them to the infantry." He became very popular.

After a few days the duds had been removed. Men by the truckload came to the brewery to fill their water cans, according to Graves. "I never had to wait in line." Smiling he added, "The MPs recognized my jeep with the red fenders and BDS on the front. But the vats were soon drained."

At another time Graves was called to an artillery unit to check out a building that contained dynamite. "There was about two tons of it there," he recalled, "and nitro was leaking all over the floor."

He knew the artillery unit was on the opposite side of the river, so it would be safe just to blow up the building. He explained to the commanding officer that it would be too dangerous to move the dynamite. "I told him it wouldn't do much damage," Graves said, grinning sheepishly.

The building went, along with two tons of dynamite and the leaking nitroglycerin. When he returned to examine the results, Graves was confronted with the CO. Rattled, he told Graves he had knocked all the artillery pieces out of kilter because they were all zeroed in.

"About that time this sergeant walks up, madder than a wet hen," laughed Graves. "He asked what the hell was going on. When I began to explain, I recognized the sergeant as Howard Smith from Midland."

Smith was crossing the bridge when the explosion was set off, and he thought the bridge was blowing, according to Graves. "We both had a good laugh over it, and parted friends."

The day he had left for duty in Europe, Graves decided he would never be broke and took with him an American dollar bill. He wrote across the face of it, every country he entered during the war. In his own pen are the words, Scotland, England, France, Belgium, Luxembourg, Austria, Germany.

"As I look back," Graves reflected, "an angel was sitting on my shoulder, guiding me. If the job didn't feel right, I'd simply blow up the bomb or whatever. If anybody objected, all I would say was, 'You do it because I want to live.' I always got my way."

Among the numerous medals and citations awarded Graves was the Bronze Star Medal. The citation used words such as, "distinguished himself," "by meritorious achievement," "high example of leadership and resourcefulness," "frequently exposed to enemy fire," "pulled ammunition away from burning trucks." It was signed by Lieutenant Colonel Walter E. Forry, commanding officer of the U.S. Army Ordnance Department.

While Graves endured many adventures not known to nearly one hundred percent of Americans, his greatest thrill was standing on the deck of a ship as it sailed into New York Harbor and passed the Statue of Liberty in September 1945. He was home.

Al Gunkler Survived a Crash Landing in China Aboard a B-25

"Yesterday we started off about 9:00 a.m. for a search mission for Japanese warships along the China coast. At approximately 12:20 we caught sight of the coast for the first time. Five minutes later, as we were flying up the coast, our left engine coughed and sputtered, and when we looked, we found it to be smoking. Flak from Japanese ground forces had damaged the plane's engine. Expecting it to burst into flames any minute, we immediately headed inland, and I picked a heading for an emergency landing strip over 100 miles inland."

Those were some of the words Lieutenant Albert (Al) Gunkler, a Midland resident for the past fifty-four years, wrote to his wife, Caroline, on 21 March 1945 during World War II. Gunkler was the twenty-year-old navigator on a B-25 bomber. He was a member of the 823rd Squadron, 38th Bomb Group of the Fifth Air Corps. He later wrote in his diary that the crew of his bomber was keeping an eye on Japanese movements along the China coast and was to bomb a ship in Amoy Harbor.

As a navigator, graduating first in his class of 250 other airmen, he did his job well. The landing strip Gunkler found with maps and navigational equipment was a dry river bed, the only place for a reasonable landing along the mountainous coastline. It would be a belly landing because the plane would tip on its nose in the soft sand if the landing gear was down.

Before heading inland, the B-25 jettisoned its two-thousand pound bomb load into the China Sea to help minimize an explosion during the landing.

Any kind of an emergency landing is a risky situation, according to Gunkler. Men can be tossed around inside the plane and/or an explosion could result from the airplane fuel. He attributes the relatively safe landing to the pilot, Lieutenant Gibson.

"Maybe it was a 'this can't happen to me' attitude," or more probably a faith in our pilot," commented Gunkler. "What a sweet landing he made!" It wasn't until after the plane began skidding sideways and the centrifugal force threw them against the side of the plane, that any fear entered Gunkler's mind, "and then only mildly," he wrote to Caroline. The six airmen walked away from the battered aircraft with only a few minor bruises.

The whole incident was mild compared to the scare Gunkler had had the first time he had flown in the B-25. In training, a year earlier in South Carolina, "two planes of us trainees took off at the same time and the other one exploded right next to us," he remembered. "Six men died," he said sadly. Sabotage was suspected but never proved.

The crew of the downed aircraft in China had options other than crash landing. They could have parachuted out, leaving the plane to find its own "landing" spot. "None of us liked that option except Lieutenant Gibson, who was not at all sure he could land the plane safely, wheels up with one engine," Gunkler says. "We had more faith in him than he did himself. Lieutenant Gibson was twenty-one, the "old man" of the crew. None of the crew had experienced jumping from an aircraft, nor had they had training to do so.

Another option was to try to return to their base at Lingayen in the Philippines. But they had been warned not to attempt such a maneuver. It was a four-hour flight with two working engines, longer with only one. Other planes had attempted it with disastrous results.

The Chinese had been at war with the Japanese for several years, according to Gunkler, and the Americans were treated royally even though their hosts knew they could be imprisoned—or worse—if caught by the Japanese. The American airmen also learned there was a $10,000 bounty on their heads if captured. The Japanese knew of their distress, as the aircraft roared over their heads with a smoking engine along the coast.

In a diary he was keeping of his experiences, Gunkler stated that he had always assumed that the $10,000 was in American money, "but upon reflection, it might well have been Chinese dollars. In that case, at 500 Chinese dollars to one American [at the time], the value of my life was only twenty bucks—oh, well." He chuckled about it.

The Americans were fed and housed in excellent conditions, Gunkler explained. Sometimes the airmen slept on bamboo mats on the floor. At other times they would sleep more comfortably in a hospital. They were even asked to speak to school groups. The airmen spent a month in China before they were able to return to base.

But the military had lost contact with Gunkler and the B-25 crew. On 9 April 1945, nearly three weeks after the crash landing, Caroline received a letter from the War Department that he was missing in action. The letter mentioned above reached her on 8 May, the day before she received a letter from Gunkler written on rice paper from China. Gunkler's safety was ecstatic news for the new bride.

Gunkler and his crew finally managed to return, partly by walking sixty miles in two days with Chinese aides, into American hands.

Before his harrowing experience in China, Gunkler had flown from San Francisco to Lae in New Guinea for more training, then on to Morotai Island, south of the Philippines. On the first day in Morotai, twenty-four planes flew to support the landing on Leyte in the Philippines. Six were lost, along with thirty-six crew members. From Morotai the group spent three months supporting the Leyte operation and then moved on to Lingayen Gulf in Luzon. There they supported the taking of Manila, the capital of the Philippines.

On an earlier mission to Hainan Island, flak from Japanese ground forces penetrated the skin of Gunkler's B-25, exploding several rounds of 50 caliber bullets in the ammunition supply. The island lies between the Gulf of Tonkin and the South China Sea, about one thousand miles west of the Philippines. Between thirty and forty pieces of metal embedded themselves in Gunkler's back and legs. Nearly sixty years later, pieces of the metal still worked themselves out as the body slowly rejected the foreign objects.

Flying out of Lingayen, the planes in Gunkler's squadron continued hammering Formosa's (now Taiwan) factories and airstrips with tons of bombs, trying to keep the Japanese from producing weapons of war and keeping their aircraft out of commission.

Gunkler flew a total of thirty-six missions during his tenure with the military, but none as adventurous as the crash landing in China just thirty miles from enemy hands. Most missions were flown so low that the bombs were dropped by parachute so the plane had time to fly to safety before the bombs hit the ground.

Even his trip home, taking thirty-five days aboard a ship loaded with five thousand other troops, was exciting. Because the ship had a change of orders in the middle of the Pacific, instead of docking in California as originally planned, it headed south through the Panama Canal and docked in Virginia. Gunkler was to have a thirty-day leave, but two mushroom clouds over southern Japan ended the war before he was to return to it. Following his leave, he was sent back across the country to California to receive his discharge.

Gunkler had married Caroline Waterfall on 19 May 1944, while he was stationed in Columbia, South Carolina. The couple has five children and eight grandchildren.

He retired from The Dow Chemical Company in 1980 as a chief process engineer.

Concentration Camp is a Painful Memory for William Hahnenberg

At twenty years of age, William (Bill) Hahnenberg was sent into an experience that would fry the memory of the average person. But Hahnenberg is far above average.

After completing his army basic training in Arkansas, he was sent to the middle of the Mojave Desert in California to train for intensive war maneuvers in the desert war in Africa. After suffering through the sweltering heat for four months in preparation, the war in Africa ended.

So it was back to Ft. Leonard Wood, Missouri, for an additional four months of training. Four days after Christmas in 1943, he began a journey he would never forget. Landing in England, he was assigned to the 7th Corps Artillery, and attached to the 1st Army.

The guns that were used were twenty feet long, and on the way to combat they had to send scouts into the towns they would pass through, just to make sure they could make all the turns. The 155 mm weapons, with 95 pound shells, would fire a distance of 15 miles. "Most of the time we were within a five-mile range," Hahnenberg explained. "But the closer we could get to the front lines, the less often we would have to move. So we might start out within a mile of the targets, and by the time the Nazis had retreated, we might be firing ten miles."

Hahnenberg was "lucky." His assignment was in the headquarters battery, working in communications. Although it was considered a relatively safe assignment, if communications broke down, the headquarters battery could soon find itself in the line of enemy fire. When asked how the ninety-five pound shells were lifted to the barrels of gun, Hahnenberg replied that the men themselves lifted them. "That was probably why I was in the headquarters battery, carrying telephone lines," he mused.

His job was to lay the communication lines for field telephones. "I had only a month of training. The job was made doubly tough due to a shortage of telephone wire, not to mention dodging enemy fire."

Each time his unit moved up, he had to pick up all the wire so they could use it again. Not only were they short of wire, but short of gasoline for the vehicles, and ammunition for the mighty 155 mm weapons of death. "At one point we were limited to just four rounds

per gun per day because the front line was outrunning the supply lines," Hahnenberg recalled.

For six weeks, Hahnenberg's outfit was in a pocket within a mile of the English Channel. "There were so many men and guns that when the Nazis fired their weapons, they would always score a hit," Hahnenberg said glumly. "Every night we had 'bed check Charlie' just to see who was still alive."

When the Battle of the Bulge began, Hahnenberg worked with the 981st Artillery Battalion, keeping the lines of communication open.

Part of that job was to keep in touch daily with those men who had to announce changes in the weather. When the temperature and humidity changed, the artillerymen would have to adjust the sightings on the guns. Hahnenberg would then relay that information to the front lines. According to Hahnenberg, the Germans cut off the men, about a hundred in all, who were watching the weather front from their battalion. They were lined up and shot in cold blood. "They were the guys I had been talking with every day on the phone, and they were only about five miles from us," said Hahnenberg, adding, "I had worked with them during that whole campaign.

"The 981st was slaughtered," said Hahnenberg flatly. "They lost fifty percent of their battalion, but that was small compared to the infantry, who lost many times that many men," he remembered. But they were on the front lines from June until the following April. "We were bombed heavily," he added with a sigh, "and then there were the mines.

"But we were prime targets," Hahnenberg went on soberly. The Germans were dug into the mountains pretty well, according to Hahnenberg. "They could see us getting set, then they would start shelling."

What made it even worse was that the Germans were wearing American uniforms, taken off dead GIs, and even their tanks bore American insignias, according to Hahnenberg. "We just didn't know who was who."

On Christmas Eve 1944, in ten-degree weather, Hahnenberg's unit retreated in its vehicles thirty to forty miles to the rear, then drove for twenty-four hours to get around to the front lines once again.

But Hahnenberg was not always carrying telephone lines. He related how he started out as an antitank gunner during his desert training that stopped when the war ended in North Africa. Hahnenberg, who wears a hearing aid, mentioned that it was at that time he suffered permanent hearing loss. With the introduction of the bazooka, he was assigned to a different position. The bazooka was a handheld, battery-operated missile launcher.

One of the most painful memories for Hahnenberg took place in the Hartz Mountains in northern Germany. It was where the Germans assembled the V-1 and V-2 rockets, deep in the tunnels of the mountains. "It was the concentration camp labor that put those things together," Hahnenberg remembered. "They could have worked back in there for the next twenty years because they were positioned back in there so far. They were tunneled back in the mountain for a mile. They had the V-1s and V-2s on a regular assembly line when we got there." These were remote controlled rockets designed to fire across the English Channel to attack London.

The mountains were also where he saw some of the atrocities created by Hitler's warped mind. Wrapped in the supposed safety of the mountains was the Nordhausen concentration camp run by the Nazis.

"The concentration camp was my worst experience of the war," Hahnenberg said solemnly, trying to choke back the memory.

I've been in combat; I had seen men shot; I had seen a lot of dead guys; I've even sat down and eaten my lunch next to dead Germans, but this really got to you. Thousands of Jews were literally starving to death, and when they were too weak or too sick to work, they were shot in cold blood, and the bodies burned. The stories about those concentration camps were not exaggerated. They were everything you've ever heard they were.

I'll never forget those guys standing out there in their prisoner outfits. This one guy went to the back of the building where the cremation ovens were and picked up some dirt and ran it through his fingers, and said, "Comrades." That was where the Germans threw the ashes from the crematoriums. These Jewish prisoners were sifting through their fingers, the ashes of their Jewish friends.

That was my most upsetting experience of the war and that will always stay with me.

"Hospital rooms were filled with both the dead and the near-dead," he recalled sadly. "Those who were still alive were starving to death. When we arrived, it took the Germans by complete surprise. There were bodies still burning in the ovens.

"We also broke open locked doors to buildings where men, women and children lay dead from starvation. At gun point, we made German civilians haul the bodies up the hill on stretchers, and bull-dozers would dig trenches to bury them in. If they slowed down, we would beat on them. We weren't in too good a mood right then."

Some memories never die.

"After that we moved on to the Elbe River, and there we sat. That was the dividing line between the American and Russian sectors. It was just a matter of a few weeks before the war ended in Europe," Hahnenberg related.

"At the end of the war we were fighting fifteen-year-old kids, and sixty-year-old men because that's all they had left," said Hahnenberg. "They were unorganized and cut off from their main forces, and as our troop trucks rolled by, they would beg us to take them prisoners. They were just plain tired of fighting."

In spite of the fighting in Europe, and the atrocities burned into his memory for life, Hahnenberg is still grateful he was not in the Pacific theater. "At least we didn't have suicide planes raining down on us," he said emphatically.

Hahnenberg earned five Battle Stars during his tenure with Uncle Sam, meaning he was in five major battles. He was in combat in the Battle of the Bulge, Normandy, Northern France, Rhineland and Central Europe.

Don Harrington Will Never Forget
His 21st Birthday

As a nineteen-year-old private first class, recently drafted into the U.S. Army, he had no idea that he would be leaving a part of his body in a foreign country before returning home, or that it would happen on 13 December 1944, his twenty-first birthday.

Donald (Don) Harrington was a member of F Company, 78th Division, 309th Infantry. The 78th Division was filled with eighteen and nineteen-year-olds who were trained for infantry combat to replace soldiers who had been killed or wounded on the battlefields of Europe. Before that took place, however, it was decided that more than just replacements were needed. The war was not going well for America and the Allies, and it was decided to ship the whole 78th Division overseas.

On a cold October morning in 1944, Harrington and his division boarded the USS *Erickson* for a stormy thirteen-day troop ship ride to Bournemouth, England for advanced training, then transported to Le Havre, France.

Living in pup tents, they were deluged with three days of rain, soaking everyone and all their equipment. Soon after, they were transported by truck to St. Vith, Belgium where they were placed in reserve for General George Patton's Third Army. Before they were through, they would be under the command of General Omar Bradley's Ninth Army.

"Two weeks before entering combat," Harrington recalled, "five of us were picked by our platoon sergeant to form a patrol, and rode in a truck into enemy territory in Hurtgen Forest to find what bunkers we could, so we could determine where F Company should attack.

"We were in a jeep trailer that had a sand duplicate of the terrain of the area. As we found the bunkers, we had them marked."

When Harrington's outfit went on the attack three days later, two German mortar rounds landed close enough to them that seventeen American men were killed or wounded.

Harrington was one of the wounded. The shell had exploded about twelve inches from his left foot, and threw him spread-eagle into a ditch.

"The ditch was about three feet wide, but went almost straight down for about fifty feet," explains Harrington. "When I landed, I was in a booby trap area where the wires had a push trigger on one end and a

pull trigger on the other end. Fortunately, I set off the explosives on the way down, so when the medic got to me he had to cut the booby trap wires off me. I was completely tangled up in them."

Harrington's left leg was hanging by the cord at the knee. He also had twenty-three holes in his right leg and five broken bones in his foot and leg. The only thing that saved his right leg was that he had his trench knife in his army boot which took the brunt of the explosion.

"Because the temperature was about twenty below zero, I didn't bleed too much before getting help from our medic, John Collins.

He untangled me from all the booby trap wires, and the fuses went off, but, luckily, I had set the explosives off when I fell into the ditch. John then pulled me up to the road and gave me a shot of morphine before I passed out."

When Harrington awoke, he was on a stretcher in a barn and waiting his turn to go to an evacuation hospital in Wurms, Belgium. Even then, the ambulances had to time it right to avoid the mortar rounds that were landing on schedule in the area every fifteen minutes. That would not be Harrington's last ambulance ride.

The trip to the hospital in the ambulance is still fuzzy for him, but he remembers he was jarred awake often by ruts in the road created by mortar rounds.

When he arrived at the hospital, his jacket had to be cut off. It was too painful for him to take it off the normal way.

"They threw it in the corner with a clunk," Harrington remembered, smiling. "The doctor asked me what I had in the pockets, and when I told him 'hand grenades,' he ordered the jacket to be removed from the room. But I knew the pins were bent, and wouldn't go off."

Five hours and three units of blood later, Harrington woke up with one leg and a stump, both in full casts to keep them in place. It was his twenty-first birthday, and in spite of everything, a day for celebration. He was alive.

Three days later the historic Battle of the Bulge began, and the hospital in which Harrington was a patient, shook from the vibrations of the battle nearby. It shook even more when an 88 mm shell wrecked an upper floor of the building.

"All the patients that could be moved were taken to a train to vacate the area. A doctor and two nurses stayed with four patients who couldn't be moved," Harrington said glumly. "I never heard what happened to them."

Harrington wrote his parents, telling them only some of his experience, and assuring them he would be up and around in six weeks.

"But that was a slight miscalculation. It was six months before I was even able to sit up on the edge of the bed for twenty seconds."

Although the train left for Paris on 16 December, it didn't arrive until Christmas Eve. Frequently his train was routed to a siding and waited until another train, loaded with war materials headed for the Bulge, could pass by.

German prisoner of war medics were on the train platform in Paris to load the wounded troops into ambulances.

"They had POW on the back of their shirts, and I had my .45 under the blankets," Harrington remembered, "and if they dropped me I was going to shoot them, but there was no problem." He grinned at his boyhood bravado.

Harrington saw Paris from the back window of an ambulance, as it carried him along the narrow streets to the hospital and safety. But "safety" was short-lived. On Christmas Night, the Germans bombed the railyards only two miles away. Harrington was finally airlifted to England on New Year's Day.

He was in England only overnight, then transferred to a hospital in Wales. "We knew England was being bombed, but felt really safe in Wales," Harrington smiled.

After he was escorted to a hospital bed, a nurse came by and closed the curtains around his bed, according to Harrington. "When I asked her why she closed the curtains, she said, 'so you can die in peace.' I assured her I wasn't going to die, so she whipped open the curtain and left."

Harrington was in traction for forty-nine days, with weights on the end of the ropes, stretching the skin over his left stump, and to keep his leg bones aligned in his right leg. A pin was placed in his right heel and attached to a rope that hung over the end of the bed.

Fate can be benevolent, even in a war hospital. According to Harrington, the head nurse entered his ward one day, and asked if anyone could identify him.

"What have I done now?" he asked. The nurse turned out to be Beatrice Bosley, his stateside girlfriend's aunt. His girlfriend was Neva Achenbach. Achenbach had asked her aunt in a letter if she was in the same hospital where Harrington was located because they both had the same Army Post Office number.

Nurse Bosley helped Harrington obtain a spot on the next plane heading for the States.

In March 1945 Harrington ended up at Percy Jones Hospital in Battle Creek. Between that date and January 1947 he would have seventeen more operations. In the past fifty years he has also had several operations to remove shrapnel, ugly reminders of his twenty-first birthday.

In between those operations Harrington and Achenbach were married on 21 September 1945. "On our honeymoon I carried two canes and Neva carried two suitcases," he mused. "She has been and still is the best thing that ever happened to me."

Ten years after his experience he finally regained feeling in his remaining big toe, and five years after that he could wiggle it, which helps his stability when standing. Since the time of his discharge, Harrington has worn a special shoe for his right foot, and in 1965 had to have the arch fused to lessen the continual pain. Nearly sixty years later, he still visits the VA hospital three to four times each year for treatments or examinations.

Harrington retired in 1982 as a research chemist for The Dow Chemical Company after a forty-year career. The Harringtons have five children and nine grandchildren.

Gerald Hath: A Member of a Special Unit

Gerald (Gerry) Hath was a senior at Michigan State University when he received his draft notice in May 1942. But Uncle Sam was compassionate, and allowed Hath to complete the final six weeks so he could graduate with a degree in animal husbandry. He was then inducted at Camp Custer near Battle Creek in July 1942.

Uncle Sam was not so compassionate, however, when it came to the length of time Hath would spend on his payroll. Hath would have a tenure of forty-seven months in the service with nearly half that time in the South Pacific.

He completed his basic training at Camp Roberts, California, then went on to officers' training at Ft. Sill, Oklahoma. There he obtained his 2nd Lieutenant's commission and was sent to Ft. Bragg, North Carolina, where he was assigned to the newly-formed 287th Field Artillery Observation Battalion Cadre.

"The 287th was a field artillery battalion without guns," says Hath. "Actually the largest guns we had were machine guns." Hath's only weapon was a .45 caliber revolver. His was a special unit with fewer than three hundred men, and little known to the public. Its purpose was to locate enemy field artillery by the flash and sound of their guns and to survey and make maps to give the artillery coordinates of the enemy.

His next assignment was to Camp Bowie, Texas, where the rest of his unit was formed. It was also there that he talked his girlfriend, Betty Parker, into joining him in marriage on 24 July 1943. "An 'enlistment,'" he added, smiling with pride, "that has lasted for sixty years."

Following jungle training in the mosquito-infested swamps of Camp Polk, Louisiana, Hath's outfit was sent to Oahu, Hawaii, for more jungle maneuvers. The war was in its prime, both in Europe and in the South Pacific.

In July 1944, Hath left Hawaii aboard an LST, on a heading for little-known Yap Island, approximately eight hundred miles straight east of Leyte, in the Philippine Islands.

Normally, an LST is used as a landing craft on beaches, but in this case it was used as a personnel carrier, for jeeps and a bulldozer, according to Hath.

The trip took nearly two months aboard the cramped quarters of the small ship because it could only travel six knots, or about five miles, per hour.

"We couldn't begin to keep up with a convoy," recalled Hath, "and although there could have been Japanese submarines in the area, we hoped they wouldn't bother with such a small ship."

Boredom was the main enemy. "We played a lot of cards and read. But the days and nights were smooth and the nights beautiful with the moon on the water and the jellyfish that seemed to glow in the moonlight."

Reaching New Guinea on their way to Yap, the military changed its plans. "Instead of taking Yap Island, General MacArthur decided to take Leyte Island in the Philippines," said Hath. "Because I had had some survey classes at Michigan State, I became a survey officer." During camp time he was the special service officer, arranging entertainment and recreation for the men of the 287th.

Going into Leyte on the LST was one of Hath's most harrowing experiences of the war. "Japanese pilots were strafing the beaches, then came out after us," he remembered. "This one plane came within fifteen feet above our heads. I could see the expression on the pilot's face," he added. "He made only one pass. He was more interested in the people on the beach."

Armed with only his survey instruments and a .45 caliber revolver he hoped he would never have to use, the surveying would take place right up to the front lines. "Sometimes we would come under sniper fire," he remembered.

Once, while on Leyte, Hath and his survey group of four men were working within a mile of the front lines, then returned to camp. "About that time all heck broke out on the front," he recalled.

"Soon they were bringing the wounded right past us. We missed the bombardment by about five minutes."

Hath recalled another historic moment on Leyte. "It was the first or second day of the invasion and General MacArthur drove past us in his jeep, waving to us."

Hath was part of a sound group. "We would put a half-mile arc in the ground with about six microphones to pick up the sound of guns," Hath recalled. "That technique never did work well because of the many hills." He explained that the flash ranging technique worked best. "That is, triangulating on the flash of guns to determine the distance and direction to the enemy from our artillery. Then we would draw maps for our artillery so they would know where to key in," he remembered. Artillery units often never saw their targets. They zeroed in on areas from the information they were given by survey units. "This was a very accurate method. We could radio in the coordinates to our artillery.

"Leyte was pretty much the turning point in the war," Hath said. "The Japanese still had control of the waters in the South Pacific, and there was rumor that we were going to be bombarded by sea, but it never materialized."

But the war was far from over when Hath arrived aboard ship. Many ships were waiting to be unloaded, and he and his crew of six were assigned to unload their ship of food and munitions when it became their turn.

They waited four days, and in the meantime, Hath recalled, "Through binoculars, and listening to the radio communications between the air and ground troops, we watched the war going on day and night."

Hath and the sound and flash crews watched for the gun flashes and sounds in order to do their survey reporting for the ground troops. Often he worked out of the command center on the ship, triangulating the information and calling it in to the artillery.

"It was a difficult job on Okinawa," recalled Hath. "Because of the terrain, the enemy would be located in caves. They would roll out their artillery, fire, then roll it back in."

It was not until he returned home after the war that they realized they had been watching one of the most fiercely fought battles of World War II.

Hath does not remember being really scared, but always being in danger. He recalled one Japanese soldier just before he was killed. "He had gotten into our outfit just before the war was over on Okinawa," he remembered. "When I spotted him, he got up and ran and the fellow next to me stood up and shot him. If I had kept still, he would have gotten away," he said, sadly. "I felt guilty because I don't think he was even armed." Hath thought at the time that the Japanese soldier was looking for his outfit and became lost.

The war was over on Okinawa in July 1945. Just prior to the signing of the armistice in Japan, Hath flew over the coast of Korea in a small Seabees plane to ensure the Japanese were not hiding any war ships.

"There were four of us on the plane, and we flew directly over the huge armada of American battleships, carriers, etc., heading for Japan. There were hundreds of ships spread out as far as you could see," Hath recalled. "I will never forget that sight."

First Lieutenant Hath remained on Okinawa for several months after the war, assigned to the base camp. He returned to his home and wife in Lansing following his discharge in June 1946. He earned his teaching degree in agriculture, as well as his master's degree.

He began teaching in the Midland Public Schools in 1949 and ended a thirty-one year career at Northeast Intermediate (now Middle) School in 1980.

Don Hawkins Returned a Hero to a Former War Zone

Every time one Midland resident watches the weather broadcast on television, or uses his microwave oven, he is reminded of a time nearly sixty years ago when those using microwaves were sworn to secrecy.

"We were in on the ground floor of leading edge electronic technology during World War II," said Don Hawkins, formerly owner and CEO of Hawkins Printing, Inc. for thirty years. "It was the forerunner of today's air traffic control system. You see it in use every night when you see the radar maps in TV weather reports, and every microwave oven contains a version of magnetrons that used to be a huge secret."

During World War II, radar was a highly classified subject, and those who were involved in designing, manufacturing and using it were not allowed to discuss it in public.

One of those tight-lipped individuals was Hawkins. He enlisted in the Quartermaster Corps on 10 November 1942. Eighteen days later, he turned nineteen.

After three months of training, he was transferred to what became known as the Signal Aircraft Warning (SAW) Battalion, a branch of the then U.S. Army Air Corps, at Drew Field in Tampa, Florida.

Hawkins' first overseas assignment was just before Christmas 1943. He was sent to Glasgow, Scotland, where wild rumors abounded regarding their designation for D day in Europe six months hence.

Before arriving overseas, he was a member of the 555th SAW Battalion. This Battalion did participate in the historic invasion of the continent, but, before that happened, Hawkins had been transferred to the 573rd Battalion. That was his good fortune. The 555th suffered heavy losses at the Battle of the Bulge.

Thirty days after D day, however, Hawkins and two hundred other men crossed the choppy English Channel on amphibious landing craft, and waded ashore on the now-famous Utah Beach in France.

"The beach was pretty much cleared by that time, with only an occasional sniper," Hawkins recalled.

It was also Hawkins' good fortune to be assigned to battalion headquarters, situated behind the front lines, where he typed up orders and promotions and kept track of battalion personnel.

"One day word came out that all vehicles, drivers and assistant drivers were to report to a certain spot behind the lines on the beach. Nobody knew why, but three days later the vehicles and their personnel returned, and we learned the reason they had left in such a hurry. General Eisenhower had a tough time keeping the reins on Patton [General Patton was Eisenhower's subordinate], and Patton advanced too far from his supply line. He was running out of fuel for his tanks, and our vehicles had to rush it to the front line," Hawkins remembered.

Each vehicle was loaded with five-gallon cans of gasoline, and it was a big race for 150 miles, getting the fuel to Patton, according to Hawkins. Because of the distance and the urgency, MPs were along the highway, keeping the traffic going in a rapid and orderly fashion, Hawkins remembered. "If any vehicle, for whatever reason, caused a delay, they were just ushered off to the side of the road so the others could move on," he said.

Hawkins knew the war was heating up, "because on the heels of the fuel situation was a big drive to donate blood from all the healthy military men," he said. "Every man in the company responded. Laughing, Hawkins added, "I'm not sure if it was loyalty or the shot of whiskey they got afterward."

Moving on through France, Hawkins' unit spent a miserable night dodging sniper fire around Paris. By the time they reached Bastogne, a small town in southeast Belgium, "you would hardly know there was a war going on," recalled Hawkins.

It would not remain that way for long. According to the American College Dictionary, "U.S. forces were besieged here during the German counter offensive, December 1944."

The movement of Hawkins' unit took it through Vlytingen and Acchen, Belgium. The latter, according to Hawkins, was a city of 100,000, and it had been leveled by Allied bombings.

While Hawkins's unit was not directly involved in the Battle of the Bulge, it was on the fringe, and close enough to hear the battle taking place.

"Everyone took his turn seriously in patrolling our area at night," Hawkins recalled. "And it was a difficult job because the Germans had confiscated American uniforms, trucks, weapons and some even knew our passwords. Many of them spoke perfect English."

When asked how the American troops would weed out the Germans from the Americans, Hawkins replied, "We would ask more detailed questions, like 'who won the World Series last year?' or, 'Who was Dick Tracy's girlfriend?'"

The primary function of Hawkins' unit was to protect their men and materials against enemy aircraft, then to direct their own aircraft to targets with radar.

Directing the fighter aircraft were specially trained Air Corps controllers. They would be directing P-51s and P-47s from centers manned by Signal Corps personnel. The center's personnel would plot radar reports of aircraft sightings on large tables or screens. Maps of the combat zones were then superimposed. The 573rd SAW, of which Hawkins was a member, took an active role in directing the fighters.

The team's job was to get within twenty or thirty miles of the front lines, and establish their radar sites. "First, it was all defensive, to protect us against enemy aircraft," Hawkins recalled. "Then when the enemy planes became diminished, we used the radar on the offensive to direct our own planes to targets."

In the summer of 1944, Hawkins and his unit were on the border between France and Germany, "and the battlefront was moving so fast, and the pilots, flying very low, were radioing back to the ground troops that the Germans were waving white flags in surrender. We were moving as fast as we could to capture them on the ground. They knew they were surrounded."

Hawkins went on, smiling at the memory. "The Germans wanted to be captured and get it over with, and it was the first time in known history that the air force took prisoners."

The first prisoner Hawkins took was a fifteen-year-old in a German uniform who turned himself in. "He had become lost from his unit," Hawkins remembered, "and had been living off berries or whatever he could find edible in the woods."

The boy-soldier was more than happy to tell everything he knew. In return, he was given all the C rations he wanted. "We hated those rations," said Hawkins, "but he ate two cans of them without hesitation." Hawkins and his men finally took them away from him so he wouldn't get sick.

On 8 May 1945, victory was won in Europe. A month later, according to Hawkins, a new unit was formed, called the 29th Tactical Air Command. Hawkins became one of its members.

En route by truck convoy to the seaport in Marseilles for France to board their ship, they received word that the second atomic bomb had been released over Nagasaki, and the war was finally over.

"Actually we didn't hear about it right then because we were on the trucks. It wasn't until we reached France that we heard about it, then rumors of Japan's surrender began surfacing," Hawkins recalled. For ten days he received various shots in preparation for transfer to the South Pacific.

"We protested the shots," Hawkins chuckled, "because the war was over, but orders were orders and we got them anyway."

All during the war, Hawkins carried with him a small Bible given to him by an elderly gentleman from his church in Bay City. "I didn't have any favorite passages," he smiled, "but just reading it when I could was comforting."

The war didn't end for Tech-4 (Sergeant) Hawkins until 10 October 1945, just days before his twenty-second birthday. He had spent a total of three years of his young life either preparing for war or in it.

Hawkins and his wife, JoAnn, have returned twice to the former war front. "In 1990 we went back on a planned tour. In 1991, Belgium held a 'Liberation Celebration,' and we were invited back." The invitations had come from Belgian officials. Those attending besides the Hawkinses were another American, a former GI from Great Britain and a Canadian, all of whom were veterans of the war in Belgium.

Acchen had been completely rebuilt, as have all the other large cities, and Hawkins noticed a big difference in the generations there.

"While the younger people were celebrating in the streets with fireworks and frivolity, the people our age were in the upper windows of the buildings with tears on their cheeks," Hawkins recalled. "They remembered what it was once like, and who came and helped regain their freedom. They really rolled out the red carpet for us, and just couldn't thank us enough for what the American troops had done for them so long ago."

The Hawkinses and the other former GIs were besieged with gifts from the local residents.

The reunion with the local residents was a bittersweet occasion, according to Hawkins. "It was a reminder of a once-ugly past, but to meet the wonderful Belgian people we once defended is a beautiful memory we will always carry with us."

Harry Hoffman Earned Five Major Battle Stars

By early 1941, Harry (Woody) Hoffman, already an old man by military standards, had served nearly a year in the army. He was twenty-eight and looking forward to ending his one-year military commitment.

"At that time everyone had to serve at least a one-year stint," said Hoffman. About halfway through the year, the rules changed. "They weren't taking anyone over twenty-eight, and those who were already at that mark could be released."

His time was up in October that year. He was released, and two weeks later he and Phyllis Robb, his girlfriend of four years, were married in Detroit. It was 25 November 1941.

Twelve days later the Japanese dropped their lethal load of munitions on Pearl Harbor. It was "a day that will live in infamy" that would forever change their lives. Hoffman had been released to the reserves, so he was immediately recalled to active duty and assigned to Camp Polk, Louisiana. This time his commitment would not end for nearly half a decade.

Going through basic training for the infantry was a pretend situation for Hoffman and his comrades.

"We had no weapons to train with," he remembered, shaking his head.

"We had to cut saplings and pretend to use them like a rifle. For bayonet practice, we sharpened one end of the sapling and stabbed at gunnysacks filled with straw placed on a vertical pole sticking out of the ground. That's how bad off the country was.

"When we finally got our rifles we were warned not to lay them down; we could get more men, but not more rifles."

Hoffman became a member of the 3rd Armored Division, and trained for several months in the Mojave Desert in California. He was then sent to Indian Town Gap, Pennsylvania. In all, he trained for two and a half years in the States and in England before shipping out to the war zone with Company B, 36th Armored Infantry Regiment

His introduction to war began shortly after D day when he landed on the shores of France. To get there, they had to cross the English Channel to Omaha Beach. In the middle of the channel, they were delayed for three days because as Hoffman put it, "They were having the worst storm they had had in twenty years."

As rough as it was—they bobbed like a cork on a whitewater journey down the Colorado River—that delay may have saved his life. By the time his outfit arrived the fighting was further inland, and in terms of opposition, the landing was relatively smooth.

In France, Hoffman received his only injury of the war. He and a buddy had dug a foxhole and had found some old boards to partially cover it for better protection.

"German fighter planes came in at low level and strafed us," Hoffman recalled. "At low level, airplanes are difficult to hear until they are nearly on top of you."

Hoffman and his buddy dove for their foxhole, and Hoffman hit his kneecap on the edge of one of the boards as he dropped in. "It tore it up pretty good," he said.

"I debated going to the medics because if I did, my wife would be notified," he remembered, "and I didn't want to worry her." His buddies patched him up as best they could, but it still bothers him sixty years later.

By the time it left France in September 1944, Hoffman's company had lost two-thirds of its men, and only one officer remained. But it regrouped with replacements and moved on into Belgium.

During the Battle of the Bulge in Belgium, Hoffman's outfit was nearly annihilated. "From a company of 190 men," he recalled, "there were only about 50 of us left, and we had to pull back to reorganize."

The 7th Armored Division came to their defense, he adds, "But they took an awful beating."

Hoffman's 3rd Armored Division was known as the "Spearhead Division." Because his unit had been in combat for awhile, his division was selected to lead the way into battle.

"We were always spearheading the attack," Hoffman said.

To confirm his comments, Hoffman has received a plaque he proudly displays on his living room wall. It reads,

The Third Armored Division of World War II, "Spearhead" Division Campaign Credits; Normandy, 6–6–44 to 8–23–44, Northern France, 7–25–44 to 9–14–44, Rhineland, 9–15–44 to 3–21–45, Ardennes-Alsace, 12–16–44 to 1–25–45 and Central Europe, 3–25–45 to 5–11–45.

By the time the war ended, Hoffman had earned a Presidential Citation Ribbon with five gold Battle Stars, indicating the five major battles mentioned on the plaque.

The division was nicknamed "Spearhead" because 1st Army orders so frequently read, "The 3rd Armored Division will spearhead the attack." It spent 231 days in combat and was credited with the decisive destruction of fourteen German divisions. Spearhead took 76,720 prisoners (five times its own total strength), and destroyed 6,724 pieces of enemy equipment, including 1,794 tanks and 942 special purpose guns while holding its own casualty figure to 10,371

While Hoffman was trained to use several weapons of war, and used most of them along the way, he was not always carrying a gun and advancing on the enemy. While he never let his rifle out of his sight, he was also trained as company cook. "I had a grocery store and meat market in Highland Park, Michigan before the war, and I always liked to work with food," he smiled. "It was easy for me." At seventeen he was operating his own grocery store, and later worked for the Kroger Company.

During the Battle of the Bulge, and when they had been pushed back into Germany, Hoffman and six other cooks prepared holiday turkeys in a horse barn. The turkeys had been sent from the States.

"It's difficult being a chef when you are only in one place two to three days at a time," he mused.

On a more sobering note, Hoffman reflected that three of the seven cooks were later killed in combat.

One night in his foxhole, Hoffman's lieutenant came by, and Hoffman told him he saw German soldiers on the ridge in the moonlight. Apparently ignoring the comment, the lieutenant came by two or three more times during the night and Hoffman gave him the same information.

At 3:30 a.m., according to Hoffman, the lieutenant returned to report that Hoffman's outfit was surrounded. At daybreak, the group retreated out of the area on trucks as American artillery fired over their heads, wiping out the German encampment on the ridge.

Hoffman could only surmise that his lieutenant had formed a platoon, scouted the enemy ridge to confirm the findings, and had ordered the artillery to pump in shells at daybreak. If his assumption is correct, Hoffman saved many lives.

Like many silent heroes, Hoffman's brain refused to recall some of the details of a war in which he fought six decades ago, but he does remember landing on Omaha Beach and seeing a boot with only part of a leg sticking out of a foxhole. And later an idle American tank on a beachhead where he found the men inside burned to a crisp, still at their battle stations. "I never looked inside a tank again," he said glumly.

One of his most stressful jobs of the war was hauling ammunition by truck to the front lines near Omaha Beach. "We knew any minute we could be hit and blown away."

The day he and his company came upon the Nordhausen concentration camp near Berlin, he helped free American prisoners of war. "I could not believe what I was seeing," Hoffman remembered. "The men looked more like skeletons than like men. At least thirty-five of them had been dying every day. On seeing that, my mind froze."

Hoffman's mind also froze the memory into his brain forever.

Roy Komachi: Of Japanese Descent, But a True American

He grew up in Portland, Oregon and was eighteen years old when he learned the Japanese had bombed Pearl Harbor. Although he was an American by birth, his parents were not, and 110,000 people of Japanese descent, of whom at least 75,000 were U.S. citizens, were held in internment camps as far east as Arkansas. Their only mistake was being Asian at the wrong time in this country's history.

In February 1942, President Roosevelt issued an executive order authorizing the removal of all Japanese immigrants and native-born Japanese-Americans in California, Washington, Oregon and Arizona.

Military authorities feared the Japanese on the West Coast could form a subversive force in the event of an invasion. There were very few voices raised, except for the Quakers and the ACLU, protesting the evacuation of U.S. citizens.

Puzzled as to why at the time, Roy Komachi, a Japanese-American Midland resident since 1958, says with fervor, "No matter what they did, I was an American citizen and no matter how badly I was treated, this was still my country."

Komachi's parents had come to America prior to World War I, but could not gain citizenship because they were Oriental, according to Komachi. "They couldn't get citizenship if they wanted to," he remembered.

"All the Japanese on the West Coast were affected," recalled Komachi, "but those in Hawaii were untouched. That would have ruined the infrastructure of the islands."

He went on, "I was interned in a camp in Hunt, Idaho, behind barbed wire with armed guards, along with my family and other residents of the Pacific Northwest." Komachi was twenty years old at the time.

In early 1943, Roosevelt and the War Department announced the formation of the 442nd Regimental Combat Team. This was to be a segregated unit made up of Nisei (pronounced Nee-say), second generation Japanese-Americans from Hawaii and the mainland.

Nearly 10,000 Hawaiian born Nisei volunteered for military service, and 1,100 volunteered from the mainland camps. Prior to this time, a unit of the Hawaiian National Guard was activated as the 100th Infantry Battalion June 1942, according to Komachi.

The men were comprised of the Hawaiian National Guard, and quite appropriately adopted the phrase, "Remember Pearl Harbor" as their motto. The 100th Battalion was later to be incorporated into the 442nd Regimental Combat Team in Italy, Komachi remembered.

He enlisted on 7 May 1943, and was sent for thirteen weeks of basic training in the sweltering, mosquito-infested Camp Shelby, Mississippi. "I'm not completely certain whether it was a spirit of patriotism or whether I wanted to get away from being imprisoned in the camp after over a year," Komachi said honestly.

He became a member of the 442nd Regimental Combat Team. "We were treated for what we were," Komachi says, "Americans." After basic training he shipped out of Newport News, Virginia, heading toward Naples, Italy.

According to information researched from the Internet, "The 442nd chose as their slogan, 'Go For Broke,' a Hawaiian slang term from the dice game, craps. It meant to risk everything, give everything you have . . . all or nothing!"

It took thirty days to arrive in Naples, according to Komachi. From the North Atlantic, into the Mediterranean Sea and finally to Italy, the huge convoy of ships ran a continual zigzag pattern in an attempt to avoid German submarines that might be searching for them. They were also delayed by landing on the war-torn island of Sicily, an island off the southwest corner of the "boot" of Italy itself. Sicily was the scene of sharp and stubborn fighting, long marches, and steep hills. "Before it was over, the American troops had a battle on their hands and blisters on their feet. Progress was often measured in yards," states a monograph offered by Komachi.

Sicily had to be taken so that when the Americans and Allies landed at Naples, they could be certain the enemy would not come up from behind them and trap them there.

"The 100th Battalion had preceded us into combat, having been assigned to the 34th Red Bull Division, which had a record number of continuous days of combat," Komachi recalled.

Among the toughest fighting for the 100th was at the city of Cassino, according to the literature. "The Germans held the Abbey of Monte Cassino, a huge castle-like building on top of a mountain," Komachi explained. "We were easy pickings for them as we tried to storm the mountain. Eventually, the abbey was bombed by the air force, but not before a lot of good men were shot," Komachi remembered.

"The Germans claimed they were not using it as a fortress, but when it was bombed by the Americans, the rubble made excellent cover for them, and it was easy to pick off our troops from there," he said. "Our men went from room to room routing them out."

Naples had already been taken by other forces, according to Komachi, so the landing there was relatively quiet. They then moved northward from Anzio and into Rome, which was declared an "open city," thus being spared any destruction of war.

It was here that the 100th rejoined the 442nd Regimental Combat Team to serve as a single infantry unit.

Just north of Rome, in the small village of Civitavecchia, on the West Coast of Italy, Komachi received his true baptism by fire. "It was somewhat ironic in that we had received our training in the swamps of Mississippi, and here we were fighting in the mountains of Italy," Komachi smiled.

Komachi was with a heavy weapons company, equipped with 81 mm mortars and water-cooled machine guns. "It was constant fighting from mountain to mountain, the whole length of Italy, continually pushing the Germans back."

He went on, "What made conditions so difficult was that the enemy was always on higher ground which meant that he always had the advantage of observing our movements. The only way to counter this was to launch the attacks against their positions at night which we often did."

Komachi was also with the forces near Milano when Benito Mussolini and his mistress, Clara Petacci, were captured. Mussolini was the Italian Facist leader and prime minister of Italy, who was directing his country against the American and Allied forces. Following a summary court-martial they were both shot, and their bodies taken to a Milan public square where they hanged until buried in unmarked graves.

Patrols were very active on both sides, according to another book Komachi owns, which is the story of the 442nd Combat Team. Because of the hedges and vineyards that crisscrossed the landscape, low visibility from ground level made patrolling extremely dangerous.

It was discovered, according to the book, that the Germans were maintaining a patrol base on the south side of the Arno River, and on the left flank of the 3rd Battalion. When the 442nd Combat Team entered the picture, Komachi's company commander was killed acting as a decoy and creating a diversion, enabling the rest of Komachi's company (Company M) to withdraw to better positions and call down artillery fire on the enemy.

Reaching a stalemate in the fighting in central Italy, the 442nd withdrew and was shipped back to Naples for provisions and replacements for the casualties.

His regiment was put aboard LSTs shortly thereafter for its next mission which was to join the 36th Texas Division up the Rhone Valley in France. The German army was slowly retreating back to the Rhine River, and bitterly contesting every foot of ground as it got closer to its homeland.

"We linked up with the 36th in the Vosges Mountains, which are in the Alsace-Lorraine region of eastern France, along the border," Komachi explained, "It was here that our unit was to engage the enemy in the bloodiest battle of its regimental history."

One of the battalions of the 36th Texas Division was isolated along a high ridge line overlooking the village of Bruyeres. The Germans had succeeded in surrounding these GIs, and all attempts to reach them had failed. The situation was getting desperate as they were running short of ammunition and medical supplies, according to Komachi.

"Numerous attempts to air-drop these items were only partially successful," he said. "All assaults by the 36th to reach their trapped comrades had been beaten back after three days of intensive battle. The commanding general of the 36th gave the order that he wanted his men rescued, come hell or high water, and the 442nd was ordered into battle.

"I remember our 3rd Battalion was to be the point unit for the attack, and moved into position in the pitch darkness of night. We couldn't see anything, so we just grabbed onto the guy in front of us as we moved forward." The attack commenced against stiff resistance and very heavy artillery fire.

Progress was measured in yards, Komachi remembered, against a well dug-in enemy. "Maneuverability was severely limited by the terrain, so it was essentially a frontal assault. Visibility was non-existent due to the huge trees and undergrowth. The casualties were so numerous that some rifle companies were commanded by platoon sergeants."

The average company in the regiment, Komachi recalled, was down to thirty-five men. After three days of continual combat, following a bayonet assault, contact was finally made with the trapped Texans.

"We rescued what came to be known as the 'Lost Battalion,'" he says. But not without a price. "We had over eight hundred casualties to save two hundred men of the 36th."

As a result of this action, Komachi's unit became "Honorary Texans." "I consider myself very lucky to have survived this battle with only minor wounds from a mortar round," said Komachi.

To honor their rescue, the commanding general of the 36th wanted to have a farewell regimental review before Komachi's unit left the general's command. But he was in for a shock when the 442nd assembled. "He barked, 'I said I wanted a regimental review. Where the hell is the rest of your outfit?' Our colonel replied, 'I'm sorry general, but that is the whole regiment.'"

After a three-day run down the Rhone Valley by truck, the combat team wound up on the French Riviera near Nice. Their mission was to hold the French-Italian border to prevent any German incursion at this point along the Maritime Alps. There was little action other than patrols on both sides, but men were still getting killed and wounded, Komachi remembered. "We called it the 'Champagne Campaign,'" said Komachi. The campaign lasted for six months.

As with all good things, this "plush" assignment came to an end. It was back to Italy aboard navy vessels, to face the Germans in the mountains once again. Their mission this time was to attack the Gothic Line, which was the last stronghold guarding the entrance to the Po Valley, then north to the Brenner Pass in the Italian Alps.

"Since the front had been in a stalemate for some time, there had been ample opportunity for the Germans to heavily fortify their positions, so the task was going to be difficult," Komachi said seriously. "The mountainous terrain made frontal assaults impossible, so any movement had to be done at night." He remembered hiking several miles in the dark, where they hid out in a small mountain village from which the attack was to be launched the next morning.

The element of surprise worked, and the 442nd was able to breach the Gothic Line that had resisted the 92nd Division for over six months.

"There was a battle for Mt. Belvedere in this sector, which is where Senator Bob Dole was badly wounded with the 10th Mountain Division," Komachi recalled. "They were moving up on our right flank during this battle."

At one point in the war, the 442nd passed through the village of Bruyeres on the western side of France, just thirty miles from the German Border.

"This town had been held by the Germans for some time," Komachi said. "We were able to liberate the town, and after the war the villagers were so grateful they erected a monument to honor the 442nd Combat Team."

With modest reluctance, Komachi shows his numerous combat medals, including the ribbon with multicampaign battle stars, two Bronze Stars for Bravery in Action, a Presidential Unit Citation, his Combat Infantry Badge and a Purple Heart. His war symbols are so numerous he does not even remember what some of them were for.

Komachi's unit was recognized as the most highly decorated unit of its size in U.S. military history, according to research on the Internet.

President Truman, according to the same research, "was so moved by their bravery in the field of battle, as well as that of African American soldiers during World War II, that he issued an American order to desegregate the Armed Forces."

Komachi was discharged from the army in November 1945, and with the aid of the GI Bill, entered Illinois Tech to become an architect. His plans changed, however, and he obtained a degree in chemical engineering. He retired from The Dow Chemical Company in 1986 after a thirty-year career.

In 1996 Komachi and his wife, Miye, had the opportunity to return to Bruyeres to see the monument and to visit the surrounding landscape. At one point he found a depression in the earth that he believes was a foxhole he once inhabited that perhaps saved his life more than half a century before. "In the town square," Komachi said, "they still fly the American flag." Proof of this was in the snapshots he had taken there. In addition, the villagers named a street after the 442nd Combat Team, and the sign indicated the month and year they arrived, "October 1944."

Going back and exploring the wooded area and former foxholes surrounding the village, a bittersweet feeling came over Komachi. He was pleased to have helped these friendly people so many years ago, and to see how they appreciated it. On the other hand, he was haunted by the fact that many of his friends ended their life's journey in this area so many years ago.

He knew the Germans had planted many mines around the area during the war, and the thought crossed his mind, wondering, as he did more than fifty years before, where they were and if some were still active. "It was a strange feeling," said Komachi.

Robert Lucas: A Well-Known Man with a Little-Known Past

Thousands of young people in the Midland community grew up knowing Robert (Bud) Lucas. The John Wayne look-alike was principal at Northeast Intermediate and Midland High School for a quarter century. Before that he was a mathematics and science teacher at Northeast for six years.

With hardly an exception, none of them knew that Lucas was in the little-known branch of the Navy known as the "Seabees" in World War II.

The first Seabees were called to action in January 1942. They were trained and skilled tradesmen, recruited from all walks of the construction trade. They included skilled artisans and masters in their own particular line of work such as carpenters, electricians, plumbers, welders, blacksmiths, masons, riggers, painters, and operators of all types of earth-moving equipment.

They built dry docks and bridges, dredged canals for ships, and worked in combat as well as in noncombat conditions.

Prior to the Seabees, construction in the war zones was accomplished by civil service employees. "But that created a problem," Lucas explained. "They weren't allowed to carry weapons." The Seabees, members of a military unit, were allowed to protect themselves during the building process, according to Lucas.

He grew up in Cleveland, Ohio, and had just turned twenty-one when he enlisted in the Seabees. At twenty-one, he was the "baby of the bunch." The average age of a Seabee was thirty-six. Some were in their fifties. Many were obviously too old to be drafted, and some had served in World War I. But they wanted to help America win this war too, so they volunteered their skills and training where they could be most useful. They were all enlisted men, and valuable to the military because they did not have to be trained to do their jobs. Already proficient craftsmen in their professions, the construction battalions eventually grew to 262,000 men.

Bud Lucas, although young, was a machinist, meaning he could run lathes, and he knew his tools. There was another reason Lucas became a Seabee. He was colorblind.

"I tried the regular navy, the marines, the army and the air force," Lucas remembered ruefully. "They all turned me down." But when the Seabees learned of Lucas's interests and abilities, they waived the

colorblindness stipulation. He signed up on the spot. It was 10 August 1942, but Uncle Sam waited two months before deciding he wanted Lucas.

His agenda for the next three and a half years looks like a resumé of someone who could not hold a job: five different military camps obtaining military training or advanced training, and five different ships to arrive at various places in the South Pacific.

The military training consisted of myriad orientation processes, then plunged into a maze of military drill, commando training, lectures and demonstrations of various phases and methods of warfare. With Lucas's prior experience, he moved two steps up on the hierarchy, and was given the rank of machinist.

At one of his advanced training locations in the Chesapeake Bay area, he saw the navy's diving school, submitted his application, and completed the month-long program.

It was a strenuous exercise for Lucas to become a certified diver. "Our diving gear, including the leaded feet, weighed 197 pounds. I weighed 157 pounds."

On 27 February 1943, Lucas boarded the USS *Mormachawk* with a thousand other members of the 44th U.S. Naval Construction Battalion, on a heading for the New Hebrides Islands in the South Pacific. The New Hebrides lie approximately 1,000 miles straight west of the Fiji Islands, 15–16 degrees below the equator and north of New Zealand by 1,500 miles.

The ship was extremely vulnerable as it traveled without escort through enemy submarine waters. Because enemy submarines often attacked at daybreak or at dusk when it is difficult to see a periscope, "all thousand of us had to stand on the deck twice a day with our life jackets on in case we were hit," Lucas remembered.

Fifteen days later they safely crossed the International Date Line, losing a day they looked forward to recovering for the next three years.

Three weeks later, the USS *Mormachawk* arrived on Espiritu Santo in the New Hebrides Islands. The skilled workers, along with other Seabee units, began their project of building a camp, hospital, docks, roads and airstrips.

The Seabees received their diving certification from the regular Navy divers. Their final test was to dive to the belly of the sunken USS *Calvin Coolidge* which lay at the bottom of a channel off Espiritu Santo. It was disabled because the captain of the ship insisted he could take it through by himself. The *Coolidge* hit a mine, according to Lucas, and the ship sank. Besides being a troop ship, it also carried quantities of the lifesaving medication, quinine, used against malaria. There were no casualties in the sinking. Lucas dove to help retrieve the medications.

It was on Espiritu Santo Island that Lucas and several other Seabees saw their first celebrity. They were using their outdoor shower when Eleanor Roosevelt, then the First Lady of the United States on a goodwill tour to the South Pacific, was touring the island in a jeep. The jeep in which she rode drove by the naked men.

"We knew she was on the island, but didn't know when she might be coming by," Lucas grinned. "It had been over a year since we had seen a woman, but the president's wife was far from a sex symbol. We just waved as her motorcade passed by."

In addition to his diving skills, Lucas was trained for everything from switchboard operator to truck driver.

The major nuisance on the island, according to Lucas, was "Washing Machine Charlie."

"Washing Machine Charlie was a Japanese fighter pilot who would come in high at night, and his plane sounded like an old washing machine," recalled Lucas. "He would drop a bomb or two, then be gone." The men on the ground, who worked around the clock, knew the raid wouldn't last, but would head for foxholes and bunkers for safety.

"One night I was on the switchboard when Charlie approached. I phoned the commanding officer to warn him, and asked what *I* should do." 'Stay right where you are!' replied the CO. I didn't have that job long," Lucas chuckled. "My mama didn't raise no dummy."

The heat of the South Pacific was oppressive. "It was always steaming with heavy rains. The annual rainfall in the New Hebrides averages four hundred inches." The annual rainfall is about thirty-three inches in mid-Michigan.

Fifteen months after passing under the trusses of the Golden Gate Bridge, and with the saddened faces of loved ones still etched in their memories, the 44th Seabee Battalion boarded the USS *James Monroe*, its bow pointing toward Manus Island. Manus is in the Admiralty group, located just two degrees below the equator, and directly north of New Guinea. This was as close to a hot war zone as they would get and Lucas did, in fact, earn his first Battle Star there.

"We didn't know where we were headed," Lucas recalled, "But when we got up the next morning, it was the most beautiful sight I had ever seen."

Surrounding Lucas's ship were Australian cruisers and American destroyers, meaning they finally had an escort.

"This was both good news and bad news. This meant we had an escort, but it also meant we were going to a hot spot, and getting close to a lot of naval action."

They pulled into New Guinea where the ships sat for two weeks. "We were waiting for moonless nights," Lucas explained, "hoping we could slip out of there unseen."

The right night finally arrived, and the convoy rushed toward the Admiralty Islands.

The major project on Manus Island was to tap the water from the mountain streams to provide Admiral Nimitz's Naval Fleet with fresh water for the upcoming invasion of the Philippines. General MacArthur and the infantry were on their way.

Before MacArthur would arrive, however, the 44th Seabees engaged in some heavy fighting, earning them their Battle Star. They were assisted by the Australian army and the U.S. Infantry. Landing on the beach, the navy ships were shooting their monster guns over the heads of the foot soldiers, churning the debris in front of them.

"There's nothing like a five-inch shell whistling overhead, splintering the trees in front of you, to make you realize just how serious the situation is," Lucas said. "We also encountered a couple ambushes we had to work through," he added matter-of-factly.

Another project for the Seabees was to clear and chart the harbor, enabling the American battle ships to enter. The ships needed a minimum of thirty-two feet beneath their hulls to enter safely. The coral reefs were a major hazard. Lucas and his crew would go below in full diving gear with a jackhammer to drill holes for explosives and blast the coral from the bottom.

Part of the hazard, according to Lucas, entailed sharks. "When we exploded the coral, it killed a lot of fish, and the sharks would come along and get an easy meal. We were told how to drive the interested sharks away using our air hose, but I wasn't about to put it to the test. I just went to another area and planted the dynamite."

At one point on that dive, Lucas came as close to death as he had ever been. "My mask began filling with water," he remembered. "I did the usual things to clear the mask, but it wasn't working. I had two choices. Either give the distress signal on the line to the men on the ship above me, or rip off my weights and go up by myself."

Lucas was in forty feet of water and out of air, so his decision was made in an instant. "I ripped off my weights and mask and shot for the top. Even though I made it, I began going into shock because I had held my breath so long. All I could do was yell, 'come and get me.'"

The shock caused Lucas to freeze in the tropical water. "They threw a buoy right in front of me, but I couldn't grab it. I began going down when someone dove in and grabbed me."

After his fellow Seabees got Lucas safely on the steel deck of his ship, he was still not out of danger. "They didn't know as much about resuscitation then as they do now," Lucas reflects. "They worked on me for a half-hour, and the next thing I heard was someone saying, 'He's breathing.'"

Even more hazardous than the job, were the illnesses with which the Seabees had to cope. High on the list was malaria and dengue (pronounced dengi) fever. Sometimes they became so severe they would cause a work stoppage. "At one time two hundred of our men had one or the other," Lucas sighs. That was twenty percent of their total work force.

The men were just wearing out, according to Lucas. "They were all older, and after two years of this in enemy infested jungles without a break, they became more vulnerable to stress and disease. Because of their age, many were suffering from prostate problems. And most of them had families who were growing up without a father," Lucas said.

At one point half his battalion was sent home; some from accidents, some from war injuries, and some from friendly fire. A few became casualties, and many suffered from illness.

On 10 January 1945, at age twenty-four, Lucas himself was burned out, and finally saw once again, the underside of the Golden Gate Bridge. He was looking forward to a much needed thirty-six-day furlough.

In May of the same year, the 44th Construction Battalion was disbanded, and Lucas was assigned to a new unit made up of much younger men with very little experience.

But while on leave, Lucas became engaged to Lee Kirkby. In 2002, they celebrated their fifty-sixth wedding anniversary.

On 17 June 1945, his second round of overseas duty led him once again below the Golden Gate Bridge. Aboard the USS *Briggs*, Lucas was headed for the Marshall Islands and Okinawa. It was on the latter that Lucas earned his second Battle Star. At that time this volcanic island four hundred miles south of Japan was one of the hottest spots of the war.

"But the two typhoons we encountered were much more devastating than the bombs of both sides. The typhoons leveled the Quonset huts, and the flying metal killed many of our men. The merchant ships were blown ashore, and our sea plane base was completely destroyed," Lucas recalled grimly.

Two weeks later Lucas spent his fourth consecutive Christmas away from home. He was in a hotel in Portland, Oregon, and longed for a steak dinner with all the trimmings.

"The best they could do," said Lucas, "was a tough bear steak."

But the best was yet to come. Eleven days later, Motor Machinist Second Class Petty Officer Lucas arrived back in Toledo, Ohio, and accepted his honorable discharge.

George Marshall's First Mission
Was His Worst

"In WWII, the mighty B-17 bomber was a crucial weapon in crush-
ing the Axis war machine. Slung beneath the belly of each B-17
bomber, hidden from marauding Nazi fighters was the ball turret—
a glass bubble armed with a high-caliber anti-aircraft gun. Crouched
inside, ball turret gunners had a notoriously short life span—with
good reason."

So reads the description of the one-hour video, *Suicide Missions:
Dangerous Tours of Duty*. The video depicts in graphic detail, the dangerous job of a ball turret gunner in World War II.

George Marshall of Midland was a ball turret gunner—one of the
lucky ones. Most of his fellow ball turret gunners never made it home.

Marshall was a member of the 96th Bomb Group in Europe, and
he raised the average life span of a turret gunner by flying and fighting on twenty-five missions. He is still sharing the story.

At age twenty-two in 1943, he applied for pilot training, made the
cut with a B+ average, and was turned down because the military had
an overload of pilots. What they really needed were turret gunners.
That was how George Marshall began and ended his military career.
Besides, his 125 pound body made him one of a minority of people
who could fit into the cramped aluminum and Plexiglas bubble
beneath the floor of the plane.

Marshall's first mission was one of his most memorable. He
remembered thinking at the time that if all his missions were going
to be like that one, he would not be making very many.

He had arrived on foreign soil just before Christmas 1944, and a
week later flew his first combat mission. "We got the hell shot right
out of us that day," he remembered soberly. Then he brought out a
book that described the twenty-five missions in which he had taken
part. The book was published in 1989 by Taylor Publishing Company,
Dallas, Texas. Unfortunately, many of the reports are in military talk,
so it makes them as difficult for the average person to understand as
a medical journal.

"We got the hell shot right out of us" was putting it mildly. It was
15 January 1945 over Augsburg, Germany, and Marshall and his crew
members flew in the "Green Parrot" over the Battle of the Bulge.
Because they were so badly shot up, they had to leave the formation,
leaving them vulnerable to Nazi fighter planes.

One inboard engine had been shot away. "There was just a hole where the engine had been," said Marshall. Another engine on the opposite side of the plane had been shot out and still another engine had been feathered due to a flak hit.

With only one engine at full power, they could not keep up the speed or altitude to stay with their group. "As soon as we got out of the flak area," Marshall added, "we were attacked by three German 109 fighters."

Fortunately, Marshall's plane could duck into some cloud cover and head out over the North Sea toward England and their home base at Snetterton.

To lighten the plane, the crew threw out everything that would come loose, including its radio, guns and floor boards of the aircraft itself. They knew if they landed in the frigid January waters of the North Sea, their lives would last about thirty seconds.

Looking for a spot to land in friendly territory, they soon learned they had few friends below them. They had mistakenly flown over the Battle of the Bulge at 1,000 feet, according to Marshall.

The Battle of the Bulge has been recorded as one of the most horrific battles of any war prior to the 21st Century. Tens of thousands of America's finest young men perished in that battle, and even more Axis soldiers met their demise there.

"The pilot had already given the 'stand by to bail out' signal," Marshall said. But that alternative soon dissolved when they realized where they were. "Even the Americans on the ground were firing at us with hand guns," Marshall added. "With all the confusion and heavy fire on the ground, they didn't know but what it was Germans coming in to bomb them."

Beating as quick a retreat as they could in the floundering eagle, they soon learned they did not have any friends above them either.

"Even if we had bailed, there were those German 109s out there waiting for us, and we would all have been hit," Marshall added, painting a deadly picture of their options. Then, down at seven hundred feet, they saw the welcoming shores of the English Channel.

The monstrous aircraft, known as the military's Flying Fortress, was now virtually helpless. It was an effort to even limp to an emergency landing near an English beach. They were approximately sixty-five miles short of its home base. But the "Green Parrot" would never see its cage again.

Water, sand and debris flew in all directions as the B-17 settled on its belly upon English soil. Like a slain dragon fighting its demise, it flopped upon the sandy beach, again and again, until it lay motionless.

The props, once faithfully responding to the thrust of the giant engines behind them, now bent to the curvature of the sand, went dead, never to feel the thrust again. The turret in which Marshall had spent so many hours defending his aircraft, was crushed beneath the weight of the huge weapon of war. The dragon was dead.

As soon as his plane settled on the beach, "We took off and ran like the devil because we still had a full load of gas and bombs," Marshall remembered. But the dragon did not explode, and they were soon picked up by a friendly truck and hauled back to a fighter base nearby. The following day they were safely returned to their home base. According to the book *Snetterton Falcons*:

> They risked death to save the lives of their comrades . . . They had only one good engine, and the ground was getting closer and closer. Ten Nazi fighters were hovering in the distance, not daring to attack the lone plane because of the intense flak surrounding it. **Get rid of the bomb load**—that was in each crewman's mind, but then came the sobering second thought. Below them were Germans— but locked with them in one of the toughest battles of the war were Americans. By common consent, pilot Lt. Homer Hamlin kept the bomb load. The bombardier, 2ⁿᵈ Lt. Frank Caskey, whipped off his heavy clothes, crawled into the bomb bay and set to work safety-ing the fuses so that a sudden jar during an emergency landing would not blow them up.

While his first mission might have been the most harrowing to him, Marshall's list of other close calls and mishaps reads like a one-man "Can You Top This?" show. Two of the B-17s in which Marshall flew were so badly shot up they were never flown again. One of his planes had such a large hole in its tail that it could accommodate a six-foot tall man standing up. Marshall knows, because that was what his tail gunner did once the plane had landed. Only the skill of the pilot brought the plane and crew back safely, according to Marshall. Two other times his plane had to make belly landings. He and his crew also saw some of the first jet rockets fired by the German artillery.

On another mission, sixty percent of the American planes were shot down. "There were one hundred planes on that raid, so sixty of them with ten men each, meant six hundred Americans went down," Marshall recalled sadly. "Sometimes the flak was so heavy you couldn't see beyond your own wing tips.

"One time an enemy 88 mm shell went up through the bottom of the plane, just missed our radio man, and up through the roof of the plane," said Marshall, "and exploded above the plane." The flak was effective up to 35,000 feet according to Marshall.

He did not remember which mission it was, but he remembered a burst of flak exploded near enough to his plane to rock the whole craft. "The pilot, over the intercom, told us to check in to make sure everyone was all right," he explained. When it came Marshall's turn, he pushed the talk button under his foot and spoke into his microphone to let the pilot know he was unhurt, but the pilot could not hear him.

"The pilot said, 'Shorty, come on in.' I pushed and pushed that talk button, and still the pilot couldn't hear me," Marshall recalled. Fearing the worst, the pilot radioed another crew member to check on him. "When I heard that over the intercom I rocked the turret to let them know I was okay."

But "okay" he was not. When he got out of the turret, he was black and blue from one knee to the ankle, and six pieces of flak were imbedded in the leg. "I didn't realize it at the time," said Marshall, "but my leg was paralyzed, and I wasn't pushing the talk button at all. I just thought I was." The extreme cold temperatures at the altitude they were flying prevented his leg from bleeding severely.

Marshall never received a Purple Heart for his wounds because he never reported them. "They would have taken me off the crew for a couple days if I had," he explained. "I wouldn't have liked that and they wouldn't have liked it." A plane crew in war time becomes very close, each knowing the abilities of the other.

"It's like a baseball team with their regular third baseman missing," Marshall added, "If a team member is missing, the team just doesn't play the same." For the sake of his "team" Marshall sacrificed the prestigious Purple Heart award.

But he did officially earn six other battle ribbons, including one for the Battle of the Bulge.

On still other missions, engines on his aircraft exploded, flak holes were so big they could accommodate a miniature truck, and bullet holes came close enough to crew members that cursing changed to praying. Marshall recalled, "We did an awful lot of praying. There are no atheists in a war plane."

At times, according to Marshall, they even had to be suspicious of American planes. "Sometimes one of our planes would make an emergency landing behind enemy lines. The crew would be taken prisoner, the plane would be fixed up, and used to fly against us by a German crew.

"When a lone B-17 or B-24 would come over the air field, the tower would give them instructions to land, thinking it was one of ours returning for an emergency landing," Marshall added. "Then with the German crew, it would fly low, strafing our planes on the ground, taking out two or three at a time."

Marshall had flown his twenty-five missions and was home on leave when the war ended in Europe. His next assignment was to train on the B-29 in preparation for the invasion of Japan. The second mushroom cloud over southern Japan ended the preparations.

Marshall left his legacy over Europe, and he is leaving his legacy in Midland. Since 1947 he has played taps for military funerals. "I've been playing trumpet since 4th grade," Marshall smiled. But that is another story.

Hollis McKeag Saw a Mushroom Cloud, But Did Not Know its Meaning

Hollis McKeag's World War II story could fill a book. Most of the following is excerpted from nearly sixteen pages of his memoirs as he set them to paper in 1992. The excerpts are primarily of one major experience, but he was a part of history that changed the world; an experience forever implanted in the brain of the young pilot.

His experience began on the evening of 5 August 1945, even though he had been in the U.S. Army Air Corps since 1942. All the events in the ensuing three years would only lead up to a steaming hot evening on Okinawa.

In the preflight briefing, McKeag and four hundred other B-25 pilots and crew members sat outdoors in a ravine, waiting for information on their mission for the following morning.

The first words out of the mouth of the group executive, Lieutenant Colonel Little were, "Tomorrow we will be going on one of the longest missions that we have made so far. It may also be the roughest." The colonel went on to warn of fighter attacks, including kamikazes. Those were the Japanese fighter pilots who were brainwashed by Emperor Hirohito into thinking that suicide attacks, with their planes crashing into enemy planes and ships, held a just reward in the afterlife.

Colonel Little concluded these comments with, "In the morning at 0700 we will be taking off to bomb USA."

He allowed the startled questions ranging from "Why?" to "How can we do that? The States are 8,000 miles away," to fade away before revealing a map showing a port city on the northern coast of Kyushu, Japan, known as Usa.

Usa was a heavy manufacturing center with steel mills, chemical plants and a large dock area. It was also known as a cottage industry city, where the manufacturing of war parts and materials took place in every home in the town.

"The problem that concerned us the most," McKeag said in his memoirs, "was the Tony. This was a newer Japanese fighter [plane] that had four 30 mm cannons, with a longer range than our 50 calibers. The Tonys were the ones that shot down so many B29s over Tokyo. The losses became bad enough, that in order to get fighter protection for the B29s, it was necessary to take Iwo Jima at the cost of 7,000

marine lives. The Tony was a much more formidable fighter than we had faced on any of our previous missions over Japan or China."

McKeag goes on to say how much more secure the crews felt, knowing they would be escorted to their target by two hundred army P-51s, plus some marine Corsairs and navy F6F Hellcats, all capable fighter planes. It wasn't until twenty years later that McKeag learned that his cousin, Don Hennings, from Stromsburg, Nebraska, was one of the P-51 pilots, and that he had flown escort for several of McKeag's other missions. His cousin was known to have remarked, "I remember those B-25s with all those naked ladies painted on the nose." Hennings was based on the island of Iea Shima, about sixty miles north of Okinawa.

Second Lieutenant McKeag pulled some strings to get high on the flying list so he could get into combat on this mission. "At times though, I had reservations about my eagerness," he said.

Sleep seldom came easily the night before a raid, according to McKeag. Thoughts of home came into play, and often they were thoughts of his childhood, and of Bette back in Iowa, to whom he had become engaged just prior to heading overseas. Another reason he could not sleep was that the enemy had been spotted just twenty miles from base, and the thought was always there that some could sneak, under cover of darkness, onto the base and cause great harm. For that reason, McKeag slept with his .45 revolver under his pillow. "To say that I was frightened would be an understatement," McKeag continued.

At 0700 the following morning the engines of McKeag's aircraft roared to life like clockwork, and McKeag's 41st Bomb Group left the runway in so much dust from the planes taking off ahead of them, the pilots had to use instrument takeoffs.

"As we rolled, I would help the pilot stay on the runway," copilot McKeag notes in his memoirs. "He was looking at his instruments and I would watch for the side of the runway, and put in as much rudder corrections as needed. As you roared down the runway you hoped with all your might that the guy ahead of you got off ok. If he did not, you might meet.

"When we finally felt ourselves airborne, it was a great relief. I did not pull up the wheels until I saw the runway disappear below us," McKeag writes. "The gunners believed that the takeoffs were the greatest danger. I shared their thoughts; however, I was busy while they were helpless."

With three other squadrons, involving a total of four hundred men, they climbed in formation as though in a ballet, to 12,000 feet, meeting pristine blue sky along the east coast of Kyushu. "But good flying weather is a two-edge sword," stated McKeag. "You could see and be seen."

Prior to takeoff the crew chief, along with the navigator, checked the bomb bay to make certain the 250-pound bombs were placed in the plane correctly. "There is nothing more exciting than to have an armed bomb hung up in the bomb bay," McKeag writes, "Especially with the VT [variable timer] fuse, which may be set to go off at fourteen feet off the ground. If you could not shake it loose, you headed out to sea and bailed out."

They kept ten to twenty miles off the east coast of Japan to avoid ground fire. Knowing they would encounter Japanese fighter planes, they intentionally flew somewhat away from their intended target so that the enemy planes that were not shot down by the American fighter escorts, would be low on fuel by the time the B-25s circled back over their target.

"Not only was this to be our deepest raid into Japan, it was going to be the first time there had ever been a four hundred plane raid from Okinawa," McKeag stated in his memoirs. But McKeag had trained for two years, and had flown twenty-eight previous missions in preparation for this historic flight.

A week before this raid, McKeag ran into a bit more history himself. He was sitting in the Island Defense Center in Okinawa, when in walked General Jimmy Doolittle. Doolittle, who flew the monster B-29 Superfortress, and McKeag exchanged pleasantries about their respective aircraft, and McKeag had an opportunity to inform Doolittle about the Japanese kamikaze planes, and what a major threat they had become.

While we digress here, it should be mentioned that history was still in the making for McKeag. There was an A-26 Fighter Squadron on Okinawa, and one of its pilots was Deke Slaten, who was later selected as one of America's first astronauts.

McKeag had earlier made the mistake of making a nice hexagon table in his tent, so his quarters became the local casino. "I recall that Slaten was very sharp at cards, as he had a remarkable memory."

Shortly after becoming airborne, McKeag could see the B-24s forming to the north, and the A-26 squadron forming to their south. When the three squadrons were formed, they picked up a heading in the direction of the target at slow cruise. "This would enable the 4th squadron to join us before we got too deep into enemy territory," McKeag wrote in his memoirs.

An hour into the mission, the pilots of each plane asked the men on their airship to check their equipment, and the gunners to fire a short burst before tightening the formation. "The smell of gun powder reminded you of what this mission was all about," McKeag said soberly.

The formation would then tighten to dangerously close distances apart. This gave each squadron more concentrated fire power in the event Japanese planes got through the American fighter escorts. According to McKeag's writings, "Often the tail gunner would get a little uneasy as one of your props would be only a few feet away. If you dropped back or got too low, you would create a real problem for the plane behind."

McKeag's tail gunner had once remarked, "Looking down on Japan reminds me of looking at a rattlesnake. Beautiful to look at, but deadly if you fell into their nest." He was referring to a B-24 crew that had bailed out over land a few days prior, and had been killed by Japanese farmers with pitchforks.

"We had heard stories of some of the atrocities," McKeag said, "and later were saddened to learn that many of them were true."

McKeag's crew knew it was approaching their target when they looked out and saw several "Dumbos." These were flying boats the navy named PBYs. They also saw a B-17 that had a sixteen-foot power boat attached to its belly which could be dropped to downed crews in the Pacific. The airborne squadrons were also advised that there were American submarines off shore that could come to their rescue if needed. This visual and radioed knowledge was comforting to the men in the air, who prayed the rescue equipment would not be needed.

As the American planes closed in on their target in southern Japan, the flak became visible. The radio chatter could be heard between the fighters and the B-24s as Japanese fighters tried to make their suicide passes only to be shot down by the escorts and the gunners on the bombers.

As the squadrons approached their targets, the surface winds were blowing the smoke away from them, putting the chemical plant in clear view. "The sight of the target increased the tension another notch," McKeag remembered.

As McKeag's squadron got closer to the target, it vectored out over the water to avoid the flak which was becoming more noticeable. Some of it was even becoming audible, and that was a bad sign.

The bombers were making a left turn to begin their bombing runs, "and several of us noticed a large high vertical cloud with a hat on." Others on McKeag's plane thought it looked like a flower or a mushroom. "It was to our north and a little to the east," McKeag stated. "It must have gone up to 40,000 feet, and someone commented that it looked like a baby typhoon. It was estimated to have been eighty miles distant. But since we had other things to think about besides cloud formations, we got back to the problems at hand."

Ten seconds from target, the signal was given from the navigator to open the bomb bay doors. "This I did and you could feel the controls stiffen up, caused by the additional drag of the doors." With the wind whistling through the bomb bay, the Japanese were sending up deadening flak at about 15,000 feet, "thinking we would be at that elevation," said McKeag. "While we began at that elevation, we went into a dive, and released the bombs between eight and twelve thousand feet."

Both of McKeag's hands struggled with the throttle and his eyes glued to the air speed indicator as the navigator sat with one hand on the toggle switch, warning about the flak and watched for the lead plane to drop their bombs.

They used a technique called "glide bombing." They crossed the target below in a shallow dive at an airspeed of 250 miles per hour, and dropped their bombs, then made a diving turn, losing about 3,000 feet and picked up air speed to nearly 300 miles per hour.

"The reason for the slower speed was because any faster and we would have torn off the bomb bay doors," McKeag stated in his written memoirs. "As copilot, I would handle the throttles to control air speed, and the pilot would keep the aircraft in a tight formation," he added, then continued, "it was one hell of a thrill to do this in a tight formation with sixty-four aircraft," McKeag wrote, "It looked like we were all tied together by some invisible wire."

When the bombs were finally away, even the plane felt relief as it lurched from the sudden loss of weight, and with the bomb bay doors closed, it reduced the drag. As they stayed in their dive their air speed picked up to more than three hundred miles per hour before they leveled it out and turned toward the safety of the sea.

It was during the bomb run itself that the crew was most at risk and that generated the greatest fear, according to McKeag. "I believe that Walter Cronkite, who rode a glider during combat on D day in Europe, said it best when describing [that kind] of fear. 'It was a lifetime cure for constipation.'"

As McKeag's mighty airship turned out over the Pacific, the crew once again observed that strange cloud formation. And again comments were made about it.

They picked up a heading that would take them out through the Bungo Straits and back home to Kadena, on Okinawa. The pilot asked McKeag to fly most of the way back as he began making notes about the mission that would be useful in the postmission briefing. Their plane had taken several hits from flak, along with a couple minor wounds to crewmembers, but all the planes returned safely.

The Japanese were not as fortunate. They lost a total of twenty aircraft and pilots on that day.

Returning from the mission, each crew was debriefed by air force intelligence and got their shot of whiskey. "Everyone wanted to report on the strange cloud formation," McKeag mentioned in his memoirs. "In fact, when it came to our turn, the debriefing officer didn't want to hear anything more about it. His comment was that he 'could not understand how a cloud could get so much attention.'"

They would not know the true facts about the strange cloud until President Truman announced to the world that an atomic bomb had been released over Hiroshima.

That wasn't the last time McKeag would see history in the making that week. Three days later a B-29 dropped the plutonium bomb over Nagasaki. The aircraft that dropped the bomb was low on fuel on its way back to the island of Tinian and was forced to land at McKeag's base. "We saw it land, and it caused quite a bit of interest," McKeag wrote, "but we were all kept away from the aircraft."

On 15 August 1945, McKeag and his crew of six were scheduled for a low-level mission over Japan. It was to be this crew's ninth mission over the islands. They sat at the edge of the runway, brakes locked, with their twin engines stretching for full power for takeoff. The churning dust flying from the aircraft taking off ahead of them made visibility near zero. The dust was then sucked up by the props on McKeag's plane, and hurled in the faces of the planes behind him. It was then they received from the control tower the sweetest words ever spoken in a tired, war-torn world. "THE WAR IS OVER! TAKE 'EM BACK TO THE BARN!"

"That was a message that will never be forgotten," McKeag wrote. "There were no cheers, or celebration, just a big sense of relief and gratitude." The planes on the ground turned in unison, having made their mark in history.

McKeag goes on to mention one noticeable change in the way the armament crews unloaded the bombs that day. "Before, when someone would bring their bombs back they would just release them and they would fall out on the ground. This time they took each one out by hand, taking no chances."

Captain McKeag remained in the air force for another eight months, checking out other pilots in the B-25 based at Tachikawa, Japan. He received his honorable discharge in June 1946 at the ripe old age of twenty-one, but flying remained in his blood. He immediately applied for a pilot's position with United Airlines, but was turned down. "United officials said I looked too young," McKeag chuckled.

"When I was twenty-one, I looked sixteen," McKeag recalled. Although he had been flying bombing missions over Japan since he was barely out of his teens, a sixteen-year-old-looking man-boy in the cockpit of a commercial airline would hardly inspire confidence in the passengers boarding the plane.

The rejection, however, didn't erode McKeag's enthusiasm for working around airplanes. For eight of the thirty-one years he worked for The Dow Chemical Company, he was responsible for aircraft and services and continued to serve in an advisory capacity for Dow air traffic. McKeag has also served on the Airport Commission for MBS International Airport for a full decade.

Service to people has always been a key for McKeag. At the time of this writing he was completing his third year on the Midland City Council.

Dale Meier Was Not a Fan of General MacArthur

No one knew it at the time, but in the summer of 1943 World War II was half over. There was a lot of fighting remaining, however, as Dale Meier, then twenty, was soon to find out.

He had enlisted in the U.S. Marines the previous year, and took training at Parris Island, South Carolina, and at Camp Lejeune, North Carolina. He was then selected for officer candidate school, and sent to Quantico, Virginia. With shiny gold bars on his lapel labeling him a second lieutenant, he was assigned to a replacement unit in the South Pacific.

The troop ship sailed south, then west through the Panama Canal. Several days later, he got his first awareness of what war was all about as the ship sailed into Pearl Harbor.

"We could look down through the clear water and see the Arizona setting on the bottom," he said with a sigh.

While in Pearl Harbor, half the troops on his ship were sent to the island of Iwo Jima in the South Pacific, one of the deadliest campaigns of the war, and only a few hundred miles south of Tokyo. Meier was in the other half, heading even further west, nearly to the edge of the East China Sea, and several hundred miles north of the Philippines, to a little-known Japanese-held island called Okinawa.

There he was attached to Charlie Company, First Battalion, 4th Marines, 6th Marine Division. It was now April 1945.

Every line officer in the initial landing of the Okinawa campaign was either wounded or killed, according to Meier. Fortunately, Meier was not among that first wave of Marines to hit the beaches.

Meier did not get off easily, however. "In each platoon, including replacements, there were one hundred men," he recalls. "In the end, there were only ten of us left. Ninety percent of the platoons were completely wiped out on Okinawa.

"War for the infantryman is horrible," Meier added, "I've tried to repress most of the worst of it, and not think about it. I try not to talk about it. I don't think my family has the slightest idea of what went on at Okinawa, other than perhaps having read that letter regarding casualties."

In a letter to his parents, Joseph and Ellen Meier in Los Angeles, dated 28 December 1945, Meier wrote:

On officers we had almost 230 percent casualties (these figures also take into account the replacement officers). The company rates seven officers and we had sixteen officer casualties, seven killed and nine wounded.

On enlisted men, I don't remember the exact figures, but it was about 150 percent casualties. At the beginning of the operation my platoon had about 50 men, and I left Okinawa with ten men. Casualties for the whole regiment were about 120 percent (including replacements).

Meier went on:

If you ever hear anyone say that we shouldn't have used the atomic bomb, that it was inhumane, etc., you can do anything you want to them as far as I am concerned. If it hadn't been for the atomic bomb and if we would have had to invade Japan next March or whenever it was planned, I'd almost certainly have been worth $10,000 to you (in life insurance).

I thought the hills and ridges of Okinawa were bad, but this country [Japan] has it beat by far. I'd have never lasted long in an operation in Japan, not unless a bigger miracle than happened on Okinawa happened here. The odds are too much against it. So you can thank the atomic bomb for that.

Surviving the holocaust on Okinawa, Meier and his division of marines were sent to Guam to train for the eventual ground invasion of Japan. But before that could happen, two mushroom clouds shot into the bright August sky over southern Japan, short-circuiting the event.

They were scheduled to land in the Tokyo Bay area in May 1946, but the atomic bomb changed the original plan. As it was, they did land there, but it was under different circumstances. And it was in August 1945, as members of the Tokyo Bay Occupation Force.

"It was for the unconditional and complete surrender of the Japanese navy," Meier mentioned casually.

"There was an agreement between Japan and the U.S. that any gun emplacements on the mountains would be covered with white sheets," Meier remembered, "an indication they would not be used when we went into Tokyo Bay. One mountain was one huge white sheet. They had disemboweled the mountain to plant their gun emplacements.

"If we had had to make a combat landing in Japan," Meier stated soberly, "it would have been disastrous. The hills of Okinawa were bad enough, but Japan was infinitely worse. The odds of surviving two battles like that were next to zero.

"The original 4th Marines were completely wiped out on Bataan in the Philippines, thanks to the stupidity of MacArthur." Meier voiced his opinion with some bitterness. "And the replacements were the first in Japan to honor the original regiment."

When asked if he can be quoted on his "MacArthur" statement, Meier said seriously, "Don't get me started on that. Let me just say that America needed a hero at the time, and MacArthur was so designated. He should have been court-martialed for his actions in the Philippines."

Meier added, "When President Truman finally fired MacArthur in Korea years later, Truman became *my* hero," and concluded with finality, "Enough about MacArthur."

Just prior to leaving Guam for Japan, Meier's outfit worked all night loading its ship. The trip to Japan was not uneventful, however. The landing was delayed due to a typhoon, and one of the U.S. cruisers broke in half, according to Meier. "It didn't sink," Meier recalled, "and they recovered at least half of it, perhaps both halves."

Anchoring just south of Tokyo Bay the night before, Meier recalled the spectacular sight of Mt. Fuji in the distance. "It was a beautiful sight."

The following morning Meier's unit loaded into landing craft, and beached at Yokosuka Air Station. "We were fully armed, waiting for anything," recalled Meier, "but it was a very peaceful landing. There were even Japanese on shore, welcoming us to Japan."

During the several months Meier was in Japan, "it was the most peaceful country in the world." He reflected:

The emperor had told them the war was over, and to behave. They looked to the emperor almost as a god. If the emperor had not said that, all hell would have broken loose. I never heard of one incident of retribution.

Despite the total devastation, it was amazing how the country held together. Southern Tokyo and Yokohama had been leveled. They were as flat as this table [pointing at the table where the interview was conducted]. The only things left standing were the steel safes that had been in the buildings. At that time, Japan was the safest place in the world—infinitely safer than San Francisco.

Meier went on, "What most people don't realize is that in March 1945, more people were killed from our bombing Tokyo in one night, than were killed by the atom bomb at Hiroshima."

World War II ended in August 1945, but the Marines were not yet through with Meier. Early in 1946 he was sent to Shanghai, China, and stationed at Tsinghao for a five-month assignment.

"We were to protect the countryside from Communists, said Meier, "but in effect we didn't do anything except once in a while parade around the city, showing our strength. Basically, we were killing time."

Nearly five months later, Meier was discharged from active duty at San Diego, but the marines had other plans. They kept him in the marine reserves to keep him prepared for combat once again if needed.

He was able, however, to return to the California Institute of Technology (Cal Tech), to continue his studies. He had attended Cal Tech three years before entering the military. There he earned both his bachelor's and master's degrees, and moved on to the University of California at Los Angeles (UCLA), completing his Ph.D. in 1951. He continued also carrying his rank of 1st Lieutenant in the Marine Reserves.

"I got to thinking," Meier smiled, "that my Marine Corps spec is as an infantry officer. An infantry officer with a Ph.D. sounds incongruous." He wrote a letter to the Secretary of the Navy, indicating his desire to resign his commission. His request was granted.

"One month later the Korean War broke out. Every reserve officer with my former status was recalled as part of the 1st Marine Division, and went off to Korea. The 1st Division got trapped near the Yalu River by an influx of hundreds of thousands of Chinese, and took numerous casualties, again thanks to MacArthur's stupidity."

Had Meier's letter reached the Secretary of the Navy a month later, he would have been fighting another war where once again hundreds of young men were being killed. "It was pure accident that kept me from being there," Meier said seriously. "I had no preconceived notion the Korean War was going to break out."

Almost as a postscript, Meier recalls, humorously, an incident that could have led him into a whole lot of trouble. "I picked up a Japanese light machine gun—we called them 'Nambus'—on Okinawa and carried it with me back to Guam, then to Japan and China, and finally home to San Diego. There I found the government was checking all the returning baggage. Not wishing to be caught with a machine gun, I got rid of it in a corner of the warehouse before they searched my baggage. I don't know what I planned to do with it anyway, other than to take it out in the desert and fire a few rounds, which I already had done. It would have made a nice trophy," he chuckled.

At the end of the interview, Meier produced two Japanese swords that were among the memorabilia he had brought to the interview.

"The short one I purchased," he explained. "The longer one I took off a Japanese officer."

When asked about the story behind the swords, Meier replied with a sigh, "Let's let it rest." That part of his memoirs remains lodged forever in his memory, where only *he* knows the story. And that's what makes Meier another of Midland County's silent heroes.

E. E. (Mike) Merrill: World War II Boat Commander at Age Twenty-two

"Give me a fast ship, for I intend to go in harm's way." When John Paul Jones made that statement he was only nineteen years old and the first mate of a slave ship in the 1760s. He did not know that his words would ring down through the centuries to a young man from Midland.

At age twenty-two, Mike Merrill was undoubtedly the youngest commanding officer of a PT (patrol torpedo) boat in World War II. With its laminated mahogany hull, held together with glue and 400,000 screws, a PT boat was the fastest ship in the U.S. Navy.

The eighty-foot, fifty-ton vee bow craft could travel at speeds up to sixty three miles per hour. It had a low profile above the water-line, and was not only fast, but extremely maneuverable. In addition to being the commanding officer of his PT boat, Merrill was also assigned as the engineering officer of his squadron of twelve PT boats. That meant he was responsible for the maintenance of the hulls and engines, and keeping the boats and equipment in top working order.

After receiving his commission as an Ensign in the U.S. Naval Reserve and graduating from Naval Officers Training School, Merrill spent an intense four months, training at the Motor Torpedo Boat Training Base at Melville, Rhode Island. Merrill had volunteered for PT boat duty. "It was the only way get into PT service," said Merrill. "Everyone was a volunteer."

Following this training, he had a brief furlough at home with his wife, Grace. It was then that their son, William (Bill), came into the world. Merrill left for the South Pacific when Bill was just four days old. He would not see his son or Grace again for another year and a half. "My wife still won't knowingly buy a Japanese product," Merrill said, only half kidding.

After receiving his promotion to Lt.(jg), and serving as the execu-tive officer, he became the commanding officer on the "Dragon Lady," better known on naval records as PT 155, and spent the next eighteen months fighting a war.

Merrill had a crew consisting of an executive officer and seven-teen enlisted men, many older. They were also highly trained, some under Merrill's tutelage, to maneuver the craft and to man the mighty firepower. It was also the same type of craft that John F.

Kennedy was piloting when it was rammed and ultimately sunk by a Japanese destroyer during the war. Merrill was more fortunate, and his craft was credited with sinking several Japanese ships and barges, and downing a number of Japanese warplanes over and around New Guinea and the Philippines.

Merrill's streamlined watercraft was armed with a 40 mm cannon, a 37 mm anti aircraft gun, a 20 mm gun, two 50 caliber machine guns, sixteen rockets, four torpedoes, six depth charges and an 80 mm mortar. It was powered by three V-12 cylinder Packard engines. Each engine produced 3,000 horsepower, and could accelerate from eight knots, or seven miles per hour, to forty knots, or thirty-five miles per hour in eleven seconds.

The ship carried 3,000 gallons of 100-octane aviation gasoline and consumed up to 1,000 gallons per hour at full speed.

"It was a fabulous craft, and the most maneuverable ship in the navy," Merrill said. "Because it had a draft of only three feet, we could get in close to the islands without running aground, damaging the hull or props."

That was a tremendous responsibility for a twenty-two-year-old chemistry graduate from Central Michigan University with a fresh officer's commission.

The small, speedy boats were dubbed the "Mosquito Fleet," because they were ambush vessels, hunters and marauders. They would normally patrol after dark in groups of two or three, seeking their targets, striking, and beating a hasty retreat. Assignments also included escort duty, spy transport, leading beachhead invasions, and laying smoke screens.

Eventually, the Mosquito Fleet was tagged as "Barge Busters" because they were sinking so many barges used by the Japanese as they hauled troops and munitions to the islands around the South Pacific. The PT boat crews also aided in rescuing General MacArthur from Corregidor when the Philippines fell to Japan.

According to naval history, PT boats were in more frequent contact with the enemy, at a closer range, than any other surface craft in all of World War II.

Like an animal that spends most of its time hunting for food, Merrill and his crew of the Dragon Lady spent most of their waking hours hunting for Japanese ships and munitions. Their waking hours sometimes covered the twenty-four hour clock. "When we weren't running missions we were loading munitions and refueling our boats at home base" Merrill smiled. "We seldom had pumps, and if we did, they were hand ones. Most of the time refueling had to be done by pouring the gas through large funnels and into the boat's tanks directly from fifty-five gallon drums. It would take hours."

Merrill recalled vividly the day they entered a Japanese-held harbor in Sandakan, Borneo. Four other PT boats and the Australian air force assisted them. Their mission was to destroy the three-mile harbor laden with Japanese ships, repair facilities and ammunition storage.

"We had been given detailed aerial photographs showing us where we could find our targets," recalled Merrill. "We went under cover of darkness, as we did on most missions."

But they did not go unnoticed. Almost immediately, the Japanese were firing at them from the surrounding cliffs. "We didn't have time to be frightened," he said. "That wasn't one of the options."

They were like ducks on a pond when the green tracer shells from the Japanese guns kept coming at them as the PT boats attacked the shore targets time after time, firing all the weapons they had on board, including their rockets and torpedoes. The muzzle blasts on the cliffs looked like throbbing flashlights in the blackness of the pre-dawn. "The barrels of our 50 caliber machine guns became so hot they burned out, and the shells were eventually just being lobbed a few yards beyond the boat," Merrill remembered.

Shortly after sunrise, with their munitions spent, they escaped the harbor under cover of a smoke screen launched from their craft. The mission complete, all four boats fled the harbor under continuous gunfire hailing down from cliffs above. Merrill's craft had numerous bullet holes lining the sides and deck.

The mission was successful, not only because the targets had been destroyed but also because there were no Americans killed. There were a few injuries, including Merrill, when he caught some shrapnel in the face. "It cut and broke my nose, but it was pretty insignificant and I never reported it." Had he done so, he would have been awarded the Purple Heart. "Insignificant" is only a relative term Merrill uses. Compared to injuries he had seen to other fighting men, he saw his as only a minor, temporary inconvenience.

That was only one of the dangerous missions the Dragon Lady undertook, but the modest Merrill doesn't elaborate. He only mentions that PT 155 was one of the most notorious boats in the squadron for all the damage it did to Japanese shipping around the Philippines.

One mission, however, he recalls with some pride. It was during the fighting in the Davao area where, according to an undated newspaper clipping, there was "savage fighting." Merrill's squadron destroyed a small Japanese naval base and a half-dozen Japanese torpedo boats and fuel and ammunition dumps.

Merrill's aging memory does not recall the details because he was pretty busy at the time, but his boat was carrying a celebrity for a couple of hours during the skirmish. Some time after the foray, he received a telegram that read, "My thanks and cordial greetings." It was signed by General Douglas MacArthur. PT 155 had taken MacArthur from a cruiser to an army base, some sixty miles distant.

While his mind does not recall the details of some of the battles he was in, he does recall something that has been reduced to trivia today. He remembers listening to the Detroit Tigers as they beat the Chicago Cubs to win the World Series in 1945. Perhaps the significant part was that he and the crew of PT 155 listened to that game as it was being broadcast to the Philippine Islands.

It was one thing to go into battle at night, according to Merrill, it was something else to return from battle amidst rough seas. "One night we had captured some Japanese soldiers and were heading back to our base at Mindanao in the Philippine Islands. We ran into twenty-foot seas." He chuckled as the memory flooded back. "We were tossed from one swell to the next, the prisoners all got sick and they regurgitated rice all over the boat. It was a wild night!"

As the engineering officer, he was readying his squadron for the invasion of Japan when the atom bomb was dropped on Nagasaki, ending the war.

Following the war, most of the PT boats were towed onto a huge sandbar off Samar in the Philippines and set afire. "Most of them were pretty beat up," Merrill reflected, "and because of the wooden hulls, they couldn't be mothballed. That was a pretty sad thing," he added, "standing on the shore watching them burn. It was really with mixed emotion."

For most of the world the war was over, but not for Merrill. He received orders to take a refrigeration ship from Samar to Pearl Harbor. "I drew the short straw," Merrill chuckled. "We got as far as Guam and I convinced my superiors that the ship was not seaworthy, and it really was not," he recalled. Instead of going home, he was sent on to Japan and assigned to the minesweeper USS *Elusive* to teach the Japanese how to sweep up the mines they had laid all up and down the eastern coast of the islands.

Merrill finally left the navy in June 1946, but the navy has never left him. After sixty years of boating, he is celebrating his thirtieth anniversary as commodore of the Saginaw Bay Yacht Club.

Following his discharge, Merrill worked for two years for Dow Corning, but retired thirty-two years later as the director of quality from The Dow Chemical Company in 1981. He then established his own successful management consulting business that ended eight years later.

A Positive Attitude Saved
Robert Mesler's Life

He would have been late for his wedding except that he and his bride-to-be, high school sweetheart, Margery Keicher from Midland, switched to "Plan B." They were married on 16 August 1942 instead of 12 August. "My furlough didn't come through in time for the earlier date," Robert (Bob) Mesler chuckled.

He had turned eighteen in January the year before, and was drafted two weeks after his graduation from Midland High School the following June. Little did he know that by the time he celebrated another birthday, he would be a prisoner of war thousands of miles from the comfort of his home in Midland.

Following basic training at Ft. Hood, Texas, and the Army Specialist Training Program at Hendrix College in Conway, Arkansas, he became a member of Company L, 393rd Regiment, 99th Infantry Division in one of the bloodiest battles of the twentieth century—the Battle of the Bulge.

"It was also one of Europe's coldest winters of the century," said Mesler. "It would be below zero for days at a time. And the days were so short that far north that time of year. It would be nearly dark until 9:00 a.m. and dark again at 4:00 p.m."

Mesler's unit was in the area of the Bulge for nearly a month before the fighting began. They had become somewhat acquainted with the terrain and the environment, with patrols going out daily in search of the enemy.

When the Battle of the Bulge began in December 1944, the Germans had the advantage. Not only did they outnumber the Americans and the Allies, but some of this territory was also the battleground for the Germans a war earlier, and they knew the terrain.

Mesler's division was stretched out over a twenty to thirty-mile area at the edge of the Ardennes Forest. Typically, a division would extend no more than five miles, according to Mesler. Although his foxhole was in Belgian territory, he could look out and see the German border.

"Along this line, the German offensive tried to drive a wedge in between the American and British troops," Mesler said, "and disrupt the flow of materials to the front."

On 12 December 1944, Mesler's unit was part of the advanced American forces that planned to take over the Rohr Valley. "On the

sixteenth, we had just dug our foxholes when the order came down that we had to go back and save our kitchens," Mesler said. "The Germans had captured our kitchens." Chuckling, Mesler went on, "It worked for a couple hours, but then the Germans brought in their tanks and overran us, so we had to withdraw."

Mesler's unit was surrounded as it huddled around its first aid station, and on the following day was able to retreat to a fallback position, to foxholes it had previously dug.

"We retreated for three days, then held our positions for several days," said Mesler. "And all the time the Germans were only one hundred yards away."

But the retreat continued with a great loss of men and machines until 20 December. In addition to the kitchens, Mesler lost half the men in his twelve-man squad. Sergeant Mesler then moved up to assistant squad leader.

Before year's end, replacements began arriving to take the places of the numerous casualties. "These guys had been home for Thanksgiving," said Mesler, "and now they were on the front line in Europe.

"I really felt sorry for these young men. They were mere teenagers who had just come from basic training with no advanced training in tactics or experience in fighting this enemy. They were just bodies."

What made it even worse, according to Mesler, was that it snowed almost every night for five consecutive nights after 16 December. America was ill-prepared for a winter war, Mesler recalled. The clothing was inadequate, the overcoats were lead-heavy, and they had only one pair of socks to wear, another in their backpacks. In addition, their khaki fighting uniforms stood out like pinecones on freshly fallen snow.

On the night of 11 January 1945, Mesler and several others were on patrol in their area near Elsenborn, Belgium. "When we returned to the outpost, some German soldiers had followed us back in the snow. They had on white uniforms and we just didn't see them," said Mesler. He and three of his fighting buddies were now prisoners of the German army.

While in the prison camp, Mesler says he tried to surround himself with other positive thinking prisoners. "Some of the guys had given up, and were certain they would never see home again." With that attitude most of them did not, according to Mesler. "After being beaten and nearly starved, with very little shelter or warm clothes, they just gave up the will to live."

During his nearly one hundred days as a POW, he was hospitalized twice—once with pneumonia. "The only difference between an ill prisoner and a healthy one, was that the sick person got a little more food. They had no medical facilities for us."

His second hospital stay was for exhaustion, and he received a blood transfusion. "It was administered in a very rudimentary way," said Mesler. "They had a glass beaker, a glass stirring rod, a funnel, a piece of rubber tubing and a hypodermic needle. They would take blood from the arm of the donor with the needle, place it in the beaker and stir it so it wouldn't coagulate. Then they would use the same needle, put it in my arm, put the funnel on the end of the tube and pour the blood from the funnel into my arm."

Mesler ended up with infectious hepatitis. For nine months following his rescue, he was recovering in a military hospital.

Every few days the prisoners were moved from one prison camp to another so they would not have time to plan an escape. "It might also have been because the camp couldn't accommodate any more men," said Mesler.

In one camp, Stalag VIG, near Bonn, Germany, the Royal Air Force (RAF) made a night raid on the city. The planes were slightly off course, and hit the prison camp.

Fortunately, according to Mesler, the Germans had provided bomb shelters because air raids were common in that area.

"The Germans took pretty good care of the French and British prisoners, even though they hated them, but they knew they would have to live with them in neighboring countries after the war," he said.

When asked how the Americans were treated, Mesler spurred his memory and said, "Not very well." One of the staples in their diet was a black bread that had been stored in sawdust that was indicative of its taste. "Each loaf was about a foot long and a few inches wide," he said, "and we would have to share it with five to eight others."

Sometimes the prisoners would get nothing to eat except rotting cabbage for several days at a time, he recalled. "On occasion we could have coffee, which was really roasted barley and chicory. That would be breakfast, and there would be no lunch. For dinner they would give us a cup of watery soup with no stock in it unless it might be a piece of cabbage." Mesler remembers. After the bombing at Bonn, the prisoners were moved across the Rhine River, and had no food at all for five days.

During his last ninety days of captivity, he lost sixty pounds, bringing him down to 106 pounds by the time he was freed from his captors.

Next to going home, the major topic of conversation among the prisoners was food. Mesler, for reasons he never knew, was allowed to keep pictures of family members, and the backs of them look like a menu from a nice family restaurant. He had written down all the things he would like to have for his meals. These pictures and the "menus" are still among his memorabilia from the war.

One time, Mesler and his fellow captives were in forced labor, unloading box cars while being prodded like cattle with rifles. "I called one of the guards an SOB, and in return got a rifle butt to the head," Mesler said with a smile that broke into soft laughter. "I didn't realize he could understand English." The blow knocked him down, but then he had to get up and return to work.

Sometimes they were housed in barns and had to sleep in the loft on straw. He can't recall where he got scraps of a blanket, but that and straw was all he had to cover himself on those subzero nights.

In January of that bitter winter, Mesler was allowed to complete and send a Red Cross card to his wife, letting her know he was a prisoner of war. Although the card was completed, the Germans never sent it. She thought he was missing in action until she heard his voice on the phone from New York on his way home.

Another frequent topic of conversation was escape. Mesler has a detailed diary of his days as a prisoner. His entry on 11 February 1945 reads, "Lice have almost eaten me up. No relief in sight unless Patton gets here soon."

On 23 March another entry says, "Moved away from Stalag XIIA. Debating whether or not to take off." The prisoners were loaded into box cars in Limburg, Germany, and to this day he doesn't know where they were headed.

The next day the train was strafed by three American P-47s. "The Germans used us as a decoy for an ammunition train which was hiding in a tunnel," related Mesler. The unknowing pilots, thinking they were above the ammo train, opened fire. Mesler and his fellow captives squinted through the slats of the box cars as the American fighter planes banked, then returned with all weapons blazing. "About ten men killed and thirty wounded," states Mesler's diary. There were forty to fifty men in each boxcar, he explained, and enough cars to carry the thousand prisoners.

While the Germans were busy firing at the pesky fighter planes, Mesler and several of his buddies kicked out some wooden slats on the floor of their boxcar, and saw freedom staring them in the face. "I still don't know how we managed to get those floor boards loose," Mesler said. "We weren't very healthy, and I had had a blood transfusion just a couple weeks before."

Once free, they went along the train setting the other captives free as well. "Anyone who was strong enough made a break for it," he recalled. But a strange thing happened. "When the guards saw what we were doing, they came along and helped us." It was the first time the prisoners had seen any compassion from their captors in over two months.

When asked why their captors assisted in their freedom, Mesler responded, "By March of 1945, the Germans knew they were fighting a war they couldn't win, and they just didn't care." He also explained that the German guards were older men who were fed up with the war, or much younger men who had been wounded, and not fit to return to the front lines.

The prisoners ran into an open field as the American planes banked once again for a second strafing run. Rapidly the newly-freed captives, with their bodies and with clothing, made a large POW on the ground. "As the planes approached us, they wagged their wing tips and flew off," Mesler related with a sigh.

"Our officer in charge (also a POW), and the German officer in charge negotiated, and the Germans allowed us to paint POW on top of the boxcars," Mesler stated, "so we spent that afternoon painting on top of the cars." Fortunately, the March weather had turned balmy. The prisoners had to load back in the boxcars for their unknown destination after the painting.

Escape was still on Mesler's mind a week later when he and two others made a break with a five-day food supply from the American Red Cross, packages they seldom received in the prison camp because the Germans would steal them.

In Wetzler, Germany, on this cloudless night, Mesler and his buddies crawled over a stone wall, and hid under some bushes until daybreak. The 28 March entry in his diary reads, "Took off last night, but made the mistake of sleeping in the front yard of a German Infantry School."

In that gray, cold March dawn, the escapees were awakened by German guards looking down the barrels of their rifles. "The wall separated the city from a German military installation," Mesler chuckled, as the irony hit home.

In broken English, one German soldier said, "We hope you realize we have to take you into custody." Mesler added, "They were almost apologetic."

Again compassion from the enemy as they explained to the three in ragged clothes that if they were kept in that location they would be in trouble. "The Germans left one guard with us, a fellow with a peg leg and an arm in a sling, the results of fighting with the Russians," Mesler recalled.

This "little man," as Mesler describes him, marched the three American prisoners into the town of Wetzler, and past a German

Panzer tank unit. "I was scared to death," he says seriously. "We had no idea what those guys might do." The Germans had a reputation for beating their prisoners, and here were three of the weakened enemy against a whole tank division.

The three American soldiers were spared everything except the humiliation of being paraded through an enemy town by an invalid. But the parade did not end there. "We walked on another seven or eight miles to Geisen where we were turned over to authorities."

Escape still on their minds, and their captors knowing the war was about over, the three made yet another break for their precious freedom. "We hid out for two days in the city of Geisen," Mesler recalled. Finally the American troops arrived, and we were repatriated."

On 29 March, Mesler had written, "8:30 a.m. Yanks are coming in—9th Armored Division. We are free men again."

But Mesler was not yet through being frightened. "We could hear the American tanks coming around the corner, and when the lead tank saw us the driver swung the turret of the tank, and we were looking right down his gun barrel."

Mesler and the dozen or so men with him were dirty and disheveled as they waved at the tanks, hoping they would not fire. The driver in the lead tank explained that he could not stop, but that someone would be coming for them. In the meantime, the ex-prisoners in their tattered and torn clothes, waved as the tanks lumbered by.

"After awhile a jeep pulling a trailer came up. It was the chaplain of the Tank Corps. He visited with us a couple minutes, then handed us a bottle of scotch and a box of Hershey bars. You can imagine what that did to our weakened systems," related Mesler. As if orchestrated, every man was shortly running for the nearest latrine.

In gratitude, the residents of Geisen prepared a breakfast for the Tank Corps and the former prisoners in an old schoolhouse. "It was just like we might have expected back home," Mesler remembered. But it had been so long since "back home" foods had been ingested, that the men were once again racing for the bathrooms. "We were sicker than dogs."

The ex-prisoners were taken by ambulance back to Limburg and to makeshift medical facilities. Their first treatment was a delousing project, as lice had been a major problem all during their captivity.

The next day they were flown to Paris and hospitalized. "We did a tour of Paris on a tour bus in our pajamas and robes," Mesler recalled. About a week later, when the men were relatively healthy once again, they were flown to New York, then to a military hospital nearest their home. For Mesler, it was Percy Jones Hospital in Battle Creek.

By the time he had turned twenty-one, Mesler had seen combat in the Battle of the Bulge, been wounded twice, been a German prisoner of war for over three months, endured the ravages of savage captors, faced starvation, and spent several months in hospitals recuperating from his experiences. Mesler was discharged, still with a positive attitude, on 6 February 1946.

Back home in civilian life, he entered Central Michigan University and earned a bachelor's degree in science in 1949. He worked for The Dow Chemical Company, and founded Mesler's Store for Men in 1973, with his son Greg. Mesler retired from Dow in 1983, after a forty-year career.

He also gives talks to high school groups about his military experiences, emphasizing a positive attitude for success in life. He is well qualified.

Duds Saved Melvin Miller's Life Twice

For a twenty-year-old soldier in 1943, who didn't carry a weapon in World War II, he lived through a lot of shelling.

Melvin (Mel) Miller, a semiretired cattleman in Hope Township, was trained to repair any weapon of war—from handguns to tanks. Specialized training followed, but in order to obtain that training he had to take a demotion from buck sergeant to private.

His training carried with it three semesters of college credit from Fordham University in New York. He felt it would be worth it when he returned from the service.

"It was a way for universities to help fill their enrollments while so many men were away in the war," Miller recalled.

Fifteen months later he was assigned to the 104th Infantry division, 329th Medical Battalion, a far cry from repairing machines of war, and then shipped to Cherbourg, France. His was the first division to go directly from the States to Europe.

From Cherbourg they were trucked to Belgium where they saw their first action as they approached Antwerp.

There, the battalion treated casualties for minor wounds, and administered plasma to the wounded. The more seriously injured were sent on to advanced aid stations for further treatment.

The fighting became fierce. "At one point we had to back the ambulance into a small ditch just to drain all the blood from the vehicle," Miller remembered. He stayed with the ambulance platoon until they discovered he was also an electrician. Before entering the army he had completed two years as an apprentice for The Dow Chemical Company.

"From then on I was assigned to keep everything running that required electricity . . . everything from the lights in the officers' quarters to the generators in the treatment rooms."

Because he was a medic, Miller did not carry a weapon. His only defense was the red cross on his helmet, and a red cross on his armband. "The Germans respected the red crosses only near the end of the war," Miller added.

After Allied troops secured Antwerp, Miller and his battalion were transported to Aachen, in southwest Germany.

"There was not a building left intact," says Miller, "Well, except for a few wine cellars," he mused.

As the Battle of the Bulge began to accelerate near the Roer River, the division on either side of Miller's was assigned to go forward to assist in this historic fight.

Miller's division was ordered to fan out, taking up the space of three divisions, to hold the front.

Although a trained electrician, Miller still assisted in the care of casualties. One of his worst experiences came while changing the bandage on the head wound of a GI. "As I removed the bandage, a part of his brain the size of my thumb fell out," he related soberly.

Another tragedy occurred when a hand grenade accidentally exploded in a man's pocket. "Mercifully, he died a short time later," Miller added.

One of a medic's assignments was to try to keep the wounded as comfortable as possible and treat them for shock. At a treatment station in Zundert, Holland, which was set up in a former bar, a GI was carried in minus one foot.

"After treating his wound as best we could, I asked if he would like a cup of coffee or some soup," recalled Miller. "This is a bar," the man said, "I'll have a beer."

With a unit they were serving on a drive to Breda, Holland, they were ambushed by machine gun fire. Instinctively, the men jumped into the nearby ditches. "The ditches had been mined by the Germans beforehand," said Miller. "A lot of men lost hands, feet and legs from that ambush."

On one clear day in late January 1945 (the first one in weeks, according to Miller), Miller and his men were on a drive toward the Roer River. While waiting for the Battle of the Bulge to wind down, a squadron of B-17s passed overhead, heading for Cologne.

"We ran around cheering!" Miller said, "Until they came back." One of the huge bombers was circling on autopilot as the crew bailed out. The other planes began unloading their cargo of death all over Miller's area. Their bombs eventually hit division headquarters where the copilot of the disabled plane had been taken. The bombs from his own planes killed him.

"Three or four bombs hit less than a hundred yards from us," Miller went on on, "Fortunately, all of them were duds.

"In the confusion we never learned why the one crew ditched their plane, or why the squadron returned to dump their bombs on us," related Miller. "The war just kept going on."

In another incident, Miller's encampment fell under the German 88 mm guns.

"These guns were deadly," Miller exclaimed, "and were often used to take out our tanks. Our tanks, armed only with 66 mm weapons, were no match for the Germans." One 88 mm shell came down through the roof of the building where Miller and his men were housed. It was 4:00 a.m. Fortunately, it too was a dud and failed to explode.

The war also had its lighter moments for Miller.

"One morning our captain told us we had nothing for breakfast. He knew I could speak a little German [until he was seven years old, Miller had been raised Amish], and he asked me to teach enough German to some of the men so they could stop at some farms and ask for eggs. They came back with their helmets full of eggs," Miller chuckled.

Near the end of the war in Europe, Miller was on a plane heading for a location in eastern France. It was announced on the plane that Germany and its allies had surrendered.

Two months later he was shipped to America to begin training for the war in the Pacific. Before his training began, however, two atomic bombs were dropped on Japan, ending the Pacific conflict. Miller was discharged on 3 December 1945, and was home in time for Christmas.

Darwin Orwig Witnessed the Bloody Battle of the Philippines Firsthand

On 16 March 1944, Darwin Orwig watched the Golden Gate Bridge fade from view as a sluggish troop transport headed out across the Pacific Ocean.

That ship would eventually take him to what had already been one of the bloodiest battlegrounds in modern history—the Philippine Islands.

Three years earlier, at age twenty-three, Orwig had enlisted in the National Guard for a one-year stint. The stint lasted nearly five years and took him halfway around the world. He carried only a Springfield rifle and his own intelligence, reinforced by three years of strict military training.

Thirty-seven days later, the unescorted ship docked at Finschafen Harbor, New Guinea. At Finschafen, Orwig and his shipmates were trained in the latest techniques of jungle warfare. Orwig was a member of XI Corps Headquarters, and he would later be partially responsible for the deployment of American troops throughout various parts of the Philippines and Japan.

Orwig's trek through the jungles of the Philippines and on to Japan became known as the "Paradise Parade." But it was anything but a paradise. There was little margin for error for an untried Corps, and the XI Corps was soon to be a veteran's Corps.

Finschafen was only the first stop in the "paradise parade" that would eventually lead Orwig and his colleagues in a northwestern direction toward the Philippines.

The XI Corps joined forces with one division and two combat regiments for a total of 50,000 men.

On 28 June 1944, the troops landed on Aitape in New Guinea among a barrage of heavy Japanese fire. When the firing subsided several weeks later, General Charles Hall, a West Point graduate, excitedly reported to General Douglas MacArthur that the Japanese 18th Army had been annihilated with only light American causalities.

On their way to Bataan, the American forces hit the beaches of Morotai, Leyte and Luzon with similar success.

It was on Leyte that the Americans heard the Japanese soldiers utter the only English they would ever know. "To hell with Babe Ruth," they screamed as they raced into bullets from the American rifles. The language of their enemy was often the last words they spoke.

Thanksgiving and Christmas of 1944 were spent on Leyte, as Orwig and his companions had renewed hope that the following Christmas they would be stateside with their families.

A month following the holidays of 1944, Orwig and the 50,000 other American fighting men continued to push toward their destination by landing at San Antonio on the West Coast of Luzon. The XI Corps' objective was to proceed east from San Antonio to Manila Bay to deny the retreating Japanese a haven in the extremely rugged terrain of the Bataan Peninsula.

Two years earlier, the Americans had retreated into the peninsula and it took the Japanese over five months to defeat them.

That defeat lead to the infamous "Bataan Death March," when thousands of American and Filipino soldiers perished from starvation and vicious beatings at the hands of the enemy. In a bloody attack, Orwig and his fighting companions conquered Corregidor and several other small islands in Manila Bay. In doing so, they wiped out what remained of the enemy foothold in the bay area.

According to "Paradise Parade," "The fighting was bizarre and hectic as the American troops clung to the rock [Corregidor] in the face of the shattering explosions . . . it was one of the few instances in modern warfare where the invading force was outnumbered two to one . . . and managed nevertheless, a quick and decisive victory."

But even as the United States flag was being raised over Corregidor in March 1945, there were still battles to be won before the Japanese were to admit total defeat.

MacArthur had made his earlier promise good by returning to the Philippines. On 9 January 1945, he and his forces stormed the beaches in the Lingayen Gulf in north central Luzon and began forcing the Japanese south into the awaiting American militia of Orwig's unit.

The Japanese, surprised at the well-trained fighting power of the underdogs, dug their heels into the caves and caverns of the treacherous terrain.

"They just wouldn't surrender," Orwig remembered. "Their basic philosophy was that giving up was loss of face, and dying was the only honorable thing to do in a situation like that.

"That's what made it so rough on our men in the Bataan Death March in '42," Orwig said. "The Japanese couldn't understand why our men, against all odds had surrendered, because giving up was worse than death to them.

"We had a group of American-Japanese attached to our outfit," Orwig related. "Their main purpose was to interrogate the few Japanese prisoners in their own language. They would go off-shore in PT boats, and with loud speakers, inform the Japanese that the area had been surrounded, that their comrades had surrendered, and if they would come out, they would be treated according to the agreements of the Geneva Convention. Still they wouldn't surrender.

"Eventually our troops scrambled over rocks, cliffs and through the jungles and debris with flame throwers in an effort to shake them loose. Some finally gave up, but many were just not to be had," Orwig said.

History points out that many Japanese soldiers and their leaders took their own lives rather than admit defeat, and within the last twenty years an occasional former Japanese military man, now in his 70s or 80s, has been found in the Luzon jungle, not knowing the war had ended over a half century ago.

After Corregidor, Orwig and his fighting companions went on with renewed confidence to conquer Manila, bringing to a close one of the bloodiest chapters of the war.

Following the cleanup operation in Manila, Orwig and XI Corps was dispatched to Tokyo. The war was winding down after the atomic bombs landed on target in Hiroshima and Nagasaki.

Orwig retired in April 1982 from The Dow Chemical Company's Saran and converted products department after twenty-seven years of service.

Author's note: This story was published in the Midland Daily News *on 27 May 1983.*

Newell Pennell Finds Fame
Under a Hay Wagon

"I was too late for the dugout. The nearest place was a wagon shed
... the rattle was right down upon us. I remember hitting the ground
flat ... then squirming like an eel to get under one of the heavy wag-
ons in the shed." These are the words of the famous war correspondent, Ernie Pyle, during World War II.

The words are from his book *Brave Men,* which tells the story of
the American foot soldiers during a bombing in France in 1944.

Attesting to the accuracy of the text is Newell Pennell of Midland,
also too late for the dugout, who dived under the same wagon just
moments after Pyle, to escape the torment of bombs raining down
from the battle-filled skies.

After the bombing stopped, Pyle, Pennell and a few others crawled
out from under the wagon, and brushed the dust and debris from
their clothing. According to Pennell, as they surveyed the destruction around them, Pyle said in a matter-of-fact voice, "That wasn't a
very secure place, was it?"

"Considering the tons of bombs that had just devastated the landscape," Pennell recalled, "a hay wagon was a very fragile place to try
to escape."

Pennell, then a private first class in the 8th Regiment of the famed
4th Infantry Division, had been one of the survivors of the landing
on Utah Beach in Normandy during the D day invasion in June 1944.

Following several weeks of inland combat, Pennell was assigned
as a clerk at regimental headquarters on the front line. He had seen
Pyle the day before the bomb raid in the farmhouse that had been
commandeered as temporary headquarters. It was noon on 23 July
1944 when Pyle entered the regiment.

That night, according to Pennell, he was on duty to answer the
telephone at headquarters, and Pyle sat at his dusty typewriter bang-
ing out, with two fingers, news columns of the war that would soon
be read in hundreds of newspapers around the world.

"Pyle could type faster with two fingers than most of us can with
ten," Pennell remembered. "He would look at you while he was working, but the only thing he saw was the story unraveling in his mind
as he put it on paper."

The columns Pyle wrote that night were to later become part of
his book, *Brave Men.*

"The sad part of the bombing raid," Pennell explained, "is that the bombs were dropped from our own airplanes. Knowing the raid was coming, our troops were ordered to retreat several hundred yards to ensure our safety. After the first wave of American planes had dumped their loads on target, the wind took an unexpected shift in direction and blew the dust and debris back in our faces. The next wave of air-craft, mistaking the sight from several thousand feet above, dropped their bombs prematurely. That's when we went for cover."

Pennell added, "There were many anxious moments before ground radios could correct the situation with the pilots."

But much harm had already been done. According to *Brave Men*, "there were more than 3,000 . . . aircraft involved in the raid, and because of the error the war was over for several dozen American fighting men who had been killed or injured by their own men."

Pyle wrote in his book, "I'm sure that back in England that night other men . . . bomber crews . . . almost wept, and maybe they did really, in the awful knowledge that they had killed our own American troops."

Pyle goes on in his book with, "Anybody makes mistakes . . . The smoke and confusion of battle bewildered us on the ground as well as in the air. And in this case the percentage of error was really very small compared with the colossal storm of bombs that fell upon the enemy. The air force was wonderful throughout the invasion, and the men on the ground were so thankful the planes were up there."

According to Pennell, "Ernie Pyle was small in stature, soft-spoken, comfortable to be with, and easy to talk to. He was just like one of us. He felt the same uneasiness and pressures all of us felt, and was willing to sacrifice whatever was necessary to get the job done. The major difference was that he could put those feelings on paper."

Following the victory in Europe, Pyle had been asked to return to the States for a rest. But according to Pennell, Pyle had said, "I've told the story here. It's time to move on to where the battle still rages."

That decision sealed Pyle's fate. On 18 April 1945, four months before the war ended, he was killed in a Japanese gun ambush while hiding in a ditch on Ie Shima in the Ryukyus Islands in the East China Sea.

When news of Pyle's death broke, Pennell had just turned twenty-one, and remembered, "It was just another death in the war. But the GIs felt it was the most devastating blow to the war effort. Pyle had informed the American public for so long what the ground troops had been going through, and in language they could understand." Pennell added, "I guess that's what made the troops feel he was like one of us."

Author's note: The above story was written for the Midland Daily News, *and published on 28 December 1981.*

Calvin Pritchard Saw Evidence of Cannibalism in the Philippines

He was nineteen years old, when on a hot, humid July day in 1944, Uncle Sam called him to defend his country. The soft spoken Calvin (Cal) Prichard was one of three sons and a sister (who volunteered for the Women's Auxiliary Voluntary Enlistment), to serve during World War II. He was both excited and apprehensive at the time, but little did he know he would carry the memories of this experience with him for the rest of his life.

Prichard's first experience in armed combat occurred on the island of Palawan, the easternmost island in the Philippines.

"When we arrived there, battleships and cruisers were shelling the beach," he recalled, "and that was a very exciting thing to watch.

"We were ordered into our landing craft with full combat gear, and headed for the beach, not knowing what we would encounter. As it turned out, the Japanese had moved back, and there wasn't any action on the beach. It was sort of a mop-up operation. Someone had misjudged the number of Japanese troops on the island. We were very fortunate."

Fortunate, indeed. The second assignment for Company L, 186th Infantry, 41st Division, of which Prichard was a member, was not as easy.

From Palawan they were taken to the large jungle island of Mindanao. "We were on the offensive there as well, and received more opposition. But the Japanese troops knew they couldn't hold us off, and dispersed into the hills and caves," Prichard recalled.

"At that stage of the war, the Japanese couldn't get any supplies to their troops, so most of the time they were just fighting to stay alive, and trying to find something to eat. Our navy had everything blocked off. At that time, the Japanese navy was almost nonexistent; they knew they were defeated."

Like a Michigan-Ohio State football game, with Michigan leading 31–6 late in the fourth quarter, the defeated were just trying to stay alive late in the game.

"They had even discarded their weapons because they couldn't get any ammunition. They were just trying to find food to survive," Prichard explained.

"We came across a dead Japanese soldier, and they had cut chunks of meat off his buttocks, just like you would slice a ham," Prichard

remarked, somberly. "I had never seen anything like that before. But they were *hungry.*

"The Filipinos were used as guides because they knew the trails back through the bush. One evening we had a little skirmish with some diehard Japanese soldiers looking for food. Several of them were shot.

"The next day one of the Filipinos was walking around with a gunny sack containing five Japanese heads. He had cut the heads off and carried them around over his shoulder," Prichard shook his head at the memory.

"Another time, there were some enemy who just wouldn't surrender. They ran into a building and wouldn't come out. We fired some rounds into the building, when suddenly we heard a big bang. A Japanese soldier had blown himself up with a hand grenade. The only thing that held him together was his spine. Everything else had been blown away."

The weather was often overcast in the Philippines, according to Prichard, and because there were no roads through the jungle, their K rations had to be air dropped. At one period, Prichard's unit itself was hard-pressed for food.

"But we got lucky one day," he recalled. "We found some abandoned, wormy rice left behind by the Japanese soldiers, so we ate that for a couple meals."

After Mindanao was secured, training for the invasion of Japan began. "With the atomic bombs on Japan, President Truman became our hero," Prichard remembered. "We sure didn't want to invade their homeland on foot."

Two months after the bombing of Hiroshima, Company L was headed for the devastated city to destroy the Japanese munitions embedded in its caves.

"The city was completely leveled except for one building, which supposedly was the target for the atom bomb. The steel structure was still standing, and it was the only thing left standing in the whole city," Prichard recalled.

The population of the seaport city of Hiroshima on the day the atom bomb was dropped was nearly 172,000, according to The American College Dictionary.

"I drove through the city every day with some Japanese who were working for me. There were tons and tons of ammunition in those caves. We picked it up and dumped it in the bay," related Prichard.

"One day we found a Japanese soldier who had hung himself. We suspected he was the one who had failed in an attempt to blow up a cave a short time before."

Prichard did not know why they wanted to blow up the cave, but the Japanese military men did not accept failure gracefully.

Prichard never held any animosity toward the Japanese. "We knew where they were coming from," he explained glumly. "They just had a different philosophy on life.

"They were under the impression that it was better to commit suicide than surrender to us."

The former Sergeant Prichard did not want to relate any more of the "gory details" as he put it, but ended the interview with, "An experience like that gives a person a different outlook toward life. I was just glad to do my part."

Roy Renwick Survived a Bullet to the Throat

The end of World War II was still a year away when Roy Renwick, a resident of Midland County for the past quarter century, received his draft notice. He was barely eighteen, and was sent to Little Rock, Arkansas for infantry training. Just a few months later, he boarded the HMS *Queen Elizabeth* in New York, and sailed for England. The plush *Queen Elizabeth* had been converted into a troop ship.

His stay in England was short-lived as Company L of the 329th Infantry, 83rd Division crossed the English Channel, heading for France.

On the French coast, they were loaded into railroad cars called "forty and eight." Renwick elaborated by saying, "They could put forty men and their equipment on those cars, or eight horses." Some of the cars still contained the stench of the latter.

"We arrived in Belgium just after the major part of the Battle of the Bulge, but there might have been some of the fighting still going on," Renwick said as he tested his memory. "I don't remember exactly where we were, but I do know the towns we went through had been leveled by the war."

He remembered crossing the Elbe River, preparing to enter Berlin, and noticing where the forests had been knocked down by the ravages of war. "There were also dead forest animals all over," Renwick recalled.

It was near there that Renwick had frostbite on his toes, a malady that bothers him yet today.

In the eighteen months he was in Europe, he earned four Battle Ribbons, including the Bronze Star for Meritorious Service. But those would not be the only citations he would receive for his service to America. There was another war just around the corner for him.

Although Renwick was never wounded, he did have some close calls, including one from friendly fire. The one that clings to his memory is the day he was following a tank when one of his own artillery forces opened up on the tank, thinking it was an enemy. The armor-piercing shell missed the tank, but landed within inches of Renwick, kicking dirt and debris all over him. "If it had been a regular shell, I wouldn't be sitting here today," he said grimly. "But there is no shrapnel from an armor-piercing shell."

Another time he was an observer on the third floor of a farmhouse
and a large artillery piece named Big Bertha lobbed a shell over the
house. A few feet lower and he would have taken a direct hit. "I heard
it coming," Renwick remembered, "and I headed for the basement
as fast as I could. It landed somewhere just over the house, but that
was a fearful sound, not knowing where it was going to land."

For three months Renwick was a member of a reconnaissance
group, hoping to draw fire so the main forces would be able to detect
the exact location of the Germans with the hope of wiping them out.
In short, he was a decoy, placing his life in jeopardy.

Going through a small town one day, Renwick attempted to take
four prisoners. "One German soldier began to run, and climbed over
a tall fence. I shot where I thought he would be an instant later, but
concluded I had missed. I turned around, and three German soldiers

were coming out of a house toward me waving white flags. They were ready to give up."

He escorted the prisoners back to confinement, "and a day or two later I happened to see another prisoner with an arm in a sling," he said. "Seeing where he had received his wound, and knowing where he had been, I was certain he was the soldier I had shot at earlier."

Renwick was a member of the occupation forces in Austria from January until April 1945, and received his honorable discharge in June 1946. He elected to enter the reserves, holding his rank as a staff sergeant.

Five years later, like a threatening cloud gathering moisture, Korea loomed over the horizon for Renwick, and he was doused in a torrent of enemy gunfire once again. By this time he had a wife and two children, the youngest only seven months old.

He was flown to Ft. Lewis, Washington, and later assigned to Company K, 24th Infantry Division, which entailed advanced training before flying on to Seoul following a brief layover in Tokyo.

Almost immediately, Renwick was engaged in the fighting. "One morning we heard the charge command of bugles from the Chinese," he remembered, "and that just about tore us apart." That meant the enemy was in full charge. Fortunately Renwick was in a backup unit and not on the front line at the time, but those who were took a pounding.

He was not without a nearly fatal wound, however. What he believes was a sniper shot him through the throat. Most people wouldn't live through that but, Renwick explained, "The bullet didn't hit anything vital." The bullet entered the left side of his throat and went out the right side. His voice box was affected temporarily, according to Renwick, "but it came back." He does not know what caliber bullet it was; he just knows "it wasn't the kind that explodes on contact."

A helicopter airlifted him to an aid station where an attending nurse was surprised he was not dead. Renwick was then airlifted to a hospital ship in the Sea of Japan that took him to a hospital in Tokyo. After he had healed for approximately two weeks and enjoyed some R & R, he was returned to his company in Korea for two more months. The scar on each side of Renwick's throat testifies to his experience.

He also realized that he had been on the verge of shell shock. "One night in the Tokyo hospital," he recalled, "I was sound asleep when a nurse came in and touched me on the arm. I sat up in bed and nearly decked her. I didn't even know where I was.

"After that she would stand in the doorway and call out, 'Sergeant Renwick, time for your medicine.'" He chuckled about that as he told the story.

But that was not the last of his wounds. In the middle of the winter he returned to the battle front. "When we could get some sleep it meant laying on the snow and covering up with whatever we could find. One night it was four below, and my feet got frostbite again."

Another time Sergeant Renwick was under a mortar attack. "The enemy had a practice of shooting one long, the next one short," he remembered with a tinge of excitement in his voice. "On the third shot you better get the hell out of there." In his scramble for the nearest foxhole, he dropped his rifle just outside. "When I finally reached for it, all that was left was the barrel. The stock had been blown away." Renwick knew it could just as easily have been him.

Renwick was discharged in October 1952, and left the Korean conflict with six more medals, including one with three campaign stars, one from the South Korean government, and a Purple Heart.

Renwick, like many other veterans interviewed, sums up his feelings by concluding, "We don't talk about it much." That is what makes them silent heroes.

Earl Sanders Guided the Planes at Omaha Beach

Twenty-year-old Earl Sanders applied for navy pilot training, but didn't pass the eye exam, one of the many prerequisites for a pilot. He was told he could go into the regular navy, and within six months they could get his eyes in shape for pilot school. Disappointed, he didn't know that the very next day he would be drafted into the Army Air Corps (later changed to U.S. Air Force). It was October 1942, as nearly as Sanders can recall.

His first few days in the military were spent at Camp Custer in Battle Creek, then he was off to South Miami Beach for instructions in close order drill.

"For young inductees, we didn't do too badly. We were housed at the Whitman Hotel," Sanders smiled.

But their situation was about to change for the worse. After only a few weeks, he was sent to Camp Crowder, Missouri for radio operator training. He was there for nearly a year in crowded barracks, then to Bradenton, Florida where he lived and trained on a baseball diamond in a tent city.

Baseball was not their game, however. The game was training in aircraft warning procedures.

After more training in a variety of Florida locations, Sanders finally shipped out from Camp Shanks, New York aboard the *Queen Mary*. The huge luxury ocean liner had been converted into a troop ship for war purposes. It was 21 January 1944, and there was a little over a year and a half left of World War II.

The ship eventually docked in Twyford, England, and once again Sanders was living in a tent city.

Sanders was an acting First Sergeant when he and a number of other high-speed radio operators were plucked from their units and taken to an air base somewhere in England. There they were locked in a room for thirty days, training and honing their radio and radar skills for the eventual D day invasion.

When D day arrived on 6 June 1944, Sanders was a member of the 573rd Signal Aircraft Warning (SAW), but was attached to the 9th Air Force Fighter Command. Another Midlander, Donald Hawkins, was also a member of the 573rd SAW, and in one of the other five battalions, but neither knew it until they were both working at The Dow Chemical Company many years later.

Sanders was in charge of ten radio operators and cryptographers aboard a First Army Headquarters ship, the USS *Achenar,* anchored just a few hundred yards off Omaha Beach. His job was to guide, via radio and radar, American planes to areas on shore that had been identified by ground troops as needing air support.

"The ground forces would radio us where they needed help from air support," Sanders stated, "then we would radio air command in England for that support. When the P-40s and P-51s came into the area, we contacted them by voice radio, and guided them to their air strikes. They would then go in to do their strafing or bombing, or whatever else needed doing from the air."

Sanders and the others worked out of the map room on the ship, next to General Hodge's quarters.

The pounding of the beaches lasted fourteen days for Sanders, after which he once again returned to England. During that time, however, the ship on which Sanders was housed came under air attack by enemy planes, "but we didn't get hit," he said matter-of-factly.

His job completed at Omaha Beach, Sanders was sent to New Castle, near the Scotland border, to rejoin the 753rd SAW. The following month, he and thirty-three others from his outfit were attached to the 566th SAW and returned to France. There they continued to guide American fighter planes to ground targets both day and night.

In a now yellowed letter sent to his stepmother, Edna Sanders, dated 20 June 1944, he explains why his family had not heard from him in several months.

> I know it's been some time since you have heard from me but of course you know why. I was assigned to one of the ships that participated in the invasion, and it was quite an experience, believe me. We were in a position only a few hundred yards off one of the beaches [Omaha], so consequently right in the midst of a little action.
>
> We were there for several days; although we underwent frequent raids by enemy aircraft we, fortunately, came out of it ok. Even England looked good to me when we got back. I wish I could tell you some of the more vivid details, but you can readily see it's impossible.

Sanders and his thirty-three colleagues were eventually sent to an air base in France where they were given the distinction of being named the First Pathfinders Squadron. "We became the ground control for the B-26 Bombers, and what they called blind bombing," Sanders explained, "We actually had a pilot and bombardier in our radar unit. We would lead the first plane of the squadron in over the target [via radar], and the bombardier in our unit would actually toggle the bomb bay on the lead plane to drop the first load of bombs. As soon as the planes following saw the first plane's bombs, they would drop theirs.

Sanders's work was not always done from the compartment of a ship, however. During the Battle of the Bulge, he and his men had assembled their radar radio equipment on the highest piece of real estate they could find to make them more effective.

"When we were disassembling the equipment [which took a day and a half] to pull out after the battle, we were still getting sniper fire," Sanders said. "But no one got hurt even though there were two bullet holes in my radio shack."

But that wasn't going to be Sanders's last close call. Going back to England, past the white cliffs of Dover, a Dutch merchant ship rammed the ship carrying him and his men. "It was a bigger ship than ours, and the navy had to bring tug boats to tow us back to Camp Top Hat in Brussels from which we had originally departed." He doesn't know why the incident with the Dutch ship took place, but he speculates it was due to someone's incompetence.

"We loaded onto another ship, and somewhere out in the Atlantic it blew a boiler. It took us a few days longer to cross than it should have," Sanders said.

Sanders had not been home for over three years. "Most of the time, no matter where we were, we were quarantined for secrecy because radar was so new at the time," he said.

The war ended in Europe while Sanders was in a small town that the Americans had just taken from Germany. "We had had a complete German division surrender to us, including a general," said Sanders, "and they could have come and taken us anytime they wanted to. But they were tired of war too, and just waited for the right time to surrender."

When asked if he was frightened at any time, he replied, "We were too busy to be frightened, but I never gave it a thought as to my dying."

Sanders received awards and citations for his participation in five major battles, including Ardennes-Alsace, Central Europe, Rhineland, Germany, Northern France. He also received the General Orders' 9th Air Force Commendation.

He carried his bravery into his civilian life as well. In 1997 he was afflicted with cancer. "I am a survivor," he said firmly. "Even though I was on chemotherapy for a year, I never gave a thought that this might take my life."

Sanders also had musical talents he used both in the military, and later in civilian life. When he was not in the war zone, he was singing at the Red Cross Club and Officers Clubs in England.

In civilian life, he has had lead roles in such productions as *Pajama Game* and *Guys and Dolls* at the Midland Center for the Arts as well as in theaters in Bay City and Saginaw.

"Wild Bill" Sinclair Became a Prominent Attorney

Making a sweeping turn, he aimed the nose of his aircraft southeast, lined up the body of the bulky bomber to port side of what would one day become Northwood University, and revved his twin engines for maximum noise.

Opening the throttle to "full," Captain William (Bill) Sinclair roared the B-26 275 miles per hour at treetop level above Main Street in Midland, Michigan.

"I had to make an abrupt swerve to the right and point the nose up sharply to avoid the Dow smokestacks," Sinclair smiled. The smokestacks no longer exist, but not because of Sinclair's antics.

Sinclair, a prominent Midland attorney for nearly forty years, smiled at the thought.

Sinclair, then a flight instructor based at Dodge City, Kansas, had flown home for an overnight visit with his family. He landed his B-26 at Tri-City Airport, which, at the time, didn't even have a control tower.

His commanding officer knew about the incident before Sinclair returned to Dodge City the next day.

"He wasn't overly happy with me," Sinclair admitted, "but we were friends, and after a few whiskies it was forgotten. But I never did anything like that again."

Still smiling, Sinclair went on, "I've never even told my kids of this foolishness."

But that was not the last incident for Sinclair and his ill-fated aircraft.

As operations officer, he had volunteered to fly the ship. It happened that "fly" was a misnomer.

"It was poorly designed," Sinclair recalled. "Its wings were too short, and the engines didn't have enough power."

On one occasion, Sinclair watched as a B-26 was burning at both ends of the runway.

"One crashed on takeoff due to stalling, and another had crashed upon landing. It could have been pilot error, but it was just a hard ship to fly," he remembered.

Sinclair himself lost power in an engine at 100 feet. "I immediately looked for a place to land because one engine was not strong enough to keep me airborne for long."

He made it back to the airfield while alerting his control tower to clear the runway.

"I kept my landing gear up until the last possible instant to reduce the air friction, and I was later told I had missed a bus under me by inches," Sinclair recalled.

On another occasion Sinclair's craft lost an engine over the Rockies at 12,000 feet.

"The question was whether to jump or find an emergency airfield. We had already divided the candy bars among the crew."

Fortunately, he was able to coax the craft as far as Flagstaff, Arizona, for another successful emergency landing.

The aircraft, however, got better, and Sinclair got luckier. He had been selected for fighter school, the dream of every aviator at the time. It also meant an opportunity to be sent to the South Pacific.

But fate had other plans for this plucky pilot. He had to remain behind due to some surgery. It was a big disappointment to the young, single, ambitious air jockey. However, he later learned that most of the men he would have been with had been killed on various missions over the Pacific.

In August 1945, Sinclair finally received his eagerly awaited orders for the Far East. His next home was to be on Okinawa. Before he had packed his duffel bag, the world had learned of the atom bomb and Hiroshima.

It was another disappointment for young Sinclair, who had looked forward to combat duty where he could use his training and skills to defend his country.

So Sinclair repacked his duffel, picked up his discharge papers and headed instead for Midland.

Author's note: This story was written for the Midland Daily News, *and published on 30 May 1988.*

Lovell Sovereen was Among the Ninety-Five Percent

He had just graduated from Midland High School in June 1944, when he was sent to San Diego for his basic Marine training, then on to Camp Pendleton, California, for additional training. Private Lovell Sovereen was pleased to be asked what choice of occupation he would like to have in the marines.

"They wanted to know what I would be interested in," Sovereen remembered with a smile. "So I said I would like to go to cook and baker's school, because I thought they probably didn't get shot at." So they made him a machine gunner.

"As I was taking my training as a machine gunner, I noticed in the administration office, a lot of marines typing and doing bookwork in an air-conditioned office. I, on the other hand, was hitting the deck and shooting, and I vowed that if I got out of this alive, I would learn to be the best typist and office worker ever." Sovereen recalled with a chuckle his fond wish to be in comfortable surroundings.

Following gunnery training, Sovereen was sent to a group for reassignment. "Each day they would take a few out until I was the only one of eight left in my tent," he recalled. "Pretty soon I was the only one left in the whole unit. They even closed down our mess hall. So, on my own, I went to another mess hall nearby.

"Finally, I went to my lieutenant and asked what I was supposed to do." That, in itself, was a rather brazen move for a buck private in the Marines. He said, "We'll tell you what to do, when to do it, and how to do it. I don't care to listen to your problems.'

"So I went back to my tent. Each morning, I went to the neighboring mess hall for breakfast, and then took it easy the rest of the day," Sovereen recalled thinking that war was going to be easier than he had expected.

A week later his lieutenant and some other marines entered his tent and asked him what he was still doing there, because no one was supposed to be in the tents at that point.

"Like it was my fault," Sovereen said, shaking his head with wonder at the incomprehensibility of officers.

Within minutes a personnel truck arrived, and Sovereen had a lonely trip by himself to rejoin his unit. By this time, the recruit was a six-month veteran in the U.S. Marines.

On Thanksgiving morning 1944, young Sovereen thought he would have a good meal, which would have been a welcome change from their ordinary fare. He knew that even the marines had good meals on major holidays. Unfortunately, that morning his unit was loaded on trucks with full fighting gear, and taken to a ship in San Diego to an overseas assignment. The bottom line was that at his camp he had missed Thanksgiving dinner with all the trimmings, and by the time he was aboard the ship, they had already had theirs. He remembered being really annoyed about it at the time, but laughed about it later.

"That was when I learned that the marines were not exactly like the movies," he grinned. The ship was heading to Hawaii, and Sovereen became seasick the first day out and for nine days afterward. "I remember thinking that maybe it was just as well I missed that big dinner."

More than a week later, the ship docked at Pearl Harbor. Already Sovereen was looking forward to a Christmas dinner. But once again, his fantasy was not to be. On Christmas morning, he once more packed his belongings, boarded another ship for another island in the Hawaiian chain, and again he missed his holiday meal.

"By this time, I was getting real disgusted and quite hungry," Sovereen said, in full agreement that an army (or marine unit) travels on its stomach.

The 5th Marine Division had been activated in November 1943, his unit became part of it, and he continued training as a machine gunner. In early February 1945, the division headed for war and one of the most historic battles of World War II—Iwo Jima. Things began to get serious.

Sovereen's unit was in the third wave to hit the beaches in the LSTs. His division was responsible for taking Mt. Suribachi. As the door of the craft dropped upon the beach, his lieutenant caught a bullet in the leg. "That was the last time I saw him," Sovereen recalled, with some envy.

The picture of four marines raising the American flag on Iwo Jima is, undoubtedly, the most reproduced photograph of the war, and several monuments have been erected in various locations in the United States to commemorate that event. Sovereen, with his usual luck, missed the whole dramatic event. He was down below in a foxhole waiting for orders for the next move.

"I wasn't scared at the time," recalled Sovereen, "everything was happening so fast. It was after I left the island and had time to reflect that I began to shake."

While it has often been repeated that "It's a small world," Sovereen had amazing evidence of it on that small island in the Pacific. While on the beach on Iwo Jima, after Mt. Suribachi had been secured, he ran into two other Midland residents, James Bandeen and Curtis Layman. After the war Bandeen became owner of Bandeen Chevrolet in Midland.

As he and Layman exchanged information about themselves, Sovereen discovered that Layman was on the burial detail. As they parted company, Layman said, "Well, I'll be seein' you." It was not a phrase Sovereen was eager to hear at the moment. "I just hoped that I'd be seeing him when he was seeing me," he recalled.

At one point, Sovereen was in a foxhole with a ranking marine, and they were catching Japanese fire in the bunker directly behind them. The ranking marine told Sovereen to "stick your head up and see where the gunfire is coming from." It was a long day in the fox-hole, Sovereen recalled, with no one willing to stick their head, or their neck, out.

Another time as his unit was mopping up after Suribachi, he heard a buzz bomb approaching. This type of bomb was so named because it made a distinctive buzzing sound, according to Sovereen.

"The louder the sound, the closer it's going to hit near you," he recalled. "Four of us jumped into the same foxhole at the same time," Sovereen said. "I rolled myself into a ball, and the shell hit in the middle of the foxhole." The shrapnel tore into Sovereen's leg and thigh, tearing up the leg badly but breaking no bones. The other three were killed.

Sovereen was taken to a field hospital, and later shipped to Guam where the shrapnel was removed. He was then sent to a hospital at Pearl Harbor, where he spent the next two months recuperating.

While he was still in Hawaii, the atom bomb ended the war, but he was about to begin another challenge—one for which he had lit-tle training.

He hoped that now that the war was over, he would be sent home and discharged. He theorized wrong. Since he was now healthy and back on his feet, he was sent to Nagasaki, Japan as part of the occu-pational forces. It had been only six weeks since the world had wit-nessed the last atom bomb ever exploded in combat.

It was really shocking to see what damage it had done. Then, shortly after that, they sent out a patrol of about twenty or twenty-five of us to "make friends" in a town of 50,000 inhabitants. Needless to say, we felt somewhat outnumbered. The first day only a few kids came out to see us, and we gave them candy bars, which was all we had. The next day, a few more kids came out to get their candy bars. Little by little, the adults began to overcome their fears and came out and we gave them what we could. By the time we left, two weeks later, the entire town was there to see us off.

Sovereen smiled at the memory. He also recalled that

there wasn't much use for a machine gunner in an occupational force so I, along with many others, was ordered to guard an empty building. There were so many of us and they had to keep us busy.

I was getting pretty bored with that when I read a notice inviting men to join the boxing team. We would box once a week, two rounds, for three minutes each. That sounded like a good deal to me, so I signed on. They then relieved me of guard duty.

Unfortunately, while I thought we would be fighting just for fun, my opponents took it seriously. And I decided it was a hell of a way to die for my country. After two fights, I went back to guarding empty buildings. It was a lot safer.

Shortly after that, I volunteered to help run a dry cleaning plant. That was a real good deal. All I had to do was to push a green button to start it and a red button to turn it off. We had local people to do the ironing and if it broke down, we called a mechanic. However, we cleaned with gasoline, and one night the dry cleaning plant burned to the ground.

Sovereen sighed regretfully. Once again, he returned to guard duty.

Nine months later, Sovereen returned to civilian life, attended the Northeastern School of Commerce in Bay City, and in 1947 opened his own tax accounting service in Midland. As of this writing, he had been in business for fifty-six years. Remembering his vow to himself during his combat training, he also learned to type.

Reflectively, Sovereen added, "At the time of the experience, even seeing men dropping on both sides of you, you still don't think it will happen to you, although maybe that is just nineteen-year-old thinking. Later, you realize you too could have been killed."

Ninety-five percent of the men and ninety-eight percent of the officers in the 5th Marine Division were either killed or wounded on Iwo Jima.

Even a War Could Not Stop the Music
for James Stark

Being a musician all his life didn't keep Midland's James E. Stark from seeing combat in World War II. In fact, that may have contributed to it.

In 1940, Stark entered his third year as a teacher near Buffalo, New York. To supplement his meager salary, he joined the National Guard and played baritone horn with the unit's band once a week.

Two months after school began, his unit was called to active duty, and Stark was headed for Alabama and combat training.

After the attack on Pearl Harbor on 7 December 1941, and just before his outfit was shipped to the Far East, Stark volunteered for the U.S. Army Air Corps, and was assigned to Maxwell Field in Alabama for basic training.

Within the next three months he was given several batteries of tests to determine his aptitude for the military. As a result, Stark was designated to begin navigator training aboard B-24 bombers.

"The tests were really senseless," mused Stark. "Unless you were really a deadbeat, they placed you where the most help was needed. Out of 120 men tested, 118 of us became navigators."

In the fall of 1942, Stark was commissioned a second lieutenant, and sent to West Palm Beach, Florida to await orders. Ten days later he found himself in a huge B-24 hangar with air force personnel from twelve other squadrons. Approximately 2,400 men listened to General Henry "Hap" Arnold, commander of the U.S. Army Air Corps, deliver an address.

The only pertinent thing Stark remembered forty-one years later is that they would not know what their mission would be until they were airborne, and that they would have to pack six months worth of personal items, such as razor blades, smokes, and toothpaste. "The suspense was both nerve-wracking and intriguing," Stark reminisced.

Leaving Florida, his B-24 first landed in Cuba to pick up supplies, then headed for China via South America, the Ascension Islands, Africa and India. His became the first bomber group in World War II to use an air strip near Kunming, on the western edge of mainland China, and just east of the Burma hump, a mountain range separating China from India.

Because of the location, Stark's squadron had to make several round trips into India, hundreds of miles away over the hump, just to obtain enough gasoline, bombs and other supplies to fly a single bombing mission over Shanghai, Hong Kong, Burma and various naval ports where there was a concentration of Japanese supply bases in China.

Stark recalled his toughest mission with pinpoint accuracy. It was on a flight over central China where he was among three other squadrons, forty-eight B-24s, assigned to bomb Japanese riverboats loaded with supplies.

"The distance to our targets and return trip was out of flying range for a fighter escort, so most of the time we were on our own," he remembered.

Once Stark had used his expertise to guide his pilot onto course, he became a gunner in the nose of the B-24, firing a 50 mm gun to protect his pilots from a frontal attack by enemy aircraft.

Over the plane's intercom, Stark heard the top turret gunner yell, "Zero at ten o'clock at our altitude!" Looking out through his unprotected glass bubble, Stark downed the Japanese airplane in a blaze of oncoming bullets, but not before his pilot had been hit in the shoulder.

"That was three minutes from our target," Stark said, "and one hundred more zeros rained down upon us out of the sun as though they knew we were coming. It was like a humming bunch of mosquitoes looking for blood and knowing where to find it."

The squadron's lead plane had been downed, and the pilot of Stark's craft was out of action. Being third in command, Stark remembers climbing into the pilot's seat, now acting as copilot, and strapping on the necessary safety equipment.

In the back of his memory he recalled praying, "Don't let anything happen to the copilot. This isn't my bag." He had had only minimal instruction in piloting the aircraft.

Overall, the entire mission was successful. Fifty Japanese airplanes were downed, eleven credited to the gunners on Stark's airplane. Eight American planes and crews were lost.

After the bombs had been dropped, and the remaining enemy aircraft had turned tail, Stark and his crew headed for the nearest landing strip to seek aid for their wounded pilot. It turned out to be a forward P-38 fighter base, three hours from their own base.

"Our monstrous aircraft, landing on a strip built for the short take-off fighters, was a novelty to the natives and American men working at the airfield," Stark recalled, "and we drew a lot of attention."

The war was not always a series of disasters and near disasters for Stark. He also remembers the time when his crew had bought a "terribly out of tune" upright piano in India for $10, and loaded it upside down in the bomb bay of the B-24 so Stark, the musician, could entertain his squadron back at their base in their off hours.

Stark also talked of "one of the best kept secrets of the war." While in training in Alabama, he met Honora Austin who was a dietitian in the local military hospital.

"The good part," Stark smiled, "is that she agreed to become my bride. The bad part," he added, "was that she worked for the civil service, and if the marriage were known, she would have lost her job."

The Starks kept their secret for nearly a year when she quit her job to be with him at West Palm Beach, waiting for his overseas orders in 1942.

In 1978 Stark retired from the Midland Public Schools after directing Midland High School bands for thirty years.

In his retirement, he went on to conduct Blast From the Past, a group of older Midland musicians who play frequently for dances at the Community Center in Midland.

Author's note: This story was written for the Midland Daily News, *and was published on 28 May 1983.*

Tom Stetler Went from Small Towns in Michigan to Remote Islands in the South Pacific

He grew up in small towns in southern Michigan. Towns like Highland Park, Grass Lake, Pleasant Lake and Jackson. Tom Stetler would soon trade them for remote islands in the South Pacific. Islands like Samoa, Guadalcanal, Tulagi, Wallis and Ieshima.

Like a lot of late teens in the early 1940s, he felt the patriotic pull of his country's plight, and joined the military.

At eighteen, he was in the U.S. Navy preparing to perform the initial amphibious assault on the beachheads of Guadalcanal in the Solomon Islands. It was 6 August 1942, and the assault was to be launched from the USS *Zeilin*, named for a Marine general.

Stetler was in Seattle, Washington, however, when he got word of the brutal attack on American soil in the Pacific Ocean. He and a friend were on leave, and at the home of friends for a typical relaxing Sunday dinner. Around noon his host turned on the radio—"television" was not yet in the vocabulary of the American public—and they learned that Pearl Harbor had been ravished by the Japanese. All military personnel were being ordered to report to their respective bases. Stetler and his friend enjoyed a hurried dinner, excused themselves, returned their rental car, and went to a movie.

"We weren't very serious about the whole thing," Stetler chuckled, "and we wanted to take advantage of our liberty. But about ten minutes into the movie, the lights went out, and an announcement was made for all military personnel to report to their bases. We were in uniform, and just couldn't slip down in our seats enough to be ignored, so we got up and headed for our ship."

By the time the two reached the ship, it was on full alert, according to Stetler. His ship headed south, and began training for amphibious landings on the beaches of southern California with the marines.

In late March 1942, Stetler's ship dispatched a shipload of Marines in Honolulu, continued training for the assault on the Solomon Islands, took aboard a shipload of infantry Marines, and set sail for a three-week training exercise in Samoa.

The devastation of the Japanese attack the previous December was still very much in evidence, Stetler remembers.

Leaving Samoa, the seagoing armada of marines was to take over the French territory of Wallis Island to give the marines experience

in amphibious landings. "Just getting through their harbor was a harrowing experience in itself. There was a coral reef all around the main
harbor, and the charts we were working from were probably dated
back in the 1700s," he chuckled. "So we had to plot our own charts,
using the technology we had on board. It was sort of fun, but at least
no one was shooting at us."

During the three trips Stetler's ship made to Guadalcanal carrying
troops, it was fired upon numerous times, and watched as four heavy
cruisers and two destroyers were attacked and sent to the bottom of
the South Pacific.

During one attack, Stetler's ship was ordered to retrieve all the
landing craft that had started for shore. "We stacked those boats as

fast as we could, and in every haphazard way imaginable," Stetler remembered. "We could see and hear the enemy guns through the night darkness, and we knew we had to get the hell out of there."

The Japanese had no losses, but had been training for night attacks, and according to Stetler, "at that time we didn't even have radar."

"The attack probably lasted only forty-five minutes," Stetler recalled, "but it seemed to go on forever."

The USS *Zeilin* had joined a task force of ships coming up from New Zealand to join the armada, which would soon strike Tulagi. Marine casualties were high that first day on Tulagi, according to Stetler.

"There was very little resistance when we landed on the island of Guadalcanal, and so the marines just walked inland." Stetler did not go ashore because he was a signalman, and was maintaining his post on the bridge of the ship. A channel of about six miles separates Tulagi and Guadalcanal.

About mid-October 1942, Stetler's ship landed the first infantry troops on Guadalcanal. There was a signal station on the island from which he helped coordinate the landings between the ships and the shore.

"Actually, the signal station was a canvas tent with a thirty-foot bamboo tower. We also had a shell casing, which was sounded for a general alarm," Stetler explained.

Stetler's job was to make radio contact with Tulagi, and warn his own ships offshore if a raid was coming from Japanese planes.

Shortly after returning to his ship, he thought they were getting bomb bursts from aircraft overhead, but soon learned that the Japanese had brought in some big guns, and were shelling the troop ships from the beach. "Fortunately, a couple of our own planes were in the area, and took out the enemy guns," Stetler said.

"We actually took on board two to three hundred prisoners from Guadalcanal," Stetler added. "They said they were Korean laborers, but they had on Japanese uniforms."

The prisoners were taken to Wellington, New Zealand, several hundred miles southeast of Guadalcanal, and turned over to the New Zealand armed forces. The men on Stetler's ship then had a two-week reprieve while the barnacles were removed from the ship's underside in dry dock.

On 11 November 1942, Stetler's ship was making its third run to Guadalcanal to unload troops for the fighting there. While the troops were unloading, Stetler was temporarily assigned to help defend them from air raids, and was positioned at a 20 mm gun as a loader. "That's the guy who slants the magazine onto the breach and taps the gunner on the head to let him know he can start firing again," Stetler explained.

Shortly after noon on that day, word came that an air attack was approaching. Among the five ships, now cruising in a circle to concentrate their firepower, Stetler's ship was the only one hit. Five dive bombers, one after another, headed for the USS *Zeilin*, Stetler's home away from home.

Stetler's ship took five near hits; meaning that the bombs came close enough that the compression of the water split the seams of the ship under water. But credit goes to the gunners aboard the ships who shot down three enemy aircraft, and took their pilots aboard, according to Stetler.

There was only one fatality aboard Stetler's ship, and the damage control people were able to secure collision mats around the ship, slowing the leaks enough for the pumps to keep up with the incoming water, and limp back to Long Beach, California for repairs.

Later in the war, the USS *Franklin Roosevelt* aircraft carrier was hit and partially disabled. Stetler's ship was dispatched to assist the *Franklin* somewhere between Iwo Jima and Japan. If necessary, they were prepared to take it under tow. By the time they arrived, another ship had already arrived, however, and was towing it to the nearest dry dock for repairs.

Stetler's last duty of the war occurred on the second day of the battle for Okinawa. His ship was sent to assist naval vessels in distress. His ship contained all the latest fire fighting equipment the Navy could muster at the time. It was his first experience of watching an airplane deliberately hurl itself into a ship. These planes were called kamikaze planes, and were flown by Japanese pilots who believed it was a great honor to die for the emperor.

After two days, his ship was dispatched to a small island west of Okinawa, called Ieshima. It was the island on which the famous war correspondent, Ernie Pyle, was killed.

The task at Ieshima was to wait for distress calls from ships that had been either been hit by torpedoes or by Kamikaze planes. During the next few days, Stetler's ship attempted three rescues, one successful, according to Stetler. "The other two had been badly beaten up, and the more water we poured on the fires the deeper they sank, and eventually they capsized," he said soberly.

One of the ships, the USS *Hugh Hadley,* had been credited with shooting down the most Japanese airplanes in the war. In return, it had been hit with three kamikaze planes. "We came alongside the *Hadley,*" Stetler recalled, "threw lines over her side, and hoped they had flooded their ammunition magazines so there would be no more explosions. Firefighters from our own ship went aboard her.

"We finally got the fires under control, and towed her back to Ieshima."

Later, Stetler's ship, with tow lines, was trying to pull a destroyer off a beach where it had become grounded in low tide. They were then attacked by Japanese dive bombers.

"That was a bit harrowing," Stetler remembered, "trying to pull another ship out of shallow water, and shooting at planes at the same time. We let loose with smoke off our fantail so the kamikazes couldn't see us, and they soon left for bigger targets near Okinawa.

"Even at that, one hit near another ship right at the water line, but didn't sink it."

After that, Stetler's ship secured the destroyer and headed south for the Philippines. He soon learned that he had been selected, through his seniority status, to return to the States for R & R.

Stetler didn't know it at the time, but he was coming home for good. His parents then lived in Dearborn.

He was sitting on a train in Kalamazoo when he got word the surrender of Japan was imminent, and for all practical purposes, World War II had come to a close. But it was not the end of his harrowing experiences in a military uniform.

When he stepped off the train in Detroit, a car came up to him, screeching to a halt, and asked where he was headed. Stetler told him he was headed home to Dearborn where his parents lived at the time. The driver then invited him to get in the car and he would drive him there.

"The driver was a madman," Stetler laughed. "The way he drove was more frightening than any of my experiences in combat. He was even stopped by the police, but they let him go when they saw me in uniform. The whole city had gone crazy with the good news."

Returning to school, he earned his degree in engineering, and became employed by the Michigan Bell Telephone Company. Nine years later, he joined the telecommunications department at The Dow Chemical Company, and retired in 1986.

A Long War for Robert Streeter

He was in a Chicago movie theater when suddenly the movie stopped, the lights came up, and members of the Shore Patrol stepped up on the stage to announce that Pearl Harbor had been attacked. They ordered everyone in the military to return immediately to their respective bases, and everyone else was encouraged to go home. He and several others were escorted in a paddy wagon back to their base at Great Lakes Naval Training Center.

That was how Robert Streeter was introduced to World War II on 7 December 1941.

He had been in the naval reserves since the previous September, and was going to machinist school at the Great Lakes Training Center. Following that, he was sent to Detroit for advanced schooling, then on to Newport, Rhode Island.

In April 1942, Streeter was assigned to the USS *Ralph Talbot,* a Navy destroyer and one of the most highly decorated ships of the war. The officers and men serving aboard her earned two Navy Crosses, four Silver Stars, two Legion of Merit medals, one Bronze Star medal, twenty Commendation Ribbons, fifty Purple Hearts and five meritorious promotions.

The USS *Ralph Talbot* had been moored in Pearl Harbor on the morning of 7 December 1941, and its crew had shot down two enemy planes, damaging a third, before it cleared the harbor.

At the time of Streeter's assignment the *Talbot* was at Mare Island, off the California coast, being equipped with larger guns. The *Talbot* then joined a convoy, and headed back to Pearl Harbor. This was also Streeter's introduction to the wrath of war.

Several partially sunken ships from the attack four months earlier were still sitting on the bottom, with their upper portions showing above the water line, still smoldering, according to Streeter. One such ship was the Oklahoma, he recalls.

"About a week later we joined the Australian fleet to strengthen their navy, and began preparations for the attack on the Solomon Islands," Streeter said. The Solomons are a chain of islands a relatively short distance directly east of New Guinea and northeast of Australia, in the Coral Sea.

For eighteen months Streeter and the men aboard the *Talbot* shelled the Solomons and nearby islands. Their ship came under fire 137 times from dive bombers and enemy ships.

On one mission near Okinawa, Streeter's ship was hit by a kamikaze plane. "A wing flew down the deck and severed the legs of eleven men," he recalls. The motor of the plane smashed through the wall next to Streeter's bunk. Fortunately, he was not sleeping because the destroyer was on fire where the motor had lodged.

A large part of the plane lay burning on the fantail. "That probably saved us," Streeter explained. "Because of the horrendous smoke, the other kamikaze planes aimed for the smoke, and missed the end of the ship."

The electrical system had been knocked out by the attack, according to Streeter. "We could only fire our guns by hitting the firing mechanism with a hammer," he remembered. They lost only eleven men out of a crew of 270.

An experience in New Guinea is one that will be forever etched in Streeter's memory. "I was strolling on a beach, drinking a beer, when a native eating white grubs appeared. He had a gunny sack containing Japanese heads. He was selling them for $1 each. They were so fresh they would still be bleeding," he said, shaking his head. "I ignored him the best I could."

Streeter's destroyer was so successful that in three-and-a-half years of combat, it chalked up twenty Japanese planes, including four kamikaze planes on its bridge scoreboard, damaged five others, and covered more than twenty amphibious landings.

At one point it had shot up so many loaded enemy barges and supply ships that Admiral Halsey himself signaled the ship and asked, "Have you fellows no regard for the bag limit?"

Streeter, and the USS *Talbot*, were also instrumental in overtaking numerous island chains in the Pacific. According to the *Quincey Patriot Ledger*, a newsletter presented at one of the ship's reunions, "On September 2, 1945, the USS Ralph Talbot, along with three other warships participated in the surrender of Truk atoll, the group of islands which were once the mightiest Japanese military and naval base in the Pacific."

Official surrender ceremonies included not only Truk and its eighty islands, both large and small, but also seventeen other islands ranging over nearly five million square miles of ocean and garrisoned by approximately 130,000 Japanese military personnel, according to the *Ledger*.

Streeter and the crew of the *Talbot* also went on to help capture Wake Island, the Marianas, the Marshall Islands and a number of Japanese bases scattered throughout the south and western Pacific.

By the end of the war, Streeter and his ship had fought in virtually every major action and campaign in the Pacific from Pearl Harbor through Okinawa, and returned to the States at least twice for repairs only to return to fight again. These included the Marshall and Gilbert Islands raids, the Philippines, Guadalcanal and Tulagi. The latter two were the first American offensives of the war.

Fighting off heavy Japanese air attacks during the first two days of the landing on Guadalcanal and Tulagi, Streeter found himself in the first battle of Savo Island. It was here that the Japanese force had sunk four U.S. and Allied heavy cruisers. Streeter and his comrades were then engaged in a one-sided duel with three enemy cruisers, scoring hits with its guns and torpedoes before being forced out of action by five hits from the Japanese cruisers. Once again the *Talbot* limped to the West Coast for damage repairs.

In nearly three years and eight months of almost continuous combat, Streeter and the USS *Ralph Talbot* were credited with the destruction of twenty-six Japanese aircraft, including four kamikaze planes.

According to the *Ledger*, the ship expended nearly five hundred tons of high explosives that sent its shells and torpedoes crashing into Japanese cruisers, destroyers and smaller vessels. It also engaged in more than twenty major amphibious landings.

Streeter and the men of the USS *Talbot* also participated in more than twenty-six different aviation rescue operations at sea, rescuing aviators from crashed or ditched planes, and rescued and treated more than forty survivors of damaged and sunken ships, including survivors from the ill-fated USS *Indianapolis*, which was torpedoed and sunk in the western Pacific.

Streeter took part in every battle of the *USS* Ralph Talbot except Pearl Harbor. Little wonder he proudly displays his dozen or more war medals.

Streeter retired as a tool and die maker in 1981.

Tommy Thompson Flew Ninety Missions Over Europe in a Tiny Cockpit

Cecil (Tommy) Thompson answered the shrill call of patriotism in March 1942. He was just eighteen. By the time he turned twenty, he was piloting a P-47 Thunderbolt Dive Bomber over the English Channel and into the air war over France. His small but powerful plane carried a half-ton of bombs and fired eight 50 caliber machine guns.

The horrors of Hitler were still fresh in the mind of this plucky young pilot as he aimed his payload at bridges in an attempt to cut off war supplies to the Germans. He was a proud member of the 358th Fighter Bomber Group, 9th Air Force. His bombing career began on D day, 6 June 1944.

Thompson's main mission was to support the ground forces in France. "We dive-bombed targets such as bridges, enemy vehicles, tanks, trains, etc.," he says. He was one of the first to fly a mission from the beachhead eleven days after D day. "We would fly a mission, land in France for refueling and ammunition, and fly another mission before returning to England over the North Sea."

The 358th Bomber Group relocated to Cretteville, France on 17 July. "We were not far from the action on the front line," Thompson related. "We could hear the roar of the guns in the background."

Eight days later, the Eighth and Ninth Air Force sent in 3,000 heavy and medium bombers and Thompson's group of fighter bombers. They blasted a gate for the ground forces, according to Thompson. "This was called carpet bombing," he said. "They would literally plow up the area. When the hole was blasted in the German lines, the infantry went in and cleaned out the remaining pockets, and General Patton's 3rd Army poured through to the south. This was called the St. Lo Breakthrough.

After the bombing, the Germans were retreating, and the roads were clogged with motorized vehicles and horse-drawn artillery, according to Thompson. "I flew three missions that day. On my last mission my guns got so hot the tracer bullets were making a slow roll as they left the gun barrel."

Following the St. Lo Breakthrough, Thompson's bomber group flew many missions as top cover for General Patton's 3rd Army of tanks as they moved quickly toward Paris.

On one of Thompson's missions, he came close to losing it all. A 150 gallon napalm tank became caught on the manual release mech-

anism. "I flew out over the North Sea, hoping I could shake it loose," he said, "but it just wouldn't budge." He now had two options: fly over friendly territory and bail out, or try to land with the bomb on the cutting edge. He chose the latter. "I've always said it was the smoothest landing I ever made," he chuckled. "Later they came out with a mechanical release, and that took care of the problem."

Thompson will never forget his twenty-first birthday on 16 September 1944. He was flying a mission over the Paris area when he had to drop down at nearby Rennes, France for refueling and for more ammunition. While waiting, he managed to talk to someone from a C-47 cargo plane that was bringing in supplies from England. They were taking back some champagne. "I managed to talk them into selling me six bottles of champagne at $2 per bottle," he says. He fit the latter around his legs and the seat in the tiny cockpit, flew another mission, then flew back to his base.

"I gave my crew chief three bottles," he chuckled, "and I shared the other three with my buddies. It was quite a celebration."

Most of Thompson's missions were flown at an altitude of four to five thousand feet, and sometimes lower, where they were not only firing on ground targets, but catching immense flak and antiaircraft fire in the air as well.

"Our orders were to shoot up anything that moved," he remembered. "I had a German antiaircraft gunner shooting at me from the side of a hill in plain sight, so I made a circle and got his gun position in my sights. I began firing all eight 50s," he went on. When I came out of the dive, I was cutting grass. Another second into the dive, and I wouldn't have made it." But his target was obliterated.

Thompson loved his aircraft, and he loved flying it. He recalls his 75th mission. His group was to fly deep into German territory, strafe an airfield and return. "If we ran into German planes on the way in, that was as far as we could go," he says. "If we ran into them on the way out, we would be in trouble. We would not have enough fuel for a dog fight," he noted.

One of the pilots in his group had to abort, leaving Thompson and nine other P-47s to complete the round-trip. Thompson soon spotted some planes in the distance. He called them in to the other pilots, and edged over in the direction of the intruders, all the time trying to gain altitude.

"I soon found out there were about twenty German ME-109s," Thompson says, matter-of-factly. In addition to being outnumbered by more than two to one, the enemy also had the sun and altitude in their favor, he noted.

As he gained altitude, he looked back and saw an enemy plane in pursuit. "I did a steep turn, went into a high speed stall to keep away from his guns. I went into a snap roll (an evasive tactic) and then into a spin from 10,000 feet."

Thompson had difficulty coming out of the spin, and recovered at about 2,500 feet while drawing antiaircraft fire from the ground.

But his troubles were just beginning. His single engine craft began cutting out. "I shut off the super charger, used for high altitude flights, and the engine regained power," he remembered. He shook his pursuer and headed west toward the front lines and into friendly territory.

At 250 miles per hour, and at treetop level, he skittered through a valley and soon recognized tracer bullets headed in his direction from the top of both hills lining the valley. Escaping with his life, he soon crossed over the front lines, wagging his wings to identify his allegiance to the American troops below.

Finally, he found the landing strip at Toul, France, approximately fifty miles from the front. "The plane just didn't feel right," said Thompson. At the far end of the runway he cut his engine, and discovered a large hole where the supercharger had been. The main spar, the basic framework of his aircraft, had been cut through by ground fire, causing the trouble coming out of his earlier spin.

On Christmas Day 1944, Thompson got the surprise of his life. He was on a mission directly over the Battle of the Bulge. "The air was full of planes from France, England, U.S. and Germany," Thompson says, "when out of the blue and the smoke came these German 262 jets. They were flying twice our speed." At that time, jets were a novelty, and mass production of the speedy birds was barely on the horizon. "It was a little scary, with all the different planes going after targets at the same time."

For two weeks in January 1945, Thompson became a radio controller between the ground forces and air support. He was assigned to the 12th Armored Division near Strasburg, Germany, close to the bulge area. The tank he was to ride in was crippled, so he established a radio headquarters in the basement of a nearby vacant building.

"The tank battalion went out the next morning, overran the infantry, lost radio contact and was captured by the Germans," Thompson said. "We didn't know what had happened to them for three or four days. We later found out from a German POW."

He went on, "For some reason the 12th Armored Division didn't want to use air support, but after I vectored a couple P-47 missions into target areas successfully, they finally began using air support often, and with much success."

When Thompson went back to doing what he loved most, the next nine of his last ten missions drew heavy antiaircraft ground fire. After each flight, ground crews patched holes in his plane.

But a person can take just so much stress. After his 90th mission, Thompson was grounded from fatigue, and sent back to the States.

"I'll never forget crying when I saw the Statue of Liberty in New York harbor," he said openly. "Even when I think of it now, I shed tears," Thompson said, choking back a lump in his throat.

First Lieutenant Thompson didn't return empty-handed, however. Among his numerous medals, the one of which he is the most proud is the Air Medal with Fifteen Clusters. He also received the Presidential Citation with Two Clusters.

Thompson was given medical treatment at Miami, Florida, and it was there he decided to give up the option of leaving the military. He still loved flying, and continued training in California and Hawaii for several weeks, then was sent to the South Pacific.

From Guam, he flew the P-47N, a larger fighter plane with greater fuel capacity. Most of these flights were training missions. It was on one of these flights that Thompson had still another harrowing experience.

"I was on a flight with three other planes, about fifty miles from base, when I smelled gasoline fumes in the cockpit," he recalled. "I radioed in that I was returning to base." On the way back the fumes became worse. He tried opening the canopy at 250 miles per hour, when he discovered airplane fuel shooting up through the floor board of the cockpit. He closed the cockpit and the fumes became worse.

"I felt myself being overcome with fumes," says Thompson, "and I was on the radio, screaming as I came in, landing right of the runway."

Somehow Thompson managed to get the plane on the ground with only the obnoxious odor of airplane fuel in his nose and on his brain.

"The next day I was on runway control when a plane burst into flames on peel off. I called the fire in and the pilot made a quick landing, getting out of the plane before it burned to the ground," said Thompson.

An inspection of all the P-47Ns found that the rubber fuel lines were crumbling due to the salt air. All the planes were grounded until the problem was resolved.

Thompson returned to the States in March 1947 for his honorable discharge, without having to fly a combat mission in the South Pacific.

But he still loved flying, and joined the air force reserve program, flying out of Flint and Selfridge Field near Detroit. But that was not to be the end of active duty for Thompson.

Korea was more than a gleam on the horizon in 1951, when Thompson's reserve group was reactivated on 1 April of that year. They were sent to Bergstrom Air Force Base in Austin, Texas. For the first time, he knew what it was like to fly a jet plane. He was awed by its speed and its quiet engine as compared to his old World War II fighter plane.

"After checking out in the F-84 jet, reading the manual, having two rides in a T-33 trainer and a cockpit check, I got the thrill of flying a jet fighter plane," he said.

Life was pretty tame for this new jet pilot, compared to his duty over Europe just one war before. He never entered combat again, but that didn't stop him from seeing more of the world. He was sent to Mauston Air Force base in England, gunnery school in Tripoli, North Africa and back to the States for more training. Part of his training was making passes at the B-29 for camera gunnery.

Thompson finally became a full-time civilian in March 1953.

He has, ever since his air force career, been active in the Berryhill American Legion Post 165, where he has served as Commander, and a member of the American Legion drill team. The team won in national competition in 1978.

Thompson retired in 1981 after a thirty-four-year career with The Dow Chemical Company.

Richard Tolly Had Enough Thrills to Last a Lifetime Before He Turned Twenty

Richard Tolly enlisted in the Army Air Force Cadet Reserves in 1942 at the ripe old age of sixteen. He was eighteen by just eleven days when the air force thought it a good idea to make Tolly a full-time employee.

After completing his air force basic training at Shepherd Field at Wichita Falls, Texas, he completed the equivalent of a college semester course in electronics in just eight weeks at Lowry Field near Denver. He was then promoted to Corporal, and sent to Naples, Florida for gunnery training on the B-24, also known as the Liberator.

It was there that Tolly first learned the difference between being responsible for shooting down enemy airplanes, and being responsible for the crew of his own plane. On one training mission, he happened to be in the cockpit, the pilot was in the back instructing some of the crew, and the copilot left to relieve himself, turning the controls of the plane over to Tolly.

"It was the first time I had been in a B-24," Tolly muses, "but I did pretty well for the five to ten minutes I was at the controls. My green coloring had nothing to do with my being scared to death," he chuckled.

"Instead of watching the instruments on the panel in front of me, I was looking out the window. In no time I had lost five hundred feet. I managed to pull it out by myself, but the pilot in the back wondered what the hell was going on." Again he chuckled.

That was not to be the last time Tolly was "scared to death" on this aerial training mission.

Shortly after that incident, one of the engines of the Liberator caught fire over the Everglades.

"The pilot told us we might as well stay as long as we can and try to put the fire out. 'There are alligators down there.'

"We had only two shots to put the fire out. Each engine was equipped with two built-in fire extinguishers. The first one didn't do the job, but when the pilot touched off the second one, the flames went out. We finished the mission on only three engines. The other alternative was to go into a steep dive, hoping the speed would blow the fire out. We were happy the fire extinguisher worked.

"It was a good thing there was someone in the cockpit who knew what he was doing," Tolly smiled gratefully.

This particular flight was nearly tainted all the way. The pilot made the mistake of flying at 1,000 feet over Cuba.

"At one point of the pass-over, we saw the roof of a building roll back, exposing ack-ack guns," recalls Tolly. "We got out of there in a hurry!"

But all those experiences made Tolly better equipped for training at Clovis Air Force Base in New Mexico where he spent the next several weeks preparing for combat.

Preparation for combat included intensive training as a turret gunner on the Superfortress, B-29. The men and the monster flew gunnery training as well as simulated bomb runs from Nevada to Detroit to Los Angles.

One night the pilot, Captain Martin Dirnbauer, got lost over Mexico. The plane's autogyro compass had gone out, and they eventually had to land on a fighter base at Biggs Field in El Paso, Texas. The aircraft was nearly out of fuel.

A fighter base is hardly a place for a B-29 Superfortress bomber. The landing field for a fighter plane is much shorter than for a bomber. A bomber weighs several tons more than a fighter, and has a wing span several times longer. Even the buildings lining the taxi-way became a hazard due to the wings that, on that occasion, seemed to go on forever.

After refueling, Tolly and the tail gunner stood in front of the plane and helped guide the bomber along the narrow airstrip with hand signals. The tips of the wings of the B-29 were missing other planes along the runway by inches. When the plane was in position for takeoff, Captain Dirnbauer locked the brakes and raced the throttle to near top speed. The Superfortress roared with deafening madness, and the plane vibrated like a house on the edge of an earthquake.

Slowly at first, then rapidly picking up speed, the giant thirty-five-ton mammoth began its short takeoff with all four engines roaring, tires hot enough to explode, straining for each inch of runway. There was only *one* problem now. Tolly was not yet in the aircraft!

"They almost lost me on takeoff as I was still hanging out the back door of the plane," Tolly chuckled. He had scrambled to make the open door as the plane sped by him.

"Thanks to Dan [Dan Hays, the tail gunner] for pulling me in as we were airborne with my butt and legs still hanging out in space." By the time Tolly was safely inside the plane, the monster craft was over 1,000 feet above the earth.

That would not be Tolly's last close call.

In mid-summer 1945, Tolly was based on tiny Tinian Island in the South Pacific, and assigned to the *Marianna's Belle*, another Superfortress. Some of their targets were to be in Japan.

"Nearly every mission we returned with flak holes in our plane," Tolly remembered. "And over Japan the flak was like popcorn exploding. It was all around us." As the command gunner, sitting in the top turret, Tolly was responsible for spotting enemy aircraft above and around the plane. Fortunately, no one in Tolly's crew was injured.

Tolly's now aging memory also recalls an air incident that almost cost him and his crew members their lives.

"I remember being on a mission over Tanube [Japan] one night, and a Japanese zero [fighter plane] did a flythrough and missed colliding with us by approximately twenty feet. I saw the fire from his nacelle [flaps on the engine] as he passed over us. I tracked him through with all six 50 [caliber machine guns], but didn't get a shot at him at all.

"Our number three engine was on fire, and the fighter tried to finish us off. We had to feather the prop and put out the fire."

Having an engine out, the mission automatically went to an alternative target, which was a town of 35,000 people near Kobe. They dropped their incendiary bombs, then headed straight for Iwo Jima for an emergency landing.

Tolly said, "We were almost out of gas by the time we reached Iwo, and had to squeeze in behind a plane already landing. We landed *between* the two runways, over the protests of the control tower. It was either land or crash, as there wasn't enough gas for another pass."

The following morning Tolly's plane was loaded, and the crew was ready for another mission. As they were about to taxi out, they received orders from the control tower to disembark and report to lead crew training. With that training would come a promotion. They disembarked, and another crew boarded the *Marianna's Belle*, and flew the mission, according to Tolly.

That was the last time Tolly would see his beloved aircraft.

"They were shot up badly," he said, "and barely made it back to Iwo Jima. They had to bail out over the island." Three men were badly hurt on that crew, but all survived. The aircraft plunged to the ocean's depths.

"That was the end of the *Marianna's Belle*, a fairly new ship, but too badly shot up to survive," Tolly recalled sadly.

Tolly is credited with thirteen missions during the war, plus seven after the war. "Actually, we flew more than thirteen official missions," he said, "but if we didn't return with bullet or flak holes in the plane, the mission didn't count."

Tolly was one of the first people to fly over Hiroshima after the atomic bomb obliterated the city, taking with it over 100,000 lives.

"We were on a mission to photograph the damage done at Hiroshima." The devastation was caused by another B-29, the *Enola Gay*.

"We made a low-level run and saw, firsthand, the devastation," he said, shaking his head.

Tolly and the crew of his B-29 did not know what their mission would be when they boarded their plane that day. "They didn't tell us much ahead of time," he said ruefully. "We just got on the plane and did what we were told."

At five hundred feet they saw the devastation. "There was just nothing there. Nothing standing for miles. It was like flying over a garbage dump, but even that was scorched."

He noted steel beams were melted and warped like cooked spaghetti. "There were some shells of buildings here and there, but everything else was totally flat. We didn't see one living thing in the whole area."

Tolly went on to say, "When the eleven of us on our plane saw the destruction, we were horrified."

It was years before Tolly could talk about the experience. Stumbling for words nearly sixty years later, he said, "I had nightmares about it for the longest time." Footage of this experience was shown on CBS television years later.

Tolly said that he felt sorry for the women and children who were killed by the blast, "but every building, including homes, was considered a factory because the Japanese military dropped off weapons of war at the houses, and the women and children would assemble them. Everyone was involved in the war just as we were on our side."

Tolly's most harrowing mission came on the last day the war. His crew was parachuting medical supplies and food to American prisoners in a POW camp near Kobe, Japan.

"As we opened the bomb bay doors, we could see the natives scattering for cover. They thought we were making another bombing run. We soon saw a roof on the POW building. On the roof was painted the words, '1,200 prisoners . . . need food and medical supplies.'"

The supplies had been packed into fifty-gallon drums, and strapped to parachutes. "We opened the front bay and one carton broke loose and dropped right through a streetcar loaded with people."

The Superfortress made two passes trying to disperse its cargo, and both times the parachute lines became caught on the bomb bay doors and the gun turrets. The chutes opened, and created a terrific drag on the monstrous plane.

"We were only at two hundred to three hundred feet. We rotated the turrets until the wind whipped off the chutes, then the bombardier and I found some hatchets on the plane and were cutting the shrouds as fast as we could." They looked down through the bomb bay doors and saw the ground screaming past at over 120 miles per hour with twelve parachutes taking the lift, speed and power out of the four massive, straining engines. They had no parachutes on themselves, and even if they had they were too low to make a safe jump should it become necessary. There was also the possibly of one of them falling out the bomb bay door. When the shrouds were finally cut through and the chutes were released, "that plane sped forward and upward as though it had been shot out of a sling shot," laughed Tolly.

"We had a good pilot or we would never have made it through," Tolly admitted. Some of the supplies found their target. Their plane was aptly named *God's Will.*

The end of the war over the skies of Japan was not necessarily the end of the threat of war from other sources.

On 29 September 1945, less than two months after the end of World War II, Tolly was in the lead plane of four hundred B-29s to fly over Korea as a "show of power" to Korea and to Russia. The fly-over was to let Korea, China and Russia know how serious America was about this situation, according to Tolly.

"Relatively few people know that the Russians stole several B-29s from us during the war," Tolly explained. "On occasion, a B-29 would make an emergency landing on Russian soil, with their permission, because the plane was either out of fuel or badly shot up. The Russians kept the planes to study and copy our electronics, bombsights and other vital secrets." Some of those crews never came back, according to Tolly, who can document the facts. "They were tortured for any vital information the Russians could get, and never heard from again." Eventually, the Russians were emulating the B-29, Tolly said.

"We had orders that if we had to land in Russia, the last man alive was to blow up the bombsight because it was top secret."

"We also had orders to shoot down any plane that pointed its nose or gun turrets toward us," Tolly added, "even an American plane. All of the men in the formation knew this, so if an American plane turned toward us, we knew it was a stolen American craft, flown by a Russian."

Staff Sergeant Richard Tolly was offered a 2nd Lieutenant's commission at the end of his enlistment on 8 December 1949. It would mean being a gunnery officer on a B-29 and an indefinite enlistment in the Korean War. He turned it down. All of one of the crews he had flown with had been killed. And in the back of his memory were all the close calls he had encountered.

"I had had enough thrills to last a lifetime," Tolly concluded.

And he had most of those thrills before his twentieth birthday.

Sheldon Turley "Didn't Do Anything"

Sheldon Turley was valedictorian of his high school class in Nanticoke, Pennsylvania in 1940. Because of his academic achievements, his school allowed him to return for another year and take classes he had not been able to take when he was a full-time student. Those included typing, shorthand and other classes in which he had an interest.

It was those extra classes that helped him obtain his first civilian job, and would later serve him as an adjutant to General Zundahl, commanding general of the 41st Division Artillery in World War II.

War was raging in Europe in 1941, and Turley had not yet been drafted. Waiting to be called for the military, he left home for Berwick, about twenty miles south of Nanticoke, and applied for a job with American Car and Foundry. The company was making tanks for the war effort.

Turley soon became the secretary to the chief chemist, and two months later moved on as secretary for the head of research. Although he could not know it at the time, all this experience was preparing him for the war.

He worked almost a whole year before he received his draft notice, and when it came, he was told he could get a deferment because his company was making war machines. "But I had three brothers in the service, and I elected to go in," Turley said, decisively. It was nearly a year after the Japanese had bombed Pearl Harbor.

Turley was sent to Camp Roberts, California, and took artillery training. At the same time, he enrolled in a preliminary course in preparation for officer's training at Ft. Sill, Oklahoma. There he received his commission.

As a 2nd Lieutenant he was assigned to mountain training in Michigan's Upper Peninsula. "Because of our mountain training, we thought surely we were headed for Europe," he remembers.

But the military was not necessarily founded on logic. Turley's first combat assignment was far from the warm security of any office, but it was warm. He was assigned to the 146th Field Artillery Battalion in the South Pacific. His land tour began on the island of New Guinea, just north of Australia, slightly west of Guadalcanal, and very close to the equator.

Turley and his battalion fought their way northwest to Leyte in the Philippines, then south to Mindanao. By this time Turley had

trained three forward observer crews of three enlisted artillery men each. These crews took turns, joining Turley at the location of the lead infantry company at the battlefront. Being a forward observer was not a job for the weak at heart. The normal life expectancy of a forward observer in action at the time was about thirteen minutes.

But Turley raised the norm, and lived to tell his story nearly sixty years later.

Near Davao, a major city on Mindanao, the Japanese were assembling a very large group of soldiers to push the American fighting men back to the coast. Turley was ordered to obliterate this assembly. He and one of his crews climbed to the top of Mount Apo in order to direct the fire of the 105 mm, 155 mm and 240 mm howitzers of several battalions. His commands were radioed to a fire direction center that computed and sent commands to each of the battalions so that the shells of all the guns landed at the same time, resulting in a deadly barrage of firepower.

"There was so much firepower, that at times it felt as though half the island of Mindanao went up and down, shaking. I had never seen anything like it before in my life! I had been given orders not to go down to see the devastation, and I never knew why. But I had seen bodies before, and wasn't particularly thrilled to see what we had done anyway."

Reflecting carefully on his experience on Mindanao, Turley adds modestly, "Nothing scared me at the time. I was young, and didn't know any better. I had three brothers fighting in Europe, and two of those would have made a better story than what I've got," Turley added. Giving credit to his siblings Turley said, "One of them landed in Europe on D day, and the other was in Patton's army. Compared to them, I really didn't do much of anything."

Following the Mindanao campaign, Turley was slated to land on the southernmost Japanese island of Kyushu, the home of Nagasaki. "I was to be dropped off at night from a submarine to direct naval gunfire onto the island from a hidden position," he recalled. But the drop-off never took place. Instead, thanks to President Truman's decision to drop the second atom bomb, Turley never saw Kyushu.

"But I did get to Hiroshima, and walked into what was once city hall. It was only a month later, and city hall was completely burned out because of the flash of the atomic bomb. Only part of the superstructure was left standing. They didn't know at that time, the lasting effects of the atomic bomb upon people who ventured there later." Fortunately, Turley suffered no ill effects.

"At the time there were pictures in the press of a man walking across a bridge, and his shadow was burned into the concrete by the blast, and that was the bridge we crossed to get into Hiroshima." Later, this area was described as the atomic desert.

This writer, while in the military twelve years later, visited the same site. City hall was still standing as Turley described it, and the bridge was still there. The entire area was still a sandy wasteland.

Turley's tour of duty as a member of the occupation troops had lasted about eight months, when he received word of his father's heart attack back in the States. When he explained this to his commanding officer, he was encouraged to stay with the military and told that he was in line for a promotion. His commanding officer understandingly let him know that his orders to return home would be typed up if he chose to leave.

"I went home and spent a year with my father before he died," Turley said with gratitude.

For someone who "didn't do much of anything," Turley's efforts may have shortened the war for the whole world.

Korean War

1950-53

After two cataclysmic world wars, the Korean War (more commonly called the Korean Conflict because war was never officially declared), appeared to be lackluster in global importance and dramatic interest.

Drained by World Wars I and II, many Americans blocked out the three tedious years of the Korean struggle. Basically, most Americans were not all that interested in another dangerous involvement in the Orient, according to some historians.

But this war was unique in our history. President Harry S. Truman entered the conflict without declaring war, calling it a "police action." Reluctantly, the United Nations approved the president's action, and fifteen nations joined America in battling North Korea and China. It was an effort to stop world communism.

According to John Toland's, *In Mortal Combat,* four million human beings, half of them civilians, died in a brutal contest marked by atrocities on both sides, raging up and down a peninsula the size of Utah.

"When an armistice was finally signed in 1953," Toland says, none of the issues that started the war had been settled," He adds that it was the first war America never won, and that it left the United States politically embittered. It also established the dangerous precedent of a president conducting an undeclared war without constitutional sanction under the guise of a police action.

Perhaps for some of the reasons above, only a few valiant Korean War veterans wanted their stories told.

History tells us that the U.S. involvement in Korea was a memorable saga of human tragedy and courage, complete with heroes on both sides, an unforgettable epic of world consequence.

Feeling Sorry For Himself is not Ken Cummins' Style

He had tried to enlist in the navy in July 1951, but he had a vision problem in one eye. The army was not quite as discriminating. They drafted him on 28 February 1952. He was just twenty years old, and America had already been in the throes of the undeclared Korean "War" for two years.

After four months of infantry training at Ft. Jackson in Columbia, South Carolina, he was sent to Korea, via California and Japan. While in Japan, however, he was given two weeks of chemical, biological and radiological warfare training. He was also assigned to the 7th Division of the 32nd Regiment of the infantry.

Ken Cummins does not remember where he docked in Korea, or exactly where he was for the first week there, but does recall being trucked to the front lines. Little did he know he would be there less than two months, then back to Japan for serious surgery.

22 October 1952. It was the Kumwa Valley in South Korea. The Kumwa Valley might be a pretty place, with its mountain ranges, rice paddies, and its occasional oasis of trees here and there. But this was war, and there is nothing pretty about a war.

Shrapnel from enemy artillery was flying all around him, but Cummins didn't see it coming. He did not even know he had been hit until he thrust his left hand forward, and found that the piece of paper he had been holding was red. It was his own blood.

"I grabbed my arm and laid down," Cummins related, "and a medic soon came by and asked if anyone had been hit." Another sergeant with Cummins had been hit by the shrapnel in the back of his legs, and in addition to both arms, Cummins took nine pieces of shrapnel across the back.

"I didn't know at the time how badly I was hit," he mentioned, "but I twisted my sleeve to reduce the blood flow. When I tried getting up by myself my legs wouldn't move." Shock was setting in.

He was taken to the nearest aid station where he saw an old friend he had met back at Ft. Custer, Battle Creek, during the early days of their war experience. His friend had become a company clerk.

"This guy knew before I did that I was going to lose my arm," Cummins reflected.

He was then airlifted to Tokyo where he left behind a part of his body that had been so useful to him for over two decades. And it was

left in a country where men only five years his senior had fought and many died in another of America's wars.

It was not until he reached the hospital in Tokyo that he realized he was going to lose his arm. Gangrene had already set in.

"They gave me a piece of paper and asked me to sign it. I asked them what it was for, and a guy said, 'We need you to sign it. We're going to take off your arm.'"

"While I trusted their judgment, I said, 'What if I don't sign it?' He said 'We're going to take it off anyway to save your life.' I signed it," he said with a chuckle. "I didn't like the alternative." Cummins' left arm was removed four inches below the elbow.

Following the surgery, Cummins spent six long weeks in the Tokyo hospital before being transferred back to the States and to Percy Jones

Hospital in Battle Creek. There he was fitted with his prosthesis and taught how to use it. Including the one in Tokyo, he was in and out of hospitals for six months. To this day he has biannual visits to the VA Hospital in Saginaw for check-ups.

"It hasn't been that bad," Cummins stated matter-of-factly, "You can feel sorry for yourself the rest of your life, or you can get on with life." That philosophy has kept him going with a smile and with optimism since 22 October 1952, when shrapnel very nearly claimed another war fatality. Missing part of his arm has never held him back. He hunts, fishes, shoots skeet and even operates a chain saw.

Cummins concluded with a touch of patriotic nostalgia, "It's an experience I wouldn't have wanted to miss, but it's something I wouldn't want to go through again."

Maynard Monson's Patriotism is Reflected in His Family

He turned seventeen on 15 May 1950. His father had signed the appropriate papers that day, and Maynard Monson of Midland, was on his way to the induction center in Detroit.

A month later the Communist North Koreans crossed the 38th Parallel, and the United States, in defense of South Korea, was plunged into an undeclared war. In just ninety days, Monson was to be very much a part of that war. And by the time he was nineteen, he had been wounded three times, awarded the Purple Heart twice, and returned home a month before the Pinconning High School class he left to join the army graduated.

Thirty-four years later, Monson is still considered forty percent disabled as the result of a bayonet wound to the shoulder, and a mortar shell shrapnel wound in his back and right leg.

"But in every war ever fought," commented Monson, "the worst enemy never wears a uniform. The worst enemy is the elements."

Korea was no different. According to Monson, the ground troops suffered more casualties from frostbite and weather-related incidents than enemy guns. During the winter months, Monson carried two pairs of socks inside his shirt so when he changed, he always had two warm pairs to put on.

"Of course, we had no way to wash them, so the odor drifting up from my shirt sometimes became a little overpowering," he chuckled.

"During the winter it was bitter cold," recalled Monson. "I can remember my teeth chattering all night in a foxhole. We weren't issued sleeping bags because too many men had been trapped in them, unable to get out in time to flee to safety when the enemy would strike at night," he explained.

"Then in warm weather," Monson went on, "it was the mosquitoes and other insects. There were times when we didn't even have a commanding officer. In March of 1951, we made a four-week assault toward Seoul. My platoon, during that time, was reduced from forty-one men to just eighteen," Monson reflected, adding, "We had more casualties from frostbite, jaundice, and hepatitis than from enemy gunfire."

Monson was assigned to the 25th Regiment, 27th Infantry Division as a trained rifleman. Soon he was promoted to platoon sergeant in a light machine gun squadron.

"The life expectancy for that job, statistically, was three minutes," Monson recalled soberly. But at seventeen, the odds didn't bother him.

During his last battle in the early winter of 1951, Monson passed out from exhaustion and battle fatigue while carrying his wounded comrades to safety. "The next thing I remember is waking up in a hospital in Puzan."

Monson speaks sincerely as he describes his allegiance to the United States. "I would do it again if it came to that," he said seriously. "Freedom is like a gigantic insurance policy, but every now and then the premiums come due. I'm proud to have helped pay them."

Before arriving home on 7 December 1951, Monson was awarded, in addition to his two Purple Hearts, the Combat Infantry Badge, the Korean Campaign Ribbon with five Bronze Stars, and the Asiatic Battle Ribbon.

Monson's patriotism is also reflected in his family. His son, Maynard, Jr., is a captain in the U.S. Marines, now stationed in Camp Lejeune, North Carolina. He pilots a Cobra helicopter, and was stationed in Lebanon in 1984, when a truck bomb rammed into a barracks, killing more than two hundred American servicemen.

Monson, Jr. was a member of the same outfit, but fortunately was aboard the aircraft carrier *Iwo Jima* off the coast of Lebanon at the time of the blast.

Author's note: This story was written for the Midland Daily News, *and was published 28 May 1984.*

Robert Robinson: By All Means, a Man of Distinction

Most people would like to have the distinction of being first at something, but Robert (Bob) Robinson of Sanford would have traded his first with almost anyone.

Robinson was a member of Task Force Smith, a task force that was the first to take up residency in the war-torn country of Korea, immediately after the conflict began.

He had been with the 6th Army Division in Korea for two years. Now twenty years old, he was on his way home in November 1949. While waiting in Tokyo for his flight home, he was stopped on the street by the Military Police to inform him his flight had been postponed for perhaps up to a year. That was like a stab to his gut, and hurt all the way to his brain where it finally registered.

The Korean conflict was just raising its ugly head above the western edge of the Sea of Japan, and every American military man on Asian soil was being given the same message. Home was only a place in one's dreams, not a place they could expect to see anytime soon.

The only reason Robinson got caught up in the change of orders was because his plane, due to head for the States, was delayed. A few hours later and he would have been home.

The MPs escorted Robinson back to Camp Drake outside Tokyo, and he remembers saying, "I just can't believe this is happening." But he swallowed his pain, and reported to headquarters. He had been a transportation specialist, and was responsible for the loading of men and strapping in of equipment into the huge transport planes heading for Pusan. "It took hours," Robinson recalled.

"General MacArthur told us to go over there, clean the place up, and he would have us home for Thanksgiving dinner," said Robinson with some irony. MacArthur was right; he just didn't say which year.

When the war officially broke out on 25 June 1950, Robinson was a convoy leader, and part of an elite group of 406 fighting men who were the first Americans to land on Korean soil to fight a war. The group was Task Force Smith, named to honor a General Smith who had been killed there some time prior.

"The Marines like to take credit for being there first," said the still feisty Robinson, "I hate to say this, but Bob Hope even beat them there." After the infectious chuckling from the two of us subsided, he added somewhat seriously, "And that's the truth! Hope had already put on a show for us when the Marines arrived."

Returning to the serious side of the situation, Robinson explained, somewhat sardonically "But this was to be a police action. We were assigned to go in there just to keep the North Koreans from invading the South Koreans. Then we would go home."

As history shows, it would not work quite that way. The fighting lasted for three years, killing nearly 34,000 young American men whose lives had barely begun, and over 103,000 would come home with battle wounds, according to the 1999 World Almanac.

But history does not say much about how the early part of the Korean conflict was operated. Task Force Smith, and the 406 men in their first fire fight, ran up against 20,000 North Koreans. Even the high command could see this was no way to win a war.

In charge of maneuvering personnel and supplies, Robinson lost four men from his platoon. Robinson was only a foot away from one of his men when he was killed. "I just don't know what saved me," said Robinson, staring down at the table.

Robinson does not know how many casualties there were in Task Force Smith. He only knows he never saw a lot of them again.

The toughest part of his job was coordinating men and materials so both were in the right place at the right time. As a leader, he would never ask a man to do something he would not do himself.

On the first day of fighting, he asked for four volunteers to take some ammunition to the front lines, something he had done himself many times. "They never made it," said Robinson. "We later found them with their hands tied behind their backs. They had been shot in the head, right through their helmets." That battle lasted for two days, according to Robinson.

A battle that lasted much longer than that, however, was their interaction with the elements. In the Osan Valley during December 1950, Robinson and his courageous crew suffered severe frostbite from sleeping on the ground during that fierce winter, ground that was too frozen to drive in a tent stake. Instead, they wrapped themselves with everything they could find, including the tents. At night the temperature would often drop to minus forty degrees Fahrenheit. "The pain from frostbitten feet was more painful than taking a shot in the gut," Robinson said emphatically.

After soaking his feet in "some purple stuff, whatever it was," Robinson recalled, "I was sent back to the front lines. There were just no replacements for us. Any man who could halfway walk was sent back to the lines."

Robinson gives credit to the American-made weapons. "Even in those extremes, our M-1 rifles worked," he remembered, "even though they were leftovers from World War II. That was what made the difference between 406 fighting men and 20,000. They only had old fashioned bolt action rifles, and not all of them had rifles at all. As the men on the front line were killed, someone behind them would come up and take the rifle of the fallen man."

Robinson's memory, reaching back fifty years, did not even recall all the battles he was in. But he remembered living in day-to-day fear for his life. "When we would get orders to 'hold at all cost,' we just knew we wouldn't be coming out," he said as his memory slipped back into the twilight zone.

Robinson also gave credit and appreciation to the navy and air force for coming to the aid of Task Force Smith on so many occasions. "The navy would bombard the land ahead of us with their eight-inch guns from offshore, and navy and air force planes would soften up the enemy with bombing and strafing," he explained. "They saved us more than once.

"You could barely see the ships, they were so far away, but you could hear the guns, and the projectiles going over us. In fact, the ships were so far away, that by the time the shells went over us, they were tumbling from lack of power. But they were effective."

It was fortunate the navy was there at all, according to Robinson. Task Force Smith had to retreat all the way to the eastern shores of the Yellow Sea on the west coast of North Korea. They were fighting both the North Koreans and the Chinese.

The day finally came that Robinson had looked forward to for four years. He had spent forty-two months overseas, and there were finally no flight delays to make him stay longer, and no military policy to change his plans. He was discharged on 30 July 1951.

On 27 May 1952, Robinson and the other members of Task Force Smith received a letter from Major General Herbert M. Jones, acting adjutant general, which read in part,

It gives me the greatest satisfaction to forward to you, . . . a Special Certificate of Valor which has been awarded by the Secretary of the Army to you and the other members of the first group of American soldiers to fight in Korea.

The courage and skill which your unit demonstrated in standing off the aggressors in Korea will never be forgotten in American history. I know that you are proud to have been a member of this group of 406 soldiers, and I want you to know that I am proud to be associated with such fine soldiers as yourself.

Enclosed with the letter was Robinson's Special Certificate of Valor which hangs in a frame on the wall of his den in his Sanford home. It describes the battle of these 406 men who so valiantly went head to head with 20,000 North Koreans.

Robinson also received a letter dated 25 June 2000, which reads in part,

On the occasion of the 50th anniversary of the outbreak of the Korean War, I would like to offer you my deepest gratitude for your noble contribution to the efforts to safeguard the Republic of Korea and uphold liberal democracy around the world. At the same time, I remember with endless respect and affection those who sacrificed their lives for that *cause*.

The letter was signed by Kim Dae-jung, President of the Republic of Korea.

Robinson ended a thirty-two-year career with The Dow Chemical Company in March 1983. He was a transportation analyst. Perhaps his military experience trained him for a successful civilian life after all.

John Shuell Experienced More Than
He Cares to Remember

A historical document provided by the Midland County Veterans Service Office, proclaims, in part, "On the 30th of November 1950, the U.S. Army suffered more battle deaths than any one day in the history of this nation. Most of the casualties were in the 2nd Infantry Division which was destined to conclude the Korean War with far more KIA [killed in action] than any U.S. Division had in the Korean War.

Two days after John Shuell's eighteenth birthday on Christmas Eve, he enlisted in the U.S. Army, and was assigned to the 2nd Infantry Division, the very one that made the infamous history mentioned in the paragraph above.

He trained with them for just over a year before being sent to Japan where he arrived just in time to be assigned to the 19th Regiment of the 24th Division. The 19th was processing to be sent on to Pusan, Korea. Ironically, it was two days after America had her Fourth of July celebration in 1950 that Shuell arrived on foreign soil, ready to defend a warring nation against the ravages of communism. He knew that was his mission, but he could have no idea how the mission would turn out.

Ten days later Shuell was fighting for his life, 160 miles north of Pusan, along the Kum River. "All hell broke loose," Shuell remembered. "It seemed all of North Korea came across the river. Our company was understrengthed with only 160 men, and by the end of the month there were only thirty-nine of us left," he said, looking off into the distance, but seeing only the horrible picture in his mind.

When asked what his emotions might have been at that time, Shuell said, "Your adrenaline level is so high, that you would not believe that when you see the sun coming up in the morning, it seems to be setting only five minutes later. You just don't have time to think about anything but the moment. I can't remember if I was scared," Shuell said honestly, "but everyone had to be."

Following that horrific and hellish day, Shuell and his remaining company withdrew to Tajon (pronounced Ta-jon). It was a village they had passed through twelve miles south of the Kum River, but 150 miles north of Pusan.

It was at Tajon that Shuell saw General William Dean less than half an hour before he disappeared. Dean was the Commanding

Officer of the 24th Infantry Division, and it is rare that a person of
that high rank disappears or is captured. Dean was a POW for a little over three years, according to Shuell.

From Tajon, Shuell's regiment focused in on the village of Anui.
The distance to Anui is now only a blur in Shuell's memory. He just
knows he got there by walking. He also knows that when they got
there no one really knew what was going on. They had just been following orders.

From there they had a steady walk to Chinju to meet up with other forces. In thirty-six hours they walked the seventy-three miles to this small listless village. Because of the fighting along the way, Shuell's company had been reduced to only twenty-five percent of its original number. The rest had become casualties.

Three days later, the 19th Regiment withdrew and followed the Chinju Pass to Mason (pronounced Ma-san) where they boarded a train toward Pusan. Shuell remembers getting on the train, but cannot recall exactly where they got off.

He also remembers that the fighting began soon after disembarking from the train. They attempted to take the cloverleaf, according to Shuell. The cloverleaf was so named because it was a cluster of three huge hills shaped like one.

It was a frustrating battle for Shuell and his fighting partners. "We would take it in the morning, then lose it at night, take it in the morning, then lose it at night," he recalled shaking his head, reflecting his frustration.

Just when Shuell's men had lost it for good, the 2nd Regiment of the 9th Infantry came to the rescue. But the rescue was not without its price. "They lost almost a full battalion on that one hill," Shuell said, pained by the memory. The typical battalion consists of 1,000 men, according to Shuell. If the American troops had not taken the cloverleaf, it would have given the North Korean troops a straight passage to Pusan. "We could have lost it all right there," explained Shuell.

Still prodding his memory for something that had been there for over fifty years, Shuell said, "I remember that vividly. The rest is a fog."

At the time, Corporal Shuell was a squad leader of ten men, leading them head-on into the conflict with a vengeance. Often the enemy rifle and machine gun fire would drive Shuell's men into the ground. Shuell had to know when it was time to pull back and to give the order.

In the meantime, Shuell's health was failing rapidly. Seven times in sixteen months he had dysentery, malaria and what they called "K fever." He lost a pound of weight a day for two months, taking him from 190 to 130 pounds

When he would reach the point where he could barely move, he would be taken to an aid station behind the front lines, treated with medication and water until his fever broke, and returned to the front.

"There was no getting out," Shuell recalled. "Every man alive was needed on the line. If you weren't bleeding right to death, you went back. We simply had no more men."

On Thanksgiving Day 1950, Shuell's outfit was just eight miles from the Manchurian border. "The frost in the ground was twenty-two inches deep," says Shuell, "and the only way you could dig a fox-hole was along the wall of the rice paddies."

Shuell's term of one hellish year and four days finally drew to an end. He would soon be in civilian clothes once again, or so he thought. Shuell arrived back in the States to receive his discharge in July 1951, only to be told his time in the army had involuntarily been extended for a year. It came as the result of Congress passing Public Service Act 22.

The words entered his mind like a dagger through his heart. He had already served his country on foreign soil in the harshest of conditions for nearly a full year. However, he quietly accepted his fate, and mentally adjusted to the fact that his uniform would not be hanging in the closet at home for another twelve months.

He was sent to Ft. Meade, Maryland and gradually made his transition from war to peace by working in the reception center for incoming recruits. He received his final discharge on 6 June 1952.

Looking back, Shuell said reflectively, "I'm glad I had to stay in. When I came back from Korea, my nerves were shot. I was as nervous as a race horse at the gate. What kind of a person would I have been to be turned loose on the street?"

Shuell had spent a great deal of time in the hospital with various diseases. He had been wounded, had frostbite on his hands, ears, nose, feet, and had sores from living and fighting in temperature extremes of more than –40 degrees Fahrenheit to 115 degrees Fahrenheit. He also found himself helpless as his buddies were shot all around him, and his nerves were shattered before leaving the war zone.

He received five battle ribbons and the Purple Heart. When asked about his wounds, Shuell refuses to talk about them. It is not just a case of modesty; it is more an attempt to put it in the past forever. "It's better forgotten," he said almost in a whisper, staring off into the distance, but showing the mental anguish that was still there.

Shuell will always remember that his introduction to combat included the loss of ninety good American men, mostly teenagers in their prime, as was he. Many of them were his friends. "My only hope is that my kids and grandkids never have to go through something like that," he said as his voice once again trailed off to a whisper.

After a follow-up telephone call to clarify some of his statements, Shuell said, "There's more I can tell you, but it becomes too emotional."

Shuell ended a more than forty year career in the plastics department at The Dow Chemical Company on 31 December 1992.

Vietnam War

1965-1973

The Vietnam War, another police action, was a tragic, ill-conceived war that ultimately claimed over 47,000 American lives, and the lives of hundreds of thousands of Vietnamese. It ended in a humiliating defeat for the United States.

According to Richard Stacewicz in his book, *Winter Soldiers,* "The generation that came of age during the 1960s is still coming to terms with the Vietnam War.

"In looking back over that turbulent era, commentators often tend to portray those who fought in Vietnam as proponents of the war, and those who eluded the draft and military service as demonstrators against the war. Yet some of the most outspoken hawks never served in uniform, while some of the most passionate doves were Vietnam veterans."

Robert S. McNamara, former defense secretary for both the Kennedy and Johnson administrations, has stated, "Both Washington and Hanoi had missed opportunities to achieve our geopolitical objectives without the terrible loss of life suffered by each of our countries."

The Vietnam War was one of the most unpopular undeclared wars ever entered by the United States. Men went by the thousands; they fought, they died, and they were injured. And those fortunate enough to come home never had a hero's welcome. In fact, they were often the brunt of disparaging retorts.

Many of Midland County's best were among the thousands, but only a few were willing to share their stories on the following pages.

Chuck Berryhill Received a Purple Heart Thirty-one Years Late

Lance Corporal Berryhill had enlisted in the marines at seventeen, but the military ruled he couldn't be sent overseas until he turned eighteen. It obliged a year later. He had joined the marines because his older brother, David, was a career Marine.

"I missed the big Tet Offensive," Berryhill explained, "but I was a replacement for someone who was killed there."

"We were on patrol in this village, and the villagers sold us whiskey and pop. We were their market," says Chuck (his given name) Berryhill of Cleveland Manor.

He was just outside Cam Lo in South Vietnam with the 2nd Battalion, 3rd Marine Regiment, 3rd Division when he encountered his first firefight.

"[The villagers] usually accompanied us on our full patrol," Berryhill explained. "But on this particular day they just stopped, but wouldn't tell us why." He hesitated and went on, "They knew what we were getting into, and sure enough we got ambushed by the Viet Cong. The villagers knew what was there, but if they had told us ahead of time, they would probably have been killed."

As soon as the firing began, Berryhill ducked behind a bush, hoping somehow it would act as a concrete barrier when the shots rang out from the distance ahead of him. As a forward observer radio operator, he was ordered to go over a berm facing an open field.

"It was like in the movies," recalled Berryhill. "The rounds were kicking up dirt all around me, but they never quite hit me."

His next experience was one that he would rather forget, but the mental pain just will not let it go. "I moved from a small bush to just around that berm and looked back. Another guy moved into my former position, and he got shot." It looked like Berryhill might be next.

He moved along the berm and into a ditch-like crevasse. At the end of the ditch was a machine gun pointing in his direction. The person controlling the trigger was not a friend. As the staccato shots of the weapon rang out, Berryhill glued his back to the side of the ditch.

As he hugged the ditch, he could feel the breeze of the bullets as they whizzed past his eighteen-year-old face. "If I had even coughed, and in so doing, moved my head forward a fraction, he would have blown my head off," Berryhill said. But that was only the beginning of his problems.

"As I tried to press my back even further into the side of the ditch, I began to feel these little pricks on my back and legs." As Berryhill tried to hug the side of the ditch even harder, he realized he had stirred up a nest of fire ants. Machine gun bullets continued to fly past his face while the ants were chewing up his backside. It gave new meaning to the cliché "between a rock and a hard place."

"Suddenly the ground around me began shaking like an earthquake," Berryhill went on, "and I heard this screeching noise coming up behind me. It was one of our tanks that had come up to take care of the machine gun."

What the tank driver didn't know, however, was that Berryhill was in the ditch just below him. "I thought he was going to run over me, but he stopped just short." What Berryhill didn't know was that the muzzle of the 90 mm gun of the tank was right over his head.

"Each time he fired, my jaw hit my chest just from the concussion," Berryhill remembered. "He did that enough times to rattle my brain, but he blew out the machine gun." The tank then backed off, never knowing Berryhill was in the ditch. "I climbed out of the ditch, stripped down, and killed the ants on my body. So the tank driver got rid of the machine gun, and I got rid of the ants. All's well that ends well," Berryhill said, now able to laugh at his life-threatening experience.

Later, Berryhill was caught in an ambush outside Khesahn. Crawling along on his belly through the thick underbrush, darkened with a canopy of trees, he sprayed the area in front of him with his machine gun, firing at muzzle flashes.

"Whoever was shooting at me was close enough to spray dirt in my eyes," Berryhill said. "He was also using a machine gun, and suddenly there was a sharp pain in my leg and it went numb. I thought he had blown my leg off."

Berryhill was relieved when he looked down, to find a small piece of shrapnel in his shin, the result of the hand grenade the enemy had thrown.

The ambush was over soon after that, according to Berryhill. "Somehow the Viet Cong would disappear back into the jungle or in tunnels without a trace," he remembered with amazement. "We wouldn't even find bodies from the battle."

Berryhill was airlifted to an aid station in a secure area. He remained there for two weeks, then returned to the front lines.

When Berryhill was not fighting an enemy, he was fighting illness. Two of the first four months in Vietnam he spent on a hospital ship trying to wipe out attacks of malaria.

On another occasion where Berryhill was attacked, it was a different kind of enemy. While still in Vietnam, he saw a fellow from Midland he once knew, David Patrick. "Actually, I was a friend of his brother's, but I knew Dave."

Patrick was a dog handler attached to Berryhill's unit and had a German Shepherd on a leash. Dogs were trained to sniff out humans and explosives in the area. "I reached out to shake Dave's hand, and the dog attacked me," recalled Berryhill. "Fortunately, I had on my flak jacket at the time. But the dog was doing what he was trained to do. He thought I was going for his handler, so he went for me."

Berryhill extended his time for six months while still in Vietnam, and by doing so, received a thirty-day leave to come home. That may have saved his life. "While I was home, my entire unit was completely wiped out," he remembered, shaking his head. "Either killed, or injured so bad they couldn't return to action. I didn't know it until I was going back, and got as far as Okinawa. That's when I got the word."

When he arrived in Vietnam once again, there was no unit for him to return to, so he was assigned to an artillery unit behind the lines, the 4th Battalion, 12th Regiment, 3rd Marine Division. "We were pretty secure there," Berryhill says, "and pretty much laid back." As it turned out his own brother Dave was his battery gunnery sergeant.

Berryhill was discharged from the Marines on 18 October 1971, exactly four years from the day he had enlisted.

It was not until September 2002 that he received the Purple Heart for his leg wound. Due to bureaucratic delays, he obtained his award through the services of the Midland County Veterans Service Office and his mother.

"My mother had saved my toe tag, and I presented it, along with other papers to the Midland County Veteran's Office," smiled Berryhill. He went on to explain that when a soldier is killed or wounded, an identifying tag is placed on the person lying there; in the case of death, it's usually on a toe. Since he was wounded, it was placed on a button on his shirt. He saved it and gave it to his mother, Ruth, when he arrived home. Fortunately, she saved it too.

Berryhill can be seen in the fall each year at Midland High School football games as a volunteer, helping in the preparation of the field for the game. In the winter he moves over to Northwood University and volunteers as a goal judge for their hockey games.

Leonard Duchene was One of the Lucky Ones

On the night of 11 May 1969, Specialist Fourth Class Leonard (Len) Duchene was with the 1st Cavalry Division (Airmobile) when its Landing Zone Jamie (LZ Jamie) was attacked by the North Vietnamese, twenty-one miles northeast of Tay Ninh.

According to the *Cavalair,* the newsletter of the 1st Air Cavalry Division, dated 11 July 1969, the battle at Tay Ninh lasted for six hours. When the sun crept over the horizon the following morning, there were seventy-five North Vietnamese bodies in and around the perimeter of the landing zone.

"I was lucky," Duchene said with a grateful sigh. "I was taking my turn monitoring the radio on that shift, when incoming mortars began impacting our area." In the dark he alerted his fighting companions, five besides himself, and they manned their six-man 105 mm gun. There were five other 105s in Duchene's unit, but his team's first responsibility was to fire flares to illuminate the area. "Just so we could see what was out there," he remembered.

"They kept this up until the spooky gunships from the army and air force arrived to drop illumination and the gun crews could go on trying to repel the invaders."

A spooky gunship is a helicopter or airplane with a mini- powered gun, similar to the Gatling gun invented in the late 1800s, except the newer version was operated by electricity instead of by hand. The gunships flew primarily at night, using night vision techniques to spot the enemy. Every fifth bullet was an orange tracer bullet, and when friendly troops saw where the bullets were going, they would also open fire on that area.

Duchene also explained that his gun crew manned the gun in the center, with five other guns and crews of six men each around the periphery. Surrounding the gun positions were members of the 1st Cavalry Infantry, who would patrol around the area trying to spot the enemy.

According to the *Cavalair,* "At 2:40 [a.m.] the men at LZ Jamie knew the attack was for real. Between then and 3:00 a.m. some two hundred rounds of 107 mm rockets, plus 60 mm and 82 mm mortars slammed into the fire-base.

"In the midst of this deafening mortar and rocket barrage, the crackling of small arms fire was barely audible. From three sides the North Vietnamese poured toward the perimeter."

In the meantime, according to the report, the enemy had used special weapons called Bangalore torpedoes to penetrate the wire fencing surrounding the American guns. The enemy then gained easy access to the men in the bunkers.

Before it ended, the Americans, now on the defense, were firing point blank. Three men in Duchene's gun crew were dead, and two others injured. Duchene was the only one who was not injured. The term "lucky" held new meaning for him.

After Duchene and his two semihealthy comrades were patched up, they returned to their gun, but commissioned some replacements for his dead friends on the gun crew.

In a letter sent to his parents in Linwood, Michigan, Duchene explained, "I took charge and had the battery mechanic, a cook and some guys from Fire Direction Control help us on the gun. We put up illumination until flare ships got there and then we worked up data and fired Cafram rounds between illuminations at a high angle." Cafram, according to Duchene, is a round that is set on a timer, and after it is fired, separates into about twelve fragmentation grenades that explode when they hit.

"All together," his letter goes on, "four guys were killed and twenty were wounded in the battery. I had about three little pieces (of shrapnel) in my arm, but I didn't notice it for a couple of days, so I took it out myself [with a jackknife]."

That was not the last time Duchene would come under fire. Less than a month later his unit came under attack again. "But it wasn't quite as bad as the other time," he said in his letter home, "This time two guys were killed and six wounded," he recalled. Everything is relative in combat.

For his valor and bravery, Duchene was awarded the Silver Star Medal, the third highest medal awarded to a military man.

Most of the time Duchene and his crews, plus equipment, would be flown into where they anticipated the next battle would be. Their guns, attached to a cable, would be dangling under the helicopter as they were air lifted to the site. Then the chopper would settle down nearby and the troops would disembark and set up their equipment and ready their 105 mm guns. The guns would set on a frame of steel spikes driven into the ground.

On other occasions, Duchene and his unit would come under fire for several hours at a time, but they seemed minor compared to what he had already experienced.

Given his preference, he would select being on the front lines rather than in a rear area. "On the front," he says "you *knew* where the enemy was and what their targets were, and you would avoid the mortars as best you could. In the rear, which was a large area, rockets would sometimes just be lobbed in, and you had no idea where they were going to hit. All you could hear was the whistle as they came in, but they could land anywhere."

One of the things that Duchene credits his life with is his training. In all his training he was taught to do things instinctively and by the book, he claims. "If we took time to think instead of what we were taught, we would get into trouble. Doing what we did became automatic."

Duchene did not enter the military to become a hero or to be awarded medals for combat experience. At nineteen, he was not excited about being drafted in April 1968, but all his friends his age were getting the same letter from Uncle Sam, and it seemed the thing to do.

When Duchene was discharged on 22 April 1970, he carried with him, in addition to the medal already mentioned, the National Defense Service Medal, The Bronze Star Medal, The Air Medal, Vietnam Service Medal with two Stars, the Republic of Vietnam Campaign Medal, and the Vietnam Unit Citation.

John Hart Lost Many Friends in Vietnam

John H. Hart joined the Marine Corps on a delayed entry program at age seventeen, before he graduated from Midland High School in 1967, near the peak of the Vietnam War.

"I was pretty gung ho, and, quite frankly, wanted to be another John Wayne. He was my hero. I thought it was my patriotic duty, and I knew I wasn't ready for college. So I joined the Marine Corps," Hart recalled.

"It seemed strange that I was looking forward to entering the military, and some of my friends were trying to keep out of it," he said, reflectively.

When Hart's father, Judge Henry Hart, asked his son if he had filed any college applications, he hadn't the heart to tell him he had already joined the marines. When he summoned the courage to tell his father what he had done, his father suggested he might better have joined the navy.

But soon young Hart was on a bus to Ft. Wayne in Detroit, was sworn in, and returned home for his high school graduation.

Shortly after graduation, Hart was sent to marine boot camp in San Diego. Unusual as it was, he was trained in three specialties; infantry (as are all marines), artillery, and much to his surprise, on his way to Vietnam, he was selected to go to language school and become an interpreter.

"By doing so," Hart recalled, regretfully, "I didn't get any leave for nineteen months because it was an additional temporary duty."

Hart was then sent from Camp Pendleton to Defense Language Institute in Monterey, California, where he learned to speak Vietnamese at the rate of fifty words per day. But the training also included vocabulary, writing and listening.

"After the first three weeks of school, we were only allowed to speak Vietnamese."

Following twelve weeks of the intensive language training, Hart was assigned to the 3rd Marine Division on the demilitarized zone (DMZ), and worked in the intelligence office.

"What it boiled down to, I was a clerk in the intelligence office," Hart said, wryly. "After a few weeks I requested mast because I did not want to be just a clerk for the rest of my military career."

Hart explained that mast was a navy term, named after the mast of a ship that goes straight up. In this case it meant that he, as an

enlisted man, could go straight to a superior officer to explain his grievance. "Theoretically, an enlisted man can request mast all the way to the president of the United States," Hart explained, "but he probably would never get that far."

Following his request, Hart was sent to Charlie 1/12, a 105 howitzer unit that flew in helicopters that dropped the men in the jungle to fight. Hart spent twenty-six missions in the field, partly as a radio operator, often landing in the LZs (landing zones), between Laos and the DMZ. He spent his twentieth birthday on one of the LZs, near Torch. His unit was sometimes in the jungle for as long as thirty days.

The second night out on LZ Torch, Hart's unit got hit and suffered fifty percent casualties, including the death of his executive officer. The perimeter unit took one hundred percent casualties, according to Hart.

The father of the executive officer, Mike Dewlen, was a writer. "One of his stories appeared in the March 1969 *Reader's Digest*. It was an emotionally packed story titled 'To Our Fallen Son' It was the story of that battle in which his son was killed," Hart remembered. "I cried when I read it."

In addition to the Vietnamese, Hart also fought the heat and humidity. "Stepping out of a plane was like stepping into a wall," Hart said. "Our drinking water was hot." During the total of Hart's two tours, he ate C rations for sixteen months. "Within the first month, most of the men had a bout of dysentery," he sighed.

Hart also explained some of the reasons some men become depressed in a war situation. "You get sick, you don't like the food, you don't have any familiar friends, you don't know where you are except you're 10,000 miles from home, and someone is shooting at you. Then you dig a foxhole to protect yourself from those shooting at you, and there are snakes, scorpions, millipedes and a myriad of bugs in the bottom of the foxhole waiting to have a go at you."

During one night in Quang-tri Province, Hart and his unit were in a howitzer contest with the North Vietnamese on the DMZ. He recalls that he used his howitzer so much that the barrel simply wore out, and had to be sent to the rear for a replacement.

In the meantime one of his comrades, Sergeant Kimura, took a bad hit, and Hart and another buddy got a litter to carry their fallen friend to a safe area where he could be lifted by helicopter and taken to medical aid. All during this scene, incoming mortars and rifle fire were a constant danger to them all.

Dropping off their burden safely, they returned to their artillery positions, again under heavy fire. "They say you don't hear the round that hits you," Hart reflected, "but I heard the round, and dove to the ground. I had a good look at the ground, and knew there wasn't much of any place else to go."

With his face buried in the ground, a mortar round exploded within a few feet of him. He was not wounded from the shrapnel, but the concussion rolled him over. As he lay there dazed, he kept wondering if he was still in one piece, and whether, in fact, he was alive or dead. He was not certain he could get up if he willed himself to do so. Artillery rounds were still coming in.

Hart's best friend, David Daniel from Macon, Georgia, noticed Hart lying there motionless, and ran to his side, picked him up and began running with him to safety. Hart, still dazed, could not yet determine if he was hurt or not.

As he slowly regained his senses, he tried to convince Daniel he was all right, "But he just kept running, yelling, 'I'm going to get you out of here! I'm going to save you!'" Hart knew that was what best friends did in war time. "He was an exceptional guy. He just wanted to save my life." It all happened at a place near the DMZ, called Camp Caroll.

Outside Camp Caroll in Quang-tri Province, at a place called C-2, Hart's commanding officer, Captain Smith, took a direct hit from a rocket. "It literally blew him apart," Hart said soberly, shaking his head. "We had to go out later and clean up the area. It was horrible. Making it even worse was knowing he had a wife and kids who would never see him again. That day we had one killed in action and four wounded."

That was not the only gruesome experience Hart had while in Vietnam. At another time, he was returning from a brief R & R to China Beach near DaNang, and heading back to the fighting area with another buddy at a place called LZ Stud (later LZ Vandergrift). They began to hear explosions fairly close, and dove for the nearest ditch. They observed one of their own helicopters three hundred yards away, and the ammunition it was carrying on a pallet began to explode. A piece of shrapnel hit his buddy between his helmet and flak jacket, killing him instantly.

"The thing that was really hard about that, besides losing another friend," recalled Hart with sadness, "was responding to a letter from his stepmother. In the letter she stated how much she loved him, and recalled the first day he had called her 'Mother,' and what a treasure he was to the family. I cried as I read her letter, and I was asked by my superior to write to her to tell her he had been killed."

In spite of the tragedies he had encountered, Hart volunteered to continue his time in Vietnam. The normal tour in the war zone for a marine was thirteen months. "I extended for a couple reasons," explained Hart. "One, I knew if I stayed on I would stay with my same unit, and I loved those guys I had fought alongside of for all that time. I had trusted them with my life every day, twenty-four hours a day. I also knew I didn't want to stay in the Marine Corps the rest of my life. I wanted to go to college when I got out. The marines got out according to priority, so those who were in Vietnam the longest had the highest priority. So that was a no-brainer."

Before he continued on in Vietnam, however, Hart was allowed to spend a thirty-day leave at home with his family. It was 1969. "While at home, I had the privilege of watching Neil Armstrong land on the moon," Hart remembered. "That was a real thrill."

He then returned to Vietnam for his second tour, only to find more personal tragedy. "One of my best friends, Lance Corporal Binks, committed suicide. He hadn't heard from his girlfriend back in the States for three weeks, and he claimed it was all over." Hart heard a shot outside his tent, and raced outside with his rifle thinking it was enemy fire, only to find his friend in a pool of blood. He had placed the end of his M-16 automatic rifle in his mouth and pulled the trigger. Hart had no idea his friend was so depressed over it. "Come to find out, he had even left his insurance benefits to his girl."

Another buddy of Hart's lost an arm with his own hand grenade through a freak accident.

In all, Hart completed twenty-six combat missions while in Vietnam; twenty by helicopter and six by truck. His second tour of duty was cut to only six months because President Nixon, in late fall of 1969, started pulling the American troops out of Vietnam.

"I was mildly disappointed," chuckled Hart. "I never got another R & R, and I really wanted to visit Australia."

But that did not stop Hart from seeing other parts of the Far East. He was sent to Okinawa for a few weeks, then on to Japan for three months where they were in continuous training on Mt. Fuji. Some of the training even included beach landings via LST.

Hart was sent home early because he had received word that his father, Henry Hart, had had a heart attack, and his condition was worsening. While that was all true, Henry Hart is still alive, living in Midland as of this writing.

In all the months Hart remained in Vietnam, he never received a serious injury. He also never used his language school training for military purposes. "Sometimes I would talk to people in the villages," he recalled, "but that was all."

Concluding the interview, he summed up his feelings at the time: "During all the shooting, and all the stuff that was going on, I was scared, but I was young. I was John Wayne, and I knew that the bad things were going to happen to someone else. I never really believed it would be me who would end up dead."

Concerning his own mortality, Hart commented, "They say there are no atheists in a foxhole. They are right. I've always been a God-fearing person, so it wasn't any different for me [to pray]. But God was in all the foxholes, trust me."

Hart was honorably discharged from the Marine Corps in September 1970, graduated from Western Michigan University in 1977, and from Cooley Law School in 1985. He began as the 75th District Judge in Midland County in January 1997, and holds that position as of this writing. It is the same court from which his father, Henry Hart, retired in 1982.

War was More Than Physical Pain for Gary Kilmer

"I was surprised when I got my draft notice for Vietnam," said Gary Kilmer of Sanford. "I was twenty-four years old."

Basic training at the armored school in Ft. Knox, Kentucky surprised him too. Most of the men there were five to six years his junior, making it difficult to keep up at times.

Three months later he was attending demolition school and advanced weapons training in Camp Roberts, California. There he was assigned to the $2^{nd}/34^{th}$ Armored, 25th Infantry Division, and sent directly to Vietnam and a two-week environmental orientation to get used to the climate and the culture. The date of his arrival there came in August 1968, just a year after beginning his military career. And in that brief career, he had become a tank driver and demolition expert.

One of Kilmer's major jobs was taking his tank group to search for personnel mines in the road. "If we hit one it would just blow the track off, and we would replace it," he stated, matter-of-factly. "The most anyone inside the tank was hurt was having his eardrums injured from the noise of the explosion."

Close calls were common, according to Kilmer. Because he had had training in demolition, he was sometimes called to detonate unexploded bombs from B-52 runs. "That could be hazardous to your health," he stated, "but if we took our time, it was pretty safe." He said that as if anyone could do it. "First we would walk in circles around the bomb to make sure it wasn't booby-trapped," he said. "We would use plastic explosives with a twenty-minute fuse so we had plenty of time to get out of there when it blew."

The most frightened Kilmer ever became, as he poked at his memory, was a time shortly after he arrived in Vietnam. "A few of us were sitting around a little camp fire, just talking," he said sadly, "and a sniper shot and killed the fellow to my immediate right."

Kilmer paused as though some memories had been triggered that he would prefer to leave behind. But he goes on, slowly, choosing his words methodically. His memory then took him to the Dong Ha Valley on 19 June 1970. It was four days before his military commitment would have ended.

There were five tanks in his group when they were ambushed by the Viet Cong with bazooka-type weapons.

"I was driving a tank at the time we were ambushed," Kilmer said slowly. "We had sandbags along the front where I was resting my hand." The incoming shrapnel ripped through the bags, and hit Kilmer in the chest and face, but not before severing his left hand on the spot.

He had a towel he used to wipe perspiration from his face in the hot, humid environment of Vietnam and in the even hotter environment of a steel tank.

"I wrapped the towel around my hand," Kilmer remembered.

Then he spun the tank around and managed to climb free. Kilmer was the only one injured. "There was a medic there, fresh from the States," Kilmer said solemnly, "and he was scared to death. He gave me a shot of morphine and applied a tourniquet to my left arm."

A nearby helicopter landed, and as the blades spun a synchronized rhythm overhead, some GIs loaded him aboard. Kilmer was taken to a field hospital in a chopper used by the top brass. Inside was General Westmoreland, commanding officer of American forces in Vietnam.

When asked for the general's first name, Kilmer hesitated in contemplation, then laughed and said, "Sir." We both enjoyed the laugh, and it took some of the sting from Kilmer's painful recollection. Minimal research revealed the general's first name to be William.

In the field hospital, "They just stapled me together," Kilmer said thoughtfully. From the field hospital, he was placed on a hospital ship that took him on to Japan.

While in Japan he was informed that his military stint was over, but if he wanted to be treated in a military hospital, with all its perks, mainly the services of VA hospitals the rest of his life, he would have to reenlist. He chose to do that. "I also did that because our company was shorthanded," he said. Smiling, he added, "No pun intended." More laughter. But the stipulation on the enlistment was that after he was healed he would receive his honorable discharge.

The helicopter experience was not his first encounter with General Westmoreland. Kilmer described the situation when his company lieutenant, who was new to combat, ordered Kilmer and several men to go on an ambush with their tanks. "Some of us refused to go, and we were demoted from specialist fourth class to specialist third class. Several of those who went were badly beaten up with gunfire and hand grenades, and hospitalized. It's hard to ambush anyone with a tank. They can hear a group of tanks coming from miles away.

"The following morning Westmoreland heard about it, and in front of us, he chewed the lieutenant up one side and down the other . . . and gave us all our former rank back. He was just a regular guy."

Following surgery and two weeks of recuperation in Japan, Kilmer was flown to Alaska, then on to a hospital in New Jersey. Less than a week later he was taken by helicopter to Valley Forge, Pennsylvania. There he stayed for three months, where he was fitted with a prosthesis and taught how to use it.

But his experiences in hospitals left him with an optimism befitting any hero. "I felt really bad about my situation until I saw so many so much worse off than I," he remembered. "Mine was a minor wound in comparison."

Kilmer never considered himself handicapped. He continued with his prosthesis to do anything he had always done, including deer hunting with bow and arrow.

In spite of all the pain and suffering he had seen, Kilmer managed to find some humor in the situation. At one o'clock one morning, near the DMZ, according to Kilmer, his tank was guarding a bridge.

The crew received fire from the other side, and opened up with its own 90 mm gun from their tank.

Unbeknown to the tank crew, they had a hydraulic leak which operated the up and down movement of the gun. The gun was in the down position when it was fired. "We blew up the bridge we were sent to guard." Kilmer stated laughing.

Kilmer has not told a lot of people about his war experiences. "We had some really bad times," he said. "There are just some things you don't talk about. It gets too emotional."

It was apparent that Kilmer was keeping something buried far back in his memory, fighting to keep it there.

Soberly, he mentions visiting the traveling Vietnam War Memorial when it went through Midland some years back.

"It was the first time I really broke up," he stated. "I was okay until the chopper flew over. That's when I lost it."

Some memories do that.

David Lackey: They Got it Right

David Lackey of Midland stood before the black granite Vietnam War
Memorial, sometimes called "The Wall," in Washington, D.C.

As he traced his fingers over the names, but not quite touching,
the painful memories, indelibly etched in his memory, of a war he
fought more than thirty years ago, came back again.

He remembered the deathly stench of corpses as they lay rotting
in vinyl body bags, and how the daily body counts kept track of the
winners and losers. He realized that he had been one of those who
had been unleashed, like an untethered animal, lashing out at an
enemy he never got to know. Upon reflection, Lackey later penned
the following words about his experience at The Wall:

THEY GOT IT RIGHT

> I trace my fingers
> across each name
> not quite touching,
> stepping over rotting corpses.
> Arranged in tight columns,
> I step carefully
> over plastic mounds
> with contorted faces behind the cloud
> of translucent vinyl.
> I grow weary
> awkwardly stepping
> barely a foot-space between rows.
> With each slow advance
> still more dead appear on the horizon.
> I struggle to keep my balance,
> each step is a stinging
> slap in the face.
> Why am I not among the dead?
> From the insulated arena
> of television news
> I had watched in silence
> the feverish dogs, untethered,
> lashing, clawing,
> jaws on jugulars, daily body counts keeping track
> of the winners and losers.

And then I was one of them.
Fitted with spiked collar and steel fangs,
dropped into the equatorial pit
of the killers and the killed,
by one I perpetuated the blood test.
Retching from the smells
of sun heated vinyl and decay
I back away, back away
and the field is gone.
Taking its place before me,
cut from the earth and laid bare,
stands the black granite scar,
of the Wall.
"They got it right," I say out loud
to no one, to my country, to myself.

In 1970, at age twenty-one, Lackey was drafted, sent to Ft. Knox, Kentucky for basic training, then on to Ft. Polk, Louisiana for training to drive armored personnel carriers (APCs). At that age, his peers regarded him as the "old man." Everyone else was younger.

Although he never used his training to drive APCs in combat, the military found in him other attributes. This got him assigned to the

C-120 Americal Division in Chuli just south of Saigon. The Americal Division was formed just for the year Lackey would be in Vietnam.

When he arrived at base camp, Lackey was given a choice of two positions; an M-60 machine gunner or a radioman. "That M-60 looked awfully heavy," Lackey smiled, "so I became a radioman. The radio was heavy too, weighing forty pounds, and our backpack with a weight of sixty pounds, I carried around about one hundred pounds, but at least I could carry it all on my back." That was a lot of weight for a man who weighed only 140 pounds.

One of his first jobs was to go into the jungle with other troops to find food the Viet Cong had hidden, to be retrieved later. "When we found some we would either radio in a helicopter to retrieve it or blow it up in place," Lackey recalled.

Lackey suggested his lieutenant go on alone because of the fear of exploding a booby trap. "For some reason the lieutenant agreed with my suggestion, and told me to go back with the others. He was lucky. He found lots of Cong food, but never a trip wire."

Trip wires were always the main worry for Lackey and his platoon. "We would always walk in a straight line," Lackey said. "And about thirty feet apart. We would be stretched out for a half-mile. One time it was the third man in line who discovered a trip wire. The booby trap blew off his foot."

Lackey tells of walking point. The point is the lead man who sees, hears and reacts first. "I avoided that every chance I could," he said. "But there were those with what I called the 'John Wayne Syndrome.' They were the young bucks who thought they could see and hear better than anyone else, and could react faster than anyone else. They thought they were invincible." And Lackey added smiling, "I was happy to let 'em."

Try as he may to avoid walking point, he wasn't always success-ful. He still had to take his turn.

"One day there I was, first one out, looking for trip wires, looking for anybody who might jump in front of me. After about two hours, a deer suddenly jumped out in front of me.

"Their deer are smaller than Michigan deer, but this one caused my heart to nearly jump out of my body.

"Later my buddies asked me why I didn't shoot it. After that I thought maybe my reactions should be faster . . . maybe I shouldn't be walking point."

On another adventure, Lackey remembers his platoon "spent the whole day hacking up the side of this mountain [with machetes]. There were trails all over this mountain, but if you use a trail there is more likely to be trip wires attached to booby traps."

It was a terribly hot day, according to Lackey, "and by the time we got to the top of the mountain, there were kids on bicycles, waiting to sell us pop . . . including Coca-Cola. And Americans think they are the only capitalists.

"We thought we were being sneaky, hacking our way up this mountain so the enemy wouldn't see us, but these kids saw us, loaded their bikes down with a block of ice and pop, and pushed them up the trails ahead of us."

It got worse for the GIs. "The kids were selling the pop for fifty cents a can. At base camp we could buy it for fifteen cents.

"We were hot and we were angry, wondering if the kids knew there weren't any trip wires on the trails. But most of us paid the fifty cents."

The nearest Lackey ever came to being injured or possibly killed was the day his platoon spooked several Viet Cong on the flatlands. After a brief exchange of gunfire, all of the Cong fled except for two who were wounded, and hid in a clump of bamboo bushes.

"Nearly all our platoon was firing in their direction, when suddenly the return fire stopped," Lackey stated reflectively.

Lackey and three others approached the bushes to check it out, when one of the men yelled, "Grenade!"

"I started to turn and run when it blew up," he said. "The concussion knocked me down unharmed, but one of my buddies was cut up by several pieces of shrapnel." Once again they approached the bamboo clump cautiously, only to find two dead Viet Cong.

Two months before rotating home, the disbanded Americal Division was sent to the 101st Airborne Division at Da Nang. "But it was in name only," Lackey explained. "I never parachuted out of a plane." When asked if he wanted to, the answer was an emphatic, "No!"

At that time he was asked if he would like to take a practice jump from a helicopter. "I liked doing that kind of stuff, but refused the opportunity just because I could," he smiled, showing relief.

Lackey, who had many close calls, considered himself lucky. He was discharged from the military in March 1972.

Clay Maxwell Crashed in an Attack Helicopter in Vietnam

As a teenager, Clay Maxwell cut firewood to pay for flying lessons at Barstow Airport. "After getting my solo license, I would sell firewood to pay for more lessons," he remembered.

Little did he know that two years after graduating from Meridian High School in 1966, he would be flying a Huey Cobra helicopter over Vietnam, loaded with rockets, a grenade launcher and a Gatling gun that could spit out nearly 2,000 rounds per minute.

The 1960s were a tough time for young men Maxwell's age. "My family was always patriotic," Maxwell said. "I didn't care for the general attitude of many of my peers, and I really felt it was my duty to help defend my country and its principles."

Having a love for aviation, he left Michigan State University, enlisted in the army and signed on as a candidate for fixed wing pilot training. "At the time the army had all the fixed wing pilots they needed," Maxwell said. He then signed up for helicopter pilot training where his skills could be utilized.

After nearly ten months of intensive training at army bases in Texas, Alabama and Georgia, he was assigned to a Huey Cobra Helicopter with the D Troop 3/4 Cavalry, 25th Infantry Division, and to a Huey Cobra helicopter. His first assignment was in the jungles of Cu Chi, Vietnam. Cu Chi is located between Saigon and the Cambodian border.

In describing his helicopter, Maxwell said, "It carried 76 rockets, each with the striking force of the 105 howitzer used by the artillery in World War II, a Gatling gun and a 40 mm grenade launcher." He added, "The Cobra was strictly an attack helicopter, and that's exactly what we did."

In the beginning of his flight career, his inclination was to be assigned to a medivac unit, airlifting downed crews from dangerous situations. "I soon learned that I was safer in an attack aircraft," he said. "At least I had fire power, and could protect myself."

One of his greatest fears was firing too close to his own ground troops because the enemy often would plant itself very near American troops, knowing the Americans would not fire on themselves. Often, the Viet Cong would dig tunnels under the American bases. "Traveling at 140 miles an hour at treetop level, it was difficult targeting the enemy," he recalled.

Another of his greatest fears was being captured. "The Viet Cong were not known for their compassion," he remembered. It was well known that American prisoners in Vietnam were tortured, even to the point of death.

Maxwell's aircraft took continual fire from his missions at treetop level as well as at 2,000 feet. One of the hazards he faced was flying over a jungle when he could not see the enemy, but they could see him. "Whenever we heard a humming noise over our FM radios, it meant we better get out of there fast. Enemy guns had us locked in on radar," he said.

Maxwell had more combat assault missions than he cared to remember, frequently under heavy ground fire from the Viet Cong. "It was an interesting education in human nature," recalled Maxwell. "One day you would feel invincible and might take all kinds of risks. Another day you would just find it harder to initiate action. You would just do your job and head back to base."

That was not the only experience Maxwell had in human nature. On one occasion, he was forced to crash-land in a rice paddy. Survival became paramount, not only for himself, but for his copilot as well. He was near the Cambodian border when he lost his tail rotor gearbox—in effect losing his center of gravity—and he began spinning toward earth. "I never found out if it had been shot by Cong gunfire or if it was due to mechanical failure," he said with a shrug. The date was Friday, 13 December 1968.

Maxwell had called the Mayday signal into his radio before the crippled chopper had fallen nearly 2,000 feet and slammed to the ground. Fortunately he could control the pitch on the main rotor to somewhat slow his vertical ascent.

Both Maxwell and his copilot, Scott Moore, suffered crushed back vertebrae. Moore was paralyzed from the waist down, as was Maxwell, temporarily. "I was in pain," Maxwell remembers, "but I had to get my copilot and myself away from there. We didn't know if or when it might explode."

An item in the *Midland Daily News* shortly after that stated that Maxwell's parents, Peter and Doris Maxwell, had received a telephone call from their son to let them know he had been injured, but was doing well. The report went on, "Another helicopter in the area saw the crash landing and went to the aid of the injured men. Maxwell helped remove Moore from the downed helicopter and he was taken to a base hospital. Then the second aircraft came back and picked up Maxwell."

It was fortunate his disabled ship, if it had to crash, found an open rice paddy in which to come down. "It was an easy rescue," said Maxwell. "If we had come down in the trees, it would have been a different story."

With a compression fracture in his back, he was flown to the base hospital, then to a military hospital in Yokohama, Japan. "After seeing some of the other men there, and the medical problems they were having, I was almost ashamed to be there. So many were a thousand times worse off than I."

After a month in the Yokohama hospital, Maxwell was given a choice. "The doc said, 'I can send you back to the States, or you can go back to Vietnam. What's your choice?' Now that was a no-brainer," Maxwell laughed. He spent the next couple of weeks in a hospital in Ft. Devins, Massachusetts.

In an earlier experience that nearly cost the lives of Maxwell and his copilot, they were saved by nature itself.

> We were coming in low from a night mission. It was during an electrical storm. On our approach, we didn't use landing lights because we didn't want to attract attention from enemy fire. Suddenly there was this flash of lightning, and we saw right in front of us, an outline of a huge dead tree. We both pulled back hard on our sticks, and we could hear the limbs dragging on the bottom of the helicopter. I can still hear that sound of the tree scraping on our aircraft. If it had not been for that lightning bolt, we would have crashed head-on into the tree.

Maxwell claimed that in a war, everyone in battle looks out for his buddies as much as he does for himself. As proof of that, he had an experience that earned for him the Army Commendation Medal for Heroism.

On 4 November 1968, a *Midland Daily News* clipping, now yellowed with time, reads, in part, "Maxwell, who served as a helicopter pilot with the 25th Infantry Division in Vietnam, was cited for heroic actions . . . in providing covering fire to protect the crews of several downed copters." And from an army newspaper, "Despite the intense enemy fire directed at his aircraft, Maxwell courageously made several low-level firing passes upon the enemy positions."

Philosophically, Maxwell believes that one of the problems of the returning Vietnam veterans was that one day they would be fighting the enemy in the jungle, then flown back to the States for discharge and would be wearing civilian clothes and walking down concrete sidewalks the next day. "There was just no time given to make the adjustment," he claimed. "In World War II, when most of the troops came home by ship, they had up to maybe three weeks to talk out their experiences with people who had also been there. Then when they got to the States, the docks were filled with people who welcomed them home as heroes. The transition was smoother."

Maxwell admits he did not sleep well for at least ten years after returning home, and that he could not even talk about his war experiences during that time.

Thinking back, Maxwell related one of his major disappointments lightheartedly. Three times he missed seeing *his* hero, and it was caused by his injuries. "I always loved Bob Hope," he smiled. "I was medivaced out of 'Nam two days before he and his entourage arrived. I had also left Saigon just before he got there, and Hope had left the Yokohoma hospital five days before I arrived." With a disappointed smile, he added, "I found out later that Hope had toured the floor I was on at the hospital." Maxwell never did see Bob Hope.

Including the Purple Heart, Maxwell earned over a dozen medals and commendations, but his most revered are two Distinguished Flying Crosses given for heroism, and certified by the president of the United States. Ironically, the first one was dated 4 July, 1968.

In August 1970, Chief Warrant Officer Maxwell returned to his family's farm in Hope. He no longer flies because, "When it's good flying weather, it's also good farming weather."

Steve Morrison Has a Hero's Painful Memories

> For gallantry in action . . . For heroism in connection with military operations against a hostile force . . . Sergeant Morrison distinguished himself by heroic actions on 8 January 1970 . . . Sergeant Morrison distinguished himself by heroic actions on 20 February 1970 . . . With complete disregard for his own safety, Sergeant Morrison continually exposed himself to the deadly barrage of enemy rocket grenades, automatic weapons and sniper fire on enemy positions . . . Sergeant Morrison's bravery and devotion to duty are in keeping with the highest traditions of military service . . . Sergeant Morrison crawled more than three hundred feet over jagged rocks and through intense enemy fire in order to deliver smoke grenades to the front element.

The above words are excerpted from the orders directed by the president of the United States to describe just some of the reasons Steve Morrison, a Midland resident for several decades, received the Silver Star, the Award of the Bronze Star Medal for Heroism, and two Purple Hearts during the fighting in Vietnam in 1970. The awards were presented less than six weeks apart.

Steve Morrison had completed work for his degree at Ferris State University, and on 13 August 1968, his twenty-second birthday, got the call from Uncle Sam that would forever influence his life.

After completing twelve weeks of basic training at Ft. Knox, Kentucky, several more weeks of advanced infantry training at Ft. Polk, Louisiana, and another twelve weeks of noncommissioned officer training at Ft. Benning, Georgia, he was sent to Tay Ninh less than fifty miles northwest of Saigon, Vietnam. Tay Ninh was nicknamed Rocket City because occasional rockets were lobbed over from Cambodia.

For the next seven months Morrison lived every day not knowing if he would get another on this earth. "We gave most of our buddies nicknames," said Morrison, "because we didn't want to get emotionally attached to any of them. We never knew if they would be with us the next day . . . and many weren't." The only thing that kept Morrison from serving the normal one-year tour of duty in Vietnam, were injuries that won for him his second Purple Heart and a trip back to the States.

"Much of the time the fighting was spent in the bush in intense heat," Morrison recalled. "Whenever we did get a chance to get back to base camp, it was a luxury to bathe in the makeshift showers."

The showers were fifty-five-gallon steel drums, painted black, and placed on wooden frames just high enough for a man to stand under. In the morning the drums would be filled with cold water, and by 1:00 p.m. the water would be warm enough to be comfortable for bathing.

"The real luxury, however, was the steam room," said Morrison. "After spending several weeks in the blistering heat in combat, we would shower, then sit in the crude steam room, and watch the filth pour out of our pores . . . and that was *after* the shower."

The Army of the Republic of Vietnam (ARVN) would have compounds near hamlets, and sometimes, more than one compound per hamlet.

Because of the language barrier, the ARVNs had to be inventive. Should they have enemy contact during the night, they formed a "T" that was parallel to the ground. Tin cans were then attached, and candles placed inside to be seen only from the air.

The device was aimed toward the enemy's positions to get fire support from the U.S. Night Hawk helicopters.

The Vietnamese are very resourceful people, according to Morrison. When tanks would leave a temporary support camp, shell casings and items of no further use were buried. "Before our troops had cleared the area the Vietnamese people were digging to find anything of value," Morrison remembered. "Shell casings were sometimes filled with earth and placed around their houses, as sandbags, for protection."

"For the most part," Morrison added, "our weapons worked as though they had already gone through a war! The first time in combat my M-16 rifle jammed. It was due, for the most part, to environment: hot, humid, and horribly dirty. After that, I was able to carry a grenade launcher. It was much easier to maintain and was much more versatile."

While much of the fighting occurred in dense jungle, some of it took place over rock and debris. Often the Viet Cong, who were clever soldiers, would burrow under the rock and, sometimes, deep under the American bases. The Viet Cong knew the Americans and their allies would never bomb their own encampments.

One day Morrison, now a platoon leader, and his radio man were leaping from one huge rock to another, their weapons ready to fire. Morrison was ready to jump from one rock to another, but his radioman misread his signal. His buddy jumped ahead of time, pushing both of them to the ground between the rocks.

At that precise moment, they heard sniper fire over their heads. "We both made like moles and avoided the gun fire," Morrison said gratefully. "His miscue saved both our lives."

Fighting also took place along the rivers and streams. Often Morrison and his platoon were in a riverboat lined with anti-shell piercing armor. "We never knew if the hamlets [villages] along the river were friend or enemy. Our first clue was whether or not we were fired upon," he continues, smiling ruefully. "Sometimes the Cong would place themselves in an otherwise peaceful hamlet, knowing we wouldn't fire on them and kill civilians."

But the GIs, in spite of being in intense danger most of the time, learned how to relax whenever the opportunity arose, according to Morrison. After the monsoon season, everything was filled with water, including the craters left by the bombing of the B-52s. Taking advantage of the newly-formed pools, Morrison and his men would take a refreshing swim.

Morrison was not very proud of his first Purple Heart. It occurred from allied groundfire. "It wasn't a major wound," Morrison recalled, "and I was somewhat embarrassed by the presentation."

His second award was a different story. Morrison had just returned from R & R in Honolulu, where he had spent a week with his wife of only six months. The Morrisons had been married just before he shipped to Vietnam.

He and his platoon were caught in an ambush. "The logistics got screwed up," Morrison said soberly. "The helicopters didn't arrive on time to pick us up at the airstrip." The Viet Cong launched rockets into the company operations, and Morrison's lieutenant was hit. "That also reduced our manpower."

While aiding his lieutenant, Morrison took some shrapnel in one leg and arm. "It was painful, and I went into shock," said Morrison. "When the medic showed up, I said, 'Tell me I'm going to be all right or I'll pass out.' 'You're going to be just fine,' said the medic." Morrison went on, "The psychology worked, and I stayed conscious." But another buddy carried him on his back to the area where the medivac choppers were supposed to pick them up.

While waiting for the helicopters to finally arrive, Morrison was standing, talking with another buddy, when an enemy rocket was lobbed behind his friend. The concussion threw him into Morrison, who struck a tree, which knocked him out. When he regained consciousness, "My buddy was lying on top of me. Both his legs and parts of both hands had been severed by shrapnel," Morrison related. "I just lay there, stroking his head, trying to console him until the medics got to us."

Morrison was able to see him before leaving the MASH bunker where base camp surgeries were performed. The wounded were then flown on to Japan for major surgery.

As they carried Morrison to the heliport to transfer him to better hospital facilities, he could see that the medivac chopper that had brought him had been riddled with gunfire, and was still on the pad. It had to be repaired before it could be flown again.

Modestly, Morrison added, "I don't talk about this much unless I'm with someone who's been there, or when friends bring it up."

Morrison felt very fortunate. "Life is good," he said, smiling. He retired from Dow Corning Corporation in 2000, and lives with Shirley, his wife of more than thirty-three years, on Wixom Lake.

Stephen Tracy: Two Wars to His Credit

Early in 1964, the 14th Cavalry Division, Troop M, of the U.S. Army, welcomed Stephen (Steve) Tracy into its fold to guard the border between East and West Germany, a position he held for eighteen months. Tracy began his military career at nineteen, just a year after he graduated from Midland High School.

In early January 1966, he volunteered for service in Vietnam. The war in that southeast corner of Asia was nearly a year old, and would not be over until Tracy was a quarter of a century old. A year later, the forces in Vietnam had mushroomed to 600,000 young men from America. Most of them were in Tracy's age group.

Tracy chuckles as he recalls why he volunteered for Vietnam. "I was nineteen, and pretty gung ho," he says. "Plus, I was tired of the frigid German winters, and wanted to try something different. I told them that if it doesn't snow over there, I'll go. I was right, it didn't snow."

Tracy was in the first armored unit in Vietnam to be in battle, according to the *Bridgehead Sentinel,* published by the Society of the First Division. In one of Tracy's first battles, his unit was outnumbered by the 272nd Regiment of the elite 9th Viet Cong Division. According to the *Sentinel,* "The 1st Squadron of the 14th Armored Cavalry [of which Tracy was a member], defeated its foes in one of the most gallant stands of the Vietnam War."

The publication goes on, "When the tanks and armored cavalry vehicles of Troop M rumbled out of the Phu Loi base on 8 June 1966, the troopers did not know that before the day was out they would have fought and won an epic battle of the Vietnam War."

The odds against them were nine to one. The Viet Cong had engaged 1,200 men, according to the *Bridgehead Sentinel.* Tracy's armored convoy contained 135 men going into battle. Fifty-one became casualties; fourteen were killed and thirty-seven wounded, according to the same paper.

"We were going down Highway 13, also called Thunder Road because of the number of mines the Viet Cong had placed there," Tracy remembered. "We could also feel an ambush coming," he added. "I really don't know how, but we could feel it approaching."

The driver on Tracy's tank had unwittingly centered the tank on the crown in the middle of the road, so neither tread touched the ground. The tank, like a turtle on its back, could not move in any direction. "and we were cut off from the main column for about five hours," Tracy said. "The main column was about a half-mile ahead of us, and they were having even more trouble with enemy fire than we were."

Tracy not only loaded tanks and served as a gunner, but at times was the tank commander, and would drive his own tank that carried four men. He also rode in personnel carriers accommodating flame throwers. "Actually, we rotated jobs because you got sick of doing the same thing day after day."

After the tank was loaded with ammunition and fuel, the loader usually rode on the outside of the tank. "We would rather take our chances with a sniper, than from being killed from a mine. If we hit a mine, it would penetrate the underside of the tank, and the risk of being killed or injured was magnified." Tracy had several friends who were disabled by a mine exploding under their tank.

While acting as tank commander, Tracy told the driver what to look for in the road and what to avoid. "I had told a certain driver for a week what to watch out for and to avoid certain marks in the road," he stated. "The only day I didn't tell him, he ran over a mine, and it tore the tracks right off the tank." Tracy and the other three were badly shaken, but none were hurt.

Tracy reflected on the philosophy of what combat experience means to the fighting man. "If a person can make it through the fighting the first sixty days," he said, "that experience could often see him through his year-long tour of duty."

He believes the reason so many American troops were lost is that President Johnson never called up the National Guard or military reserves, "men who had more maturity, combat experience and extensive training. Most of the men sent there were inexperienced eighteen-year-olds."

It was experience that taught the troopers to seek self-sufficiency on the battlefield. "They knew they would be reinforced if they started a battle, but they also knew the reinforcements might be slow in coming," according to the *Bridgehead Sentinel.* "Thus they carried an astounding load of ammunition."

Tracy is aware of how fortunate he is that his only injuries were some burns on his legs from the empty shells of his tank's 90 mm guns. "Normally we would dispose of the shells outside the tank," he recalled, "but this one day there were snipers outside, and the shells remained inside. When they are first ejected from the guns, they are so hot you could boil water on them."

Tracy's tour of duty in the jungles near Cambodia finally ended a year after his arrival. He was discharged from active duty just in time to be home for Christmas 1966.

But his military career and battlefield experiences were not over. In February 1980 he joined the Michigan National Guard. Ten and a half years later, he was activated and sent to Saudi Arabia as a member of the Michigan National Guard's 460th Supply and Service. The unit is located in Midland. It began training for the invasion of Iraq with the 24th Infantry.

His assignment in Desert Storm was as head of a water purification program, and he was reassigned to the 24th Infantry Division.

For the five months from January to May 1991, Tracy's main purpose was to get purified water to the front lines. The 460th transported and distributed supplies from the States. "We often had to get the supplies there before our men got there," Tracy said. "One of the reasons we win wars is because our logistics are far superior. That gives us a jump on our enemies."

The logistics included trucking the water, fuel and supplies down a country two-lane paved road. "It had every kind of traffic on that road one could imagine, including tanks," said Tracy." Traffic jams were common, according to Tracy, "It was bumper to bumper, and I'm sure there were more men killed in the traffic than in the war itself."

While Tracy and his men were never fired upon in Saudi Arabia, they saw firsthand some of the results of that war.

"Iraqis were surrendering all over the place," Tracy remembered. "We had no way of handling prisoners, and so we just confiscated their weapons, and told them to go on to Baghdad. And for some reason, while they were surrendering to us, they would remove their shoes. I guess it was a gesture to let us know that if we took them prisoners, they would not run away."

The Iraqis in that war had effective and sophisticated weapons, according to Tracy, "But they just weren't very motivated to fight. Most all of them had been drafted," he recalled. "Their troops were poorly led, poorly fed and poorly trained."

Tracy went on to say that in some cases, the male fighter would bring his whole family into the fighting zone.

"I really don't know why," he said, shrugging. "I don't know if it was because their culture demanded that wherever the man went, the whole family followed, or if they thought they wouldn't be fired upon if we saw women and children in the truck."

On a less serious note, Tracy mentioned that the young American fighting men in Desert Storm were good soldiers. "I didn't like their music," he chuckled, "but they were damn good soldiers."

In addition to the wars in which he participated, Tracy has spent over two decades with the National Guard in Midland. But his total military time spans a period of thirty-eight years. He holds the rank of Command Sergeant Major, the top rank for a non-commissioned officer in the U.S. Army.

Tracy enjoys the annual patriotic parades through Main Street, and as the veteran's counselor for Midland County for the past twenty-five years, he helps organize them.

Watching the veterans of our many conflicts marching in the parade gives him a sense of community and a feeling of pride in those who risked their lives to protect our way of life.

Bibliography

Armstrong, Frank A. "One Day In History." Supplement to the *Bridgehead Sentinel* (summer 1988).

Doherty, Robert E. *Snetterton Falcons.* Dallas, Tex.: Taylor Publishing Company, 1989.

Donahue, Michael. "Moment of Glory." *2nd Division Air Journal* (May 1982).

DuPuy, General William E. Untitled essay. *Bridgehead Sentinel* (summer 1988).

Eisenhower, General Dwight D. *Crusade In Europe.* Garden City, N.Y.: Doubleday, 1948.

Gordon, Dennis and Hayes Otoupalik. *Quartered In Hell: The Story of the American North Russia Expeditionary Force, 1918–1919.* Missoula, Mont.: Doughboy Historical Society, G.O.S., 1982

McNamara, Robert S. *In Retrospect: The Tragedy and Lessons of Vietnam.* New York: Vintage Books, 1996.

Morgan, Robert. *The Man Who Flew the Memphis Belle.* New York: Penguin, 2001.

Pyle, Ernie. *Brave Men.* New York: H. Holt and Company, 1944

Shirey, Orville C. *Americans: The Story of the 442nd Combat Team.* Washington, D.C.: Infantry Journal Press, [1947].

Stacewicz, Richard. *Winter Soldiers, An Oral History of Vietnam Veterans Against The War.* New York: Twayne Publishers, 1997.

Toland, John. *In Mortal Combat.* New York: Morrow, 1991.

United States Army. *The Story of the 442nd Combat Team.* Monograph published by Information-Education Section, MTOUSA, Compiled by members of the 442nd Combat Team, n.d.

United States Army. Untitled newsletter. Washington, D.C.: Department of the Army, 30 September 1954.

Zastrow, Captain Peter. "NVA Onslaught Fails at LZ." *Cavalair,* 11 July 1962.

50 Tons of Fast Fighting Fury. Brochure. Germantown, Tenn.: PT Boats, Inc., n.d.